Giallo Cinema and
Its Folktale Roots

Giallo Cinema and Its Folktale Roots

A Critical Study of 10 Films, 1962–1987

MICHAEL SEVASTAKIS

McFarland & Company, Inc., Publishers
Jefferson, North Carolina

LIBRARY OF CONGRESS CATALOGUING-IN-PUBLICATION DATA

Names: Sevastakis, Michael, author.
Title: Giallo cinema and its folktale roots : a critical study of 10 films, 1962–1987 / Michael Sevastakis.
Description: Jefferson, North Carolina : McFarland & Company, Inc., Publishers, 2016 | Includes bibliographical references and index.
Identifiers: LCCN 2016023919 | ISBN 9780786495016 (softcover : acid free paper) ∞
Subjects: LCSH: Motion pictures—Italy—History. | Film genres—Italy.
Classification: LCC PN1993.5.I88 S48 2016 | DDC 791.430945—dc23
LC record available at https://lccn.loc.gov/2016023919

BRITISH LIBRARY CATALOGUING DATA ARE AVAILABLE

ISBN (print) 978-0-7864-9501-6
ISBN (ebook) 978-1-4766-2418-1

© 2016 Michael Sevastakis. All rights reserved

No part of this book may be reproduced or transmitted in any form or by any means, electronic or mechanical, including photocopying or recording, or by any information storage and retrieval system, without permission in writing from the publisher.

Front cover image from *Opera*, 1987 (Photofest)

Printed in the United States of America

McFarland & Company, Inc., Publishers
  Box 611, Jefferson, North Carolina 28640
    www.mcfarlandpub.com

To Philip Zeller,
who has been of enormous aid
in the preparation of this manuscript,
and a big brother
for his help in all things technical.

And to District of Eastern North America
for their assistance in financing this project.

Table of Contents

Introduction: A Crime Waiting to Be Committed	1
1. In the Beginning Was the *Giallo* Mario Bava's *La ragazza che sapeva troppo* (1962)	5
2. A Vice in Common Sergio Martino's *Lo strano vizio della Signora Wardh* (1970)	26
3. Wrap Your Troubles in Dreams (and Dream Your Troubles Away) Lucio Fulci's *Una lucertola con la pelle di donna* (1971)	45
4. Murder According to the Good Book Umberto Lenzi's *Sette orchidee macchiate di rosso* (1972)	66
5. His Blindness Is His Sight Sergio Pastore's *Sette scialli di seta gialla* (1972)	87
6. No Irises for Miss Landsbury Giuliano Carnimeo's *Perche quelle strane gocce di sangue sul corpo di Jennifer?* (1972)	108
7. Jealousy as Cruel as the Grave Andrea Bianchi's *Nude per l'assassino* (1975)	130
8. The Shadow of Guilt Antonio Bido's *Solamente nero* (1978)	151
9. A Night at the Opera … Without the Marx Brothers Dario Argento's *Opera* (1987)	171
10. The Return of the Repressed Lamberto Bava's *Le foto di Gioia* (1987)	192

Conclusion: A Postscript of Sorts, Not a Requiem for a Genre   212
Chapter Notes   217
Bibliography   222
Index   227

Introduction: A Crime Waiting to Be Committed

Commit a crime, and the earth is made of glass.—Ralph Waldo Emerson's *Compensation*

Any dissection of a subject, whether sacred scriptures or motion pictures, is a process of investigating a text by explicating it, for "meaning" is not intrinsic in the text itself.[1] A director's work cannot simply speak for itself, just the same way that a passage in scripture cannot simply speak for itself, Fundamentalism notwithstanding.

The interpretation of a film's text, as with scripture, is therefore problematic, capable of being construed in diverse ways, and an argument has to be made for one reading over another. If a film, as well as the Bible, could speak for itself, then everyone would agree on what it means, but each type of analytic study has its own hermeneutics to contend with. One conclusion to be drawn, therefore, is that "there is no direct way to the author's meaning in any given text, other than by the capacity of the reader … to discern analogies to his … own inner experience, as suggested by the text."[2] This stratagem will be pursued in assessing ten *gialli*'s set pieces in order, according to Friedrich Schleiermacher, "to understand the text … even better than its author."[3] To meet this formidable challenge both a structural analysis of the films' violent scenes and an investigation into prototypes of the films' characters found in 19th-century folk tales will be employed.

The word *giallo* in Italian means "yellow," from the inexpensive paperbacks with yellow covers, first issued by Mondadori in 1929, from translations of Agatha Christie, S.S. Van Dine and Earl Derr Biggers. The *giallo* film was cinematically influenced by the '60s German *Krimi* sensation, originally in black and white and likewise based on literary murder mystery models especially those of Edgar Wallace. The Italian *giallo*, branded as "exploitation cinema," where artistic merit is sacrificed for a sensationalistic display of sex, misogyny and violence, came into prominence in the early 1970s with the relaxing of cinematic taboos in Europe. But the problem with such formulaic movies is the propensity to stigmatize them as a subordinate form of the literature on which they were based instead of viewing them "as aspects of an artistic type with [their] own purposes and justification."[4] Some critics even refuse to label them as a genre since they cut across a variety of styles, but are closely related to crime and horror fiction in their depiction of femmes fatales and innocent women at the mercy of an unknown assailant. Essentially the *giallo* is a fabricated classification by critics rather than the movie industry and has withstood a straightforward designation as a genre.[5] According to Philippe Met, their classification is "a perfect illustration of the degree of arbitrariness [and] ambiguity ... inherent in any given generic categorization, theoretical systematization or notional definition."[6]

The *giallo* is one of the anomalies in moviemaking since its directors were encouraged to experiment and so radicalize '70s Italian filmmaking. These low-budget whodunits were free from restrictions imposed on the more prestigious commercial pictures and, as a result, could be quite creative. Long after their heyday in the late '80s and '90s, the *gialli* were raised to the status of classics like the American B films of the '40s and '50s that were fetishized by French cinephiles of the *Nouvelle Vague*. Being looked upon as "poor cousin" to Italy's award-winning festival movies, the *giallo*, despite its "Euro-sleaze" epitaph, exhibits a flair for aesthetic ingenuity. When the *giallo* was first seen abroad, its content was butchered and in some countries, like Britain and the United States, denied theatrical release. It had to wait for a renaissance first through VHS and then through DVD technology where its richness could be appreciated. Academe branded it as "paracinema," a dignified term for delegitimizing the *giallo* by segregating it from mainstream films.

This brief flashback now brings us to the body of works analyzed here. The *giallo*, since it is a genre formed by common thematic interrelations principally determined within its subject matter[7] dealing with crime, eroticism and mystery, embodies a comparable style and content, irrespective of the director, whose similarity can basically be observed through the films' set pieces constituting "situation[s] ... where the narrative function ... gives way to 'spectacle' playing on far longer than what is strictly necessary for the narrative purpose,"[8] sharing mutual traits involving sexuality and hyper-violence.

The book's ten chapters cover the years of the *giallo*'s rise to its eventual waning, using Mario Bava's 1963 *The Girl Who Knew Too Much* as a point of departure and ending in 1987, when the genre was in decline with Dario Argento's *Opera* and Lamberto Bava's *Delirium: Photos of Gioia*. The selection is purely personal and the films are readily available to readers who might wish to view them. The task ahead is first to probe the *giallo*'s text through a shot analysis of the formal qualities of each film's set pieces that generate suspense, paranoia and ambiguity, and second to consider the principal characters involved in those set pieces which have affinities to 19th-century folk tales found in Vladimir Propp's functions of the dramatis personae. This latter analysis can best be accomplished at the film's conclusion once the reader is acquainted with the characters and the convolution of the plots. Propp discovered that the actions of the characters, the most elemental forms of which he called functions, mandate the generic structures for a system based on narrative subject matter to delineate the way the story is told.[9] These *gialli*, with the hero/heroine in pursuit of or victimized by an unknown killer, are, according to Alan Dunes, modern fables well adaptable to Propp's 1928 *Morphology*.[10] Of Propp's 30 functions, approximately ten will be applied at the chapter's conclusion to each film covered and will include a brief summary of the function, how the character function operates within the particular story, and any subcategories within that function that pertain to a specific character. Although no formal comparison will be made linking the functions of one film with another, by reiterating these functions from film to film, the reader will recognize the affinity among the dramatis personae in the ten *gialli* analyzed. Consequently, through the analysis of the set pieces and character functions, the constitutive elements of the *giallo* will be identified. This type of close reading basically argues that the art of the *giallo* is quite extraordinary in its arrangement of formal and literary devices "encouraging the viewers' active intelligence."[11] To maintain that they are "Euro-trash" and their enjoyment "guilty pleasures" are no longer feasible positions to hold. The extent to which this has been achieved, however, is left up to the reader.

It is time to turn to the films themselves, and witness crimes committed in a world of glass where a condign punishment is meted out, despite the law's ineffectiveness, to bring the murderer to justice, where the hero, heroine or couple find tentative closure if not happiness at the conclusion, and where the very society that is so vibrantly portrayed is also so viciously criticized. The investigation begins with the picture credited for jump-starting the *giallo* in Italy, Mario Bava's *La ragazza che sapeva troppo*.

1

In the Beginning Was the *Giallo*

Mario Bava's *La ragazza che sapeva troppo* [*The Girl Who Knew Too Much*, 1962]

> *I was the world in which I walked, and what I saw*
> *Or heard or felt came not but from myself;*
> *And there I found myself more truly and more strange.*
> —Wallace Stevens, *Tea at the Palaz of Hoon*

La ragazza che sapeva troppo, considered the prototype *giallo* film, is a combination murder mystery and Gothic thriller that takes place in modern Rome. Its relationship to Gothic literature is in tune with the disposition of its heroine, Nora Davis, who is brought up reading melodramatic thrillers, like the *gialli*, and to whose heroines she bears more than fleeting resemblance. Like them, Nora is so beset by villainy that she becomes the parody of her own story. Indeed, *La ragazza* might be looked upon as a burlesque of the woman-in-distress novel of the 18th and 19th centuries, and a blueprint of things to come in a prolific breed of '70s Italian moviemaking.

My intent is to launch this study with Mario Bava's early foray into the *giallo* and its subsequent spread over a 25-year period by a host of Italian directors who made this genre a worldwide cult favorite. The *giallo* dethrones reason not only because the world presented is determined by a perversely unstable killer's dominance over it, but also because its purpose is to dramatize the irrational, at least until the finale where reason instead of chaos has to be imposed on a celluloid world to satisfy bourgeois conventions. The villain's death and the rationalization for his/her crimes serve to suture this conclusion so that the characters might reorder their lives, and the audience might be reassured that normalcy is once again established in a fictive world that bears little resemblance to their own.

La ragazza's central character is a naive young American woman, Nora Davis (Leticia Roman), brought up on lurid murder mysteries. She comes to Rome to visit a family friend (in the Italian version, an "aunt" in other versions),[1] Mrs. Ethel Windell Bartocci (Chana Coubert). One is reminded of Jane Austen's Gothic fiction parody, *Northanger Abbey* (1798). Its heroine, Catherine Morland, has been brought up on Ann Radcliffe's *The Mysteries of Udolopho* (1794) with its swooning heroine, Emily St. Aubert. Austen has the book's impressionable Miss Morland reading and imitating *Udolopho*'s heroine. The author subverts Gothic conventions on every occasion by first suggesting some frightful happening at Northanger Abbey only to deflate it afterwards with prosaic truth. Austen's pivotal theme centers on the danger of confusing life with Gothic literature. This is also true of Bava's Nora Davis,[2] but with this difference: her confusion of reality with the *gialli* she has been reading turns out to be stranger than fiction. Moreover, Bava's parody and the metatextuality of his film's title with that of Hitchcock's *The Man Who Knew Too Much* (1934, 1956) are done lovingly as an homage. Generally Bava foregrounds the style and themes of the American director's thrillers: the lighting and camera at once recalling Hitchcock's '40s films which, through their own cinematographic peculiarities, eschewed realism for artifice.[3]

To mention but one instance of intertextual transtextuality relating to Hitchcock, one needs to consider his "wrong man" motif and how Bava reworks this idea. While Nora is characterized as young and innocent (referencing Hitchcock's Erica Burgoyne in *Young and Innocent*, 1937), and does not have to prove that the man she falls in love with isn't a murderer as does Erica, Bava's heroine is forced to prove her credibility as a witness to a crime, a feat that is as difficult as Roger Thornhill's in *North by Northwest* (1959). The uncertainty of Nora's believability is even acknowledged at the conclusion by the heroine's own dubiousness about what she saw the night of the murder, thinking that the pot she smoked on the plane might have contributed to her fantasizing.

The film begins on a jet plane with the catchy if downbeat song, "Furore," by Adricel (Adriano Celentano) and Piero Vivarelli. "Furore" is a love song much like Catullus's poem "Odi et Amo" to Lesbia. But the male singer's voice is aggressively strident, bitter, and overbearing in tone which has been exacerbated by the wail of saxophones. Nora (sporting the blond hair preferred by Hitchcock) becomes a Jamesian center of vision, creating a third-person limited filmic point of view. Yet because we experience everything through her, she seems an unreliable witness to narrative events. And since she seems unreliable, the viewer can easily be deceived because, while young and innocent, we are captivated with her and face the paranoia she experiences. Soon the viewer, like Nora, begins to blur the distinctions between real and imagined fears created through spatial distinctions between on and off-screen space, editing, point of view, camera placement and movement. The irony becomes more obvious as the film progresses, for this heroine's world is both created by her imagination through the novels she reads, and an aspect of her ego through the persona she assumes, and we are submerged into that ego.[4] This irony is transferred to the viewer in the form of a paradox: while the signifiers point to an unreliable witness, the film's limited viewpoint enables the audience to identify more fully with the heroine.

Adding to this identification with Nora, the heterodiegetic male narrator supplies, in novelistic fashion, her thoughts in voice-over allowing us more closely to share the heroine's intimate feelings. But the audience relates to her story in still another way. Built into moviegoing, it must appear that images are the expression of the viewer's own desire so that we, the "subject-spectator," supplant the "subject-producer" (contributors to the film's production), and the story can appear as the moviegoer's own desire by our taking the extradiegetic narrator's place in the production of the filmic discourse.[5] This psychological method of representation wedded to point of view and the male narrator's voice-over make identification with the heroine complete.

At the same time, the viewer is forced to examine *how* that information is communicated and by *what agent* it is communicated, placing the spectator in a bind to take the events either as real or as filtered through a woman's over-excited imagination. The male narrator informs us that Nora is a 20-year-old romantic and wants to escape reality through murder mysteries. In fact she is reading *The Knife*, and so addicted has she become that Nora, we are told, has promised her mother that this will be the last novel of its kind she will read. This heterodiegetic narrator, privileged through vococentrism so that no sound on the track other than his authoritative voice is heard, creates a fiction of its own, namely, a stabilizing frame of reference out of which meaning is generated. The device imitates 18th and 19th century novelists who "took great pains to disguise their fictions as fact so they would not be accused of spreading lies."[6] The heterodiegetic narrator is similarly implemented to report on Nora's feelings, creating a verisimilitude that is, however, prejudicially patriarchal through its tone and inflection. Nora's imagination becomes the pivotal structure on which the plot revolves, and while the heterodiegetic narrator's words are spirited in tone, they are foreboding in significance, informing us that her obsession with reading *gialli* has predisposed her to regard life as a dangerous adventure, like Ann Radcliffe's heroine, Catherine Morland. Besides the marijuana she has taken, her aunt has unexpectedly died with Nora powerless to help, and alone in a foreign country she is unable to trust the opposite sex from her chance encounter with a drug dealer. These particular circumstances mitigate her credibility in authenticating a believable story.

So, in effect, the film's title is a misnomer. The heroine only thinks she knows the killer's identity, but is misinformed about what she sees. Rather than knowing *too much*, it is a question of her knowing too little too late. Like Hitchcock's *The Man Who Knew Too Much*, *La ragazza* deals with a woman on vacation in a foreign land just like Dr. Ben McKenna in Northern Africa. Whereas Nora is single, McKenna is married; whereas the American film opens on a bus, the Italian one opens on a plane. Where the central issue in Hitchcock is the exploration of the relationship between Ben and his wife Jo, the central issue in *La ragazza* is the relationship between Nora and the handsome doctor, Marcello Bassi (John Saxon). Where they both agree is that capricious and hostile happenings inform the two films.[7] *La ragazza* opens with a stranger (Milo Quesada) on the plane offering Nora a cigarette, allowing her to keep the pack. She discovers his cigarettes are not only laced with marijuana, but that he is carrying cocaine and is arrested. The plane scene references Alfred Hitchcock's *Strangers on a Train* (1951), but whereas in the American film a cigarette lighter causes Guy Haines' problems, we are led to believe that cannabis produces similar problems for Nora in misconstruing the murder to which she is a witness.

When Nora arrives at Mrs. Ethel Windell's home, she meets Dr. Bassi, which leads them eventually into becoming amateur sleuths. Ethel is introduced with a sheet over her head sitting up in bed like a ghost to welcome Nora. This apparition, quickly dispelled to provide a rational and humorous justification as in Austen's Gothic fiction parody, serves the ominous function of a shroud foreshadowing not only Ethel's sudden death from a heart attack, but a harbinger of the deadly occurrences Nora encounters. Other Gothic motifs also emerge: one being the trope of having a young woman visit a friend or relative whom she has either never seen or not seen in many years. This plot device occurs in Sheridan Le Fanu's *Uncle Silas* (1864) whose young and naive heroine, Maud Ruthyn, much like Nora, is sent to live with her reclusive Uncle Silas. The novel, like Bava's film, undermines the principles of reality and illusion and explores terror through the exploitation of the psychological frissons within the story. The interior of Mrs. Ethel's apartment is Gothic in style with dark rooms and musty, ornate, heavy furniture. Nature also contributes to the Gothic atmosphere with the cosmic elements of rain, thunder and lightning serving as objective correlatives to convey the heroine's emotional conflicts. In contrast to the tropes of the Gothic Romance, however, the action occurs in an urban setting by the Scalinata di Piazza di Spagna in Rome as opposed to an isolated, country house.

Lighting plays an essential role here, one of the last of Bava's black-and-white films. At Ethel Windell's home, with an electrical storm in progress, the utilization of low-key lighting casts ominous shadows on the otherwise unsophisticated Nora and her elderly aunt. Low-key lighting seldom creates a realistic *mise-en-scène* with sources of light springing from improbable directions, projecting ambivalent cues with which to read the characters' faces and motivations. In the case of Ethel's death, the lighting equivocally invites the audience to read the scene in a menacing way. A pin light, at one point, is directed to the tumbler with Ethel's medication, but Nora's hands clasping the glass are silhouetted by the light passing through it, giving her fingers a clawlike appearance. When Ethel abruptly dies, the glass slips out of Nora's hands and falls to the floor in shimmering incandescence. The emphasis on the illuminated glass recalls Johnny Aysgarth's walk to his wife's bedroom with a supposed glass of poisoned milk in Hitchcock's *Suspicion* (1941). The director placed a light *in* the glass to focus attention on it, while in *La ragazza* lighting is *on* the glass with its myriad reflective surfaces to suggest similar implications. Light from two sources illuminates both sides of Ethel's face, but leaves dark patches around her left eye as though it were the empty socket of a skeleton. With low-key lighting, visual objectivity gives way to stylistic paranoia. As Nora looks at Mrs. Ethel, her body appears to move as though her corpse would rise. This is immediately followed by the cause: the cat pulling at the dead woman. The reverse order, showing effect before its cause, is startling, a visual hysteron proteron, where an apparent supernatural event is deflated by unmasking the natural cause. Close shots of Nora's eyes, the dead woman's face, and the cat simulate a claustrophobic space around the images, giving the character no place to turn. Even the cat seems frozen in time, its arched back like some stylized Halloween decoration.

Because the phone is dead, Nora hurries down the Spanish Steps to St. James Hospital where Dr. Bassi works. Positioned in the background of the frame and shot with a wide-angle lens, she appears small and vulnerable, the deep focus creating an enormous distance between her and the foreground, leaving the ensuing space exposed and ominous. A man follows her, stealing her handbag and knocking her down during the resultant struggle. With a time-lapse dissolve, Nora, groggy from the experience, rises, her face lit from her left while much of the location is in semi-darkness. With the ringing of the bells of Santissima Trinità al Monte Pincio on the Spanish Steps, the young woman turns to the sound. From a subjective viewpoint, the edifice, through a distorting lens, goes in and out of focus mimicking the state of the distraught victim. As she looks up, a woman's scream segues into the sound of the bells. From Nora's viewpoint, a female emerges from the background's darkness and unsteadily walks to the midground, the camera, for a second time, distorting the focus to stress Nora's condition. There ensue crosscuts between objective shots of Nora's alarmed face and point-of-view shots of the unknown woman as she falls forward with a knife in her back. The second half of this scene parallels the first. From the same direction of the murdered woman, a man approaches from the background. Crosscutting between the stranger and Nora in hiding continues as it did between her and the victim. Bava first prolongs the suspense by backlighting the man's movement toward the corpse so that in silhouette his face is impossible to see; then from a rear shot the man turns his face to screen right, revealing the profile of a middle-aged individual with a mustache and small beard. In a reverse shot he bends over the body, pulling out the knife and throwing it away. A close-up to Nora's face, exhibiting both terror and enthrallment at the man dragging the body off, is seen through a double-vision soft-focused image. For a woman who devours murder mysteries, she now observes an event that fascinates her even as she attempts to suppress the pleasure from watching it. Freud believed that suppression of scopophilia might lead to actual disturbances of vision which Nora seems to be experiencing.[8] Add to this Otto Fenichel's theory that one "who is looking for libidinous purposes ... wants to look at an object in order to 'feel along with him,'" and that looking could substitute for acting in those anxious to avoid guilt.[9] The scene, therefore, can be read as a complex psycho-sexual portrait of Nora Davis who, confronted with her guilty pleasure, must finally faint to maintain her psychic equilibrium.

It isn't quite clear whether the subjective viewpoint with its distorting lenses is meant to convey that Nora (1) is still under the effects of marijuana or (2) is suffering from the effects of being pushed to the ground or (3) is traumatized by Ethel's sudden death or (4) her over-active imagination, exacerbated by her reading, has brought up feelings she is incapable of handling or (5) all of the above. What is important is that the visual effects communicate Nora's unreliability as a witness to the event filtered through her impressionable, misshapen viewpoint. The audience recognizes this because she tells the authorities and the doctor that she saw a man murder the woman. Yet the viewer has not seen the actual murder through Nora's limited viewpoint. She verbalizes only what she has surmised has occurred. Therefore, the focalizer, the agent who sees, is at odds with the agent who tells the story, the extradiegetic narrator, presenting a dichotomy of viewpoints. It is this narrator who has limited the audience's view by limiting what the focalizer sees. The manner in which Nora "sees" the murder is based on several facets of focalization. The perceptual facet of the heroine's sensory range involves a psychological one dealing with cognitive and emotional factors, that is, the way she processes the information she sees. But these psychological facets[10] are based on the ideological facet that concerns Nora's general system of values, and here is where the ambiguity lies. With these pre-existing conditions, her reliability as an eyewitness is tenuous at best.

Three more points about this sequence ought to be considered, the first being its erotetic nature. The term, used by Noel Carroll, refers to "situations ... that appear earlier in ... a story ... which proceed by generating a series of questions that the plot then goes on to answer."¹¹ Although the man who has pulled the knife out of the woman's body seems like the murderer, and although Nora has seen his face and can identify him, he is not the murderer but is destroying the evidence. In the final confrontation between the heroine and the real killer, Mrs. Laura Craven-Torrani (Valentina Cortese), this scene will be recalled, but now under the actual circumstances in which it transpired. Second, this "wronged man" theme resonates in the films of Hitchcock, although, in this case, Mr. Torrani is not the central character but a peripheral "red herring." Third, the mistaken identity motif in Bava's film is imitated in Argento's *L'uccello dalle piume di cristallo* (*The Bird with the Crystal Plumage*, 1970), even though Argento denies identification with Bava.¹² Since the Bava film came out seven years before the Argento picture, there is only coincidental evidence that Argento appropriated this concept from Bava. In the Argento film, Sam Dalmas, an American writer living in Rome, sees Monica Ranieri being attacked at night in an art gallery by a mysterious man. It is later learned that Carlo Ranieri, the husband of the woman, was in fact attacked by his wife. In the process, Monica was wounded. Her husband had attempted to cover up for her. Like Sam Dalmas, Nora is an American visiting Rome. She is not a novelist but is an avid novel reader. She believes she sees a murder being committed, and also believes, like Sam, she knows the murderer's identity. Dalmas is positive he has witnessed an attempted murder of a woman. While he is unable to come to the woman's aid because of the locked art gallery doors, Nora in Bava's film is prevented from coming to the aid of the woman because of her physical and emotional condition. In the Bava rendition, as in Argento, a husband attempts to cover up the murders his deranged wife has committed. Whereas Argento ties the murders to a psychosexual trauma suffered in childhood by the wife (a typical Bava trope), Bava's insane woman kills those, including her sister, who want to put her away in order to inherit their father's wealth. These parallels are strong enough to suggest that Argento had a passing acquaintance with Bava but, perhaps, wanted to divorce himself from Italian influences and attribute his inspiration to directors like Lang, Hitchcock, Lewton, and Godard.

Nora, lying by the Spanish Steps, is attemptedly revived by a man with a whiskey flask who, upon seeing a police officer, runs away. The officer, smelling alcohol on her and noticing her hysterical condition, takes her to St. James's Hospital, where she was originally headed. Shooting from low-angle close-ups, simulating Nora's perspective, Bava makes the doctors, sisters, and police loom vauntingly over her. The close shots of Nora taken from their perspective are from a high angle causing her to seem defenseless. The police officer, believing she has dreamed the murder, is abetted by the utilization of Nora's blurred double-vision shots that call into question her physical and mental state. The officer, knowing her reading habits, cautions her, like her mother, to give up such books. This, coupled with the photography, bolsters again the sentiment of her undependability as observer. To further cast doubts on Nora, a doctor believes she has mythomania, losing sense of time and place. More importantly, mythomania, known as false memory syndrome, results in the sufferer believing that fictitious events or fantasies have really taken place. Indeed, for all the trauma that Nora has already undergone, together with her highly imaginative nature, it is possible that she can mentally mythologize herself and the events around her to mimic the situations in her books. The doctor concludes that Nora is a victim of delusion.

The next sequence is meant to pit the rational against the fanciful and to draw Nora and Dr. Bassi together in their pursuit of truth. We return, in a long, low camera angle shot, to the Spanish Steps with Nora and the doctor in the foreground, their backs to the audience looking at the Trinità al Monte Pincio in the background. Both are not centered in the frame, but rather are to left of frame creating an imbalance that connotes their divided opinions. The young lady's life has been turned upside down, and Marcello remains skeptical about what she has witnessed. The dichotomy is set up between reason and feeling where the doctor, as scientist with his rational intellect, is pitted against the individual "Romantic" with her "irrational" fears. The doctor believes in rules that nature must conform to, not the delirious opinions of a frightened and impressionable woman. The doctor's life is governed by singleness of mind, normality in behavior and orderliness in his work. Consequently it is logical for Bassi's analytic mind to assume that if the police have uncovered no clues, it is Nora who must be wrong. Thus begins the overriding aspect of the plot's structure: *to prove Nora's veracity in order to justify her sanity*. This infinitive phrase propels the story forward and unites the couple in romance through sleuthing.

Nora wants to convince Marcello of her truthfulness by reconstructing the murder scene. Bava brackets her remarks by two seemingly inconsequential incidents: a photographic shot and two children playing a game. As the heroine runs up the Spanish Steps with the doctor, the camera reveals a fashion photographer setting up models for a shoot. The foregrounding of this event reinstates the notion of the camera as a recording device that creates a fictive reality of an event by hyper-idealizing it. The models are glamorized for magazine consumption through their positioning in the frame and the use of various lenses, much like the director's use of the film camera for the movie audience. Nora, being the focalizer of the crime scene, becomes the audience's camera, filtering, through her memory, a version of the reality before her. If the photographer's camera can "lie the truth" and make the scene and the models more flawless than they are, hasn't Bava's camera done the same by contorting reality through various lenses to make us believe that Nora was possibly hallucinating? This is the first half of the director's brack-

Nora (Leticia Roman) mimes, in histrionic fashion, for Dr. Bassi (John Saxon), the murder she witnessed, but proves to be unreliable and must earn his respect regarding her veracity (Mario Bava's *La ragazza che sapeva troppo*).

eting strategy. The second half occurs when a shot is heard and Nora throws herself, like the heroine of a romance, into Marcello's arms. Bava zooms in to a house on the Spanish Steps allowing the tension to increase, the zoom intimating that something momentous is to unfold. The anticipated violence is dissipated when, in still another example of hysteron proteron, two little boys playing cowboys and Indians appear from out of the door. Marcello laughs saying that these are the only crimes she'll see in Rome. Yet at the film's conclusion, gunfire will ring out again from this house as Professor Torrani shoots his wife before she has a chance to kill Nora.

Together with the fashion photo shoot, the scene with the children bookends Nora's statements by deflating her argument and making her look rather ridiculous, although she has already done so by her sensational reconstruction of the murder, histrionically miming the victim's reactions to the accompaniment of melodramatic music with heavy drumbeats, woodwinds and base violas. What the bracketed scenes create is a *mise-en-abîme* by symbolically reduplicating the contrasting motifs of reality and artifice in referencing the textual whole of Nora's reconstruction of events. Her "reconstruction" has been linked to playacting giving a preferred reading to Dr. Bassi's interpretation of crime in Rome. The gestural codes Nora employs to describe the murder disconnect her from concrete reality, placing her in the fanciful world she has constructed out of her readings. All along the extradiegetic narrator sets up situations in which the heroine is given a chance to prove her point to a second party only to have that proof discredited by a variety of signifiers that make her appear foolish. One of the characteristics of the *giallo* is to deny credibility to what the focalizer witnesses, thereby precluding an authoritative viewpoint for the moviegoer. The paranoia created in the character must in turn be transferred to the audience, fabricating in them a moral/emotional anxiety.

Unbeknownst to her, Nora fleetingly meets the murderer, the beautiful Mrs. Laura Craven-Torrani, whose nephews have just left with their nanny. Asking if she can be of help, Nora replies that now she "sees." Her "seeing" recalls the voyeuristic experience the previous night, but the heroine only thinks she "sees," and is mistaken in trusting this woman, just as she is mistaken in trusting her judgment surrounding the murder she has witnessed. Nora places confidence in the domestic signs surrounding Laura, because the female sex appears guiltless to her, having been deceived by men since she came to Rome and having read so many mysteries where the heroine is the victim of male aggression.

As Nora and Marcello walk away, a man, his back to the camera, observes their departure up the Spanish Steps. As part of the film's erotic function and in keeping with the *giallo*'s ambivalency, this character's presence generates questions about his narrative function that are eventually answered. His voyeuristic inclinations are emphasized by a jump cut to a cemetery where Nora's aunt is being buried, and where he is seen concealed behind a tree. It is here Nora meets Laura Craven-Torrani for a second time. She takes Nora to her home saying that Ethel was a friend of hers. The man watching Nora also follows. Discordant cords from a harp are plucked as he walks up the Spanish Steps, predisposing the audience to read the scene negatively. Laura invites Nora to house-sit while she visits her husband in Switzerland, remarking that her husband's study is the only locked room to which her spouse has the key. As they leave the frame the camera emphasizes the locked room with a dolly to the doorknob followed by a quick cut and a zoom in to a photograph of Laura's husband on the baby grand that Nora has not seen. He is the same man observed pulling the knife out of the murdered woman's back, making an emphatic linkage between the locked door and the man who possesses its key. Although *La ragazza* is not a locked-room mystery, the director amusingly borrows the basic trappings of the locked-room mystery and conflates them with the prohibition found in Perrault's *Bluebeard* (1697).

Mario Bava's La ragazza che sapeva troppo *(1962)*

The manner in which the hands are clasped and Nora's (Leticia Roman, right) passivity as she is led on by the villain (Valentina Cortese, left) with her penetrating look and deceptive smile indicate who controls the scene's perceptual facet (Mario Bava's *La ragazza che sapeva troppo*).

At the film's conclusion a murder is committed in this locked room and the solution to the original murder, as well as all the others committed, is clearly explained by the perpetrator herself.

When the image dissolves from the photo of Laura's husband to the empty frame, the time lapse indicates that Laura has gone to Switzerland and Nora is now in possession of the house. The housekeeper feels it's nice to have Nora living there because the apartment is always locked up. She hasn't seen Mr. Torrani in years, and Laura can't bear to be here since her sister was stabbed to death ten years ago in front of the house. Once more the erotetic elements come into play. We have moved from the locked room to a locked house. The master of the house, who hasn't been seen in many years, is the man Nora saw the night of the murder, and the 10-year-old murder of Mrs. Craven-Torrani's sister recalls what Nora had seen the night before. When the domestic leaves, the same man who has followed Nora, his back again to the camera, watches the house. A heterodiegetic narrator's voice (male) reproduces Nora's thoughts about news of the murder committed 10 years ago, but while conflating it with the one Nora witnessed, the narrator presents a woman unsure of what she has seen, her ruminations peppered with words like "what if," "perhaps," "could" and "maybe." The creation of this mimetic stratum authenticates the heroine's uncertainty, the words themselves being conditional and the sentences mostly interrogative ("But what?"), questioning whether the recent crime could have been perpetrated under the same circumstances. Once again the heroine's reliability is mitigated, even though Nora is the audience's primary interpreter of the sign transmitting the information. The film tracks female subjectivity and desire in both subject matter and modes of address in terms of fantasies traditionally and stereotypically related with the feminine. Nora, for example, manifests signs of hysteria through her consumption of murder mysteries, through anxiety about male strangers (on the plane, on the Spanish Steps, in the hospital), through phallic knives and cigarettes and finally through the film's optical devices[13] conveyed by camera placement, distorting lenses and angles.

Nora accidently discovers a box of news clippings by the reporter, Andrea Landini (Dante Di Paolo), on murders alphabetically committed according to the victims' surnames and of an anonymous call that precedes each crime. The customary male narrator[14] gives way to Nora's own voice-over (homodiegetic narration) as she speculates upon the clippings. She also discovers alphabet blocks and picks up the letter *D*. A phone suddenly rings and a woman's voice asks who is on the line. The heroine gives her name as Davis and the voice answers, "as in death?" As Nora puts down the phone there is a cut to a turkey being carved at a restaurant table where a professor is talking to Nora and Marcello. Here, Nora is humorously likened to a turkey ready to be carved up like the Craven-Torrani woman ten years ago. Although in American slang "turkey" carries an additional meaning of "stupid" or "inept" (1951) that an Italian director might not be cognizant of, it seems suited to Nora who's eyes widen when she talks about witnessing a murder while the professor tells Nora that she hasn't been hallucinating but "psychic travel[ing]." Marcello, the voice of reason, just laughs. Over a close-up of a wide-eyed Nora, the heterodiegetic narrator adds that only the truth, at the risk of her life, could restore her sleep. The narrator amplifies the melodrama by verbally foregrounding her facial expression, hyperbolizing Nora's character as a woman who enjoys playing the dramatic role of "heroine" in her own story. The idea of a female solving a mystery unaided harkens back to 19th-century literary heroines and a biologistic determination that pits her against the traditional rules of feminine dependence while simultaneously mocking her credulity.

From the restaurant there is a cut to Nora alone at night by her house in the frame's background, taken from an extreme high-angled long shot. Menacing mysterioso music of oboe and strings is heard while hands appear in shadow at the frame's bottom right foreground lighting a cigarette; the figure moves forward a bit so that he is seen in medium shot blocking out Nora's figure in the background. This configuration of sound, lighting, music and blocking is used in visual reply to the words just voiced: "alone ... at the risk of her life." Seen this way, she cuts a Lilliputian figure which is increased by the angle and her placement in the frame. The hand coming suddenly from the frame's foreground is indeed horrific in appearance due to its proximity to the camera, much like the appearance of hands on bannisters in James Whale's *The Old Dark House* (1932) and Jacques Tourneur's *Night of the Demon* (1958). What makes matters more dire is the man completely obliterating Nora's figure as though annihilating her simply by his physical presence. The mood music attempts to give weight to the melodramatic situation and to confirm his seemingly nefarious intentions. Since screen space, with its noir lighting, more readily becomes an extension of the darkened theater space, the viewer is invited to enter the *mise-en-scène* and participate in a regime of belief, but is incapable of warning Nora.

Over an anxious shot of Nora entering the house, the male narrator asserts her isolation, providing a chance for assault. The director's antic behavior is obvious in using the narrator to express Nora's delusional theatrics by presenting her unremitting conflict that incapacitates her judgment. Interestingly, the director has seen fit to tell the story from Nora's limited perspective and from a character-narrator who doesn't appear in the story but whose voice is heard. This limitation is crucial in creating suspense and breeding melodramatic paranoidal feelings pointing to Nora's persecution complex where everything seems against her, a characteristic of the Gothic heroine whose disorder is expressed as a conflict between the overly suspicious self and the external world. Adding to this the locked door is emphasized a second time with a zoom in to it and Nora's attempt to open it. Pushing the handle down, it remains in that position until she is a short distance away. Then Bava creates a frisson by having it snap back loudly; the third and final time the handle will be emphasized is at the conclusion.

Nora's isolation engenders her eccentric behavior. To protect herself, she devises a plan by calling upon her "old friends" such as Edgar Wallace, Mickey Spillane and Agatha Christie. She covers the floor with talcum powder, the histrionic narrator's voice hissing the word as though not to be overheard. Suddenly the film's melodrama descends into intentional bathos becoming even more effective in satirizing the mystery genre. Nora's idée fixe, to protect herself at all costs, is rendered monumentally facetious through the voice-over. The narrator has jettisoned his role in creating a melodramatic effect and is now overtly making sport of the character,[15] invoking a novelistic set of visual images of delusion within Nora. We are told that spreading talcum powder over the floor and booby-trapping the room with strings is naive, but that fortunately Italian murderers wouldn't have read mysteries like *Ariadne's Terrible String* since they haven't as yet been translated. The shadow of a cloaked figure appears outside her bedroom window, moves around to the front of the house, opens the door, and walks in. He is one of the *polizia* and is attacked from behind by Marcello who, ensnared by the string, falls into Nora's trap as various bric-a-brac come tumbling down on him when he hits the floor. Once again the *hysteron proteron* device sets up a threatening situation only to deflate it while culminating in comic relief. Much of what occurs in *La ragazza* is only the appearance of actuality, as though we are watching two films: one that deals with the reality of a crime and the other that seems to deny its ontological reality. Here Nora is conflated with the mythical Ariadne and her ball of string, but this Ariadne, instead of helping her lover, Theseus/Marcello, has entangled him in the labyrinth of twine, reversing the mythological story and providing the audience a laugh at the heroine's expense. Likewise, the law officer is first observed as shadowy horror film stalker, and until he is seen at the front door, the impression is terrifying.

At night Nora receives a phone call and takes a taxi which stops at an apartment building. She enters an unfurnished and deserted apartment with bare white walls and ceiling lights swaying by a wind from an open window. A man's voice tells Nora to reach the corridor's end, warning caution since she has seen too much for one whose name begins with *D*. A lit room at the corridor's end suddenly is darkened at Nora's approach. These composite signs form a narrative tactic of equivocation through the joining of truth with deception, for while focusing attention on the mystery, the signs also help to deepen it. Momentarily unanswered is the fact that someone has watched her enter the building, someone has summoned the elevator after her, and someone's disembodied voice speaks to her. In the darkened room she almost faints but is caught by Marcello, telling him that the message she received said the murder was real, and for her to meet the caller. Pulling Marcello away from the door she injures his index finger again, which he has in a cast since he was booby-trapped in her home. This rigidly phallic finger, a running joke, is the sign of his impotence and the price he must pay for being associated with a single-minded woman. The story now swings in a different direction: Marcello finally believes Nora has witnessed a murder, and her feelings of isolation are put aside now that the couple is a team.

The pair straightaway searches out the newsman, Andrea Landini, who wrote about the "alphabet murders." During their search, the scene on the beach at Ostia reveals more of Nora's phobias through the continued employment of *hysteron proteron*. Marcello menacingly moves toward her as the music underlines this danger; she yells for help and he tells her that it's time to end this as though he is about to kill her, but instead he kisses her. After all the time she has spent with Marcello, after he has proclaimed his belief in her, she nonetheless cannot fully trust him, and through him, other men. It is assumed that her repressed fears, brought about by her addiction to mystery stories and her negative encounters with men, are the cause: she has been given marijuana by one, beaten by another, had liquor poured down her throat by a third and her credibility defamed by a doctor who called her a neurotic. But once this scene at Ostia has passed, Nora looks to Marcello for help, and this comes immediately. An elliptical match cut from Marcello's kissing Nora on the beach is segued to his kissing her at the door to her house. The couple's "playfulness" recalls Hitchcock's lovers and partners: Richard Hannay and Pamela in *The 39 Steps* (1935), Richard Ashenden and Elsa in *Secret Agent* (1936), Robert Tisdall and Erica Burgoyne in *Young and Innocent*, and L.B. Jeffries and Lisa Fremont in *Rear Window* (1954). Marcello wants to make love, but she tells him he will know by the way she pronounces his name. Humor, at the heroine's expense, deflates her romantic plea because, upon opening her door, she calls out Marcello's name in terror when she discovers Andrea Landini in her house, closely connecting terror with the ludicrous.[16] The search for the newsman has served the function of uniting Nora and the doctor, confirming their tenuous love and increasing the tension surrounding the elusive Landini.

Landini recounts his investigation of the "Alphabet Murders" so that while the story has been, up to this point, chronological, there now appears an external analepsis or flashback covering a period ten years prior to the present events at the launching of the murders. Back in the present, Landini concludes that the presumed killer, Straccianeve, is innocent while the journalist keeps returning for clues to the crime scene despite Professor Torrani's assertion of the murderer's guilt. At this point the analepsis becomes internal, filling the gap in the primary narrative. The journalist begins where he found Nora unconscious on the steps and tried to revive her with liquor, running away when a policeman approached. He followed Nora because she had witnessed a murder and he had to speak to her. The story's erotetic structure has now cleared up one important point, the identity of the stranger spying on Nora and his reason for doing so. Consequently, he is no longer viewed as a threat, but a potential support in solving the mystery: not only Marcello but Landini believes her story.

Subsequently, Landini unearths information from a cleaning lady at the Foro Italico who knew Straccianeve's sister and telephones Nora to come to his hotel where he will explain everything. His response to Nora creates a suspended answer, an aphasic stoppage of the disclosure, which hints at a significant revelation only to veer away from the revelation until the film's finale. When Nora arrives at Landini's she hears his typewriter. This progressive diegeticization of sound starts in the hallway outside Landini's rooms and continues within and on through a slow pan across the room. The camera zooms in to the typewriter to underscore that no keys are moving and continues its pan until it comes to rest on the audiotape machine. The suspense and eeriness created by the off-screen sound is acute, reminding us of the disembodied voice on the tape in the empty apartment. Nora, unsettled by the noise, reads an unsigned confession to the alphabet murders on Landini's typewriter. She also spies several folders each with a consecutive letter of the alphabet. The fourth folder, with Nora's photo, has a question mark after the letter *D*. She then discovers Landini's body with a bullet to his head, but isn't convinced that he killed himself. Back at her apartment, she notices a news article entitled "Murder Victim Found Stabbed in the Back." The camera zooms in to the woman's face inserted in the article. The heterodiegetic narrator, in a half whisper as though not to be overhead, is quick to point out that Nora recognizes the female who was murdered in the Piazza di Spagna. This patterned progression vindicating Nora's veracity begins with Marcello, then Landini and ends with a news article that confirms Nora's claim so that the very group she needs to win over, the police, now have objective evidence.

In the morgue Nora identifies the body of Straccianeve's daughter as the victim she saw that night. Laura Craven-Torrani killed her because she had been blackmailing her. The inspector then shows Nora a button, which she steals, that the woman had ripped off the jacket of the man who pulled the knife from her back. The narrator tells us that Nora had seen it before and was willing to go to any length to discover the truth. The erotetic structure that imposes itself on the narrative comes full circle from the time Nora was asked to house-sit. The viewer is brought back to the locked study door which seemingly holds the key to the purloined button. Nora observes "the threatening door with its invisible hinges ... that was forever locked." The words themselves contribute to the plot's heightened emotions becoming the linguistic signifiers of melodrama with their charged adjectives: "threatening" and "invisible" together with the adverb "forever." The voice-over continues reporting that Nora had to find the courage to open the door which contained the answer to all her fears and the solution to the mystery that lay behind it. The imperatives in the narration build up an urgency to action: "must open," "had to find." They underscore the justification to violate the implied interdiction of Laura Craven-Torrani not to open the study door. The repetition of the word "solution" is used to accentuate its importance in relieving Nora's troubled mind. But again this develops into a suspended answer as Nora, instead of trying to open the door, phones Dr. Bassi.

Ironically, after this buildup, Nora discovers the study door unlocked and that a maddened Laura has stabbed her husband in the back. As is the case in all *gialli*, everything is revealed in the conclusion, this time by the villain who, in alphabetical order, murdered others indiscriminately, throwing police off the track. She kills her sister who wanted to inherit the family fortune because Laura is insane, she kills Landini's daughter who wanted to blackmail her, and finally she kills her husband who wanted to incarcerate her. Now Nora has to be murdered. In a sensational concluding scene, the dying Professor Torrani shoots his wife through the closed door from the anteroom he is in. Light streams through the bullet holes in the door as his wife drops to the floor. In *La ragazza che sapeva troppo*, the villain's death comes from an unexpected source other than the protagonist.

In the concluding coda of the Italian print, Nora and Marcello are together on the Pincio gazing out in the distance to St. Peter's. He looks for cigarettes, and she unintentionally gives him the marijuana laced ones, but realizing it knocks it out of his mouth and throws the pack away. A priest walking by below, picks the pack up and Bava slyly suggests that another adventure might begin.

One more detail needs to be discussed in light of the film's structure and in view of the other films that will be analyzed. Bava's narrative underpinnings are consistent with those of folk tales as defined by Vladimir Propp in his *Morphology of the Folktale*. Propp arrived at the conclusion that there were 31 generic "narratemes" (smallest narrative unit) in Russian folk tales.[17] Naturally not all these characteristics need apply to *La ragazza* to qualify, but enough of them do to warrant the assumption that the *giallo* has the necessary attributes of a folk tale.

1. **A member of the family leaves home (I).**

Nora Davis is an American visiting Rome to stay with an aunt, but this form of absentation does not have to be as significant as a trip abroad. Propp lists more commonplace occurrences which will be spoken of in relation to other films. Absentation includes any circumstance that takes the character away from his/her own dwelling regardless of the distance.

2. **An interdiction is addressed to the heroine (II).**

Interdictions can be in the form of "requests," "advice," an "order/command" or even a "suggestion" given to the protagonist. The first interdiction is given by Nora's mother as a command before the film begins but repeated by the narrator: not to read any more murder mysteries. Once her aunt dies, the absentation of elders creates an opportune moment for Nora's misfortune. The second interdiction takes the form of advice from Dr. Bassi to forget all that has happened to her since her arrival in Rome. After the burial of Mrs. Windell, Nora meets the villain, Mrs. Laura Craven-Torrani, and this brings on a third interdiction in the form of a request: Nora is given free rein over Laura's house with the exception of one room that she is not allowed in—the study of Laura's husband, Professor Torrani. The villain, at this point, has entered the story.

3. The interdictions are violated (III).

Propp states that "a fulfilled order corresponds ... to a violated interdiction." Nora, while fulfilling the order not to read further murder mysteries, violates its spirit by using the lessons she has learned from them in an attempt to discover the identity of the murdered woman and clear herself from being considered delusional, but finds herself involved in a real-life mystery. This also contravenes Dr. Bassi's advice. An additional interdiction is also attemptedly violated by Nora who is provoked at least twice into opening the door to Professor Torrani's study, and eventually, in the story's resolution, does open it. If this were one of Propp's folk tales, Laura Craven-Torrani would be considered a "witch" who, behind the scenes, manipulates the heroine by frightening her as Nora becomes too inquisitive.

4. The villain receives information about her victim (V).

After Ethel's burial, Laura Craven-Torrani meets Nora in the cemetery. The young lady has been telling the priest at the service about the murder she has witnessed. Laura, the murderer, hearing this information, asks Nora if she is alone in Rome. Nora recognizes the woman she saw by the Spanish Steps, but before she can answer the villain's question, the priest intervenes saying that Nora needs friends and he feels he can count on Laura's help. In this case the careless act of the priest and Nora's disclosure allow the villain to know her victim is alone in Rome and that she has witnessed a murder.

5. The villain attempts to deceive the victim in order to take possession of her (VI).

Craven-Torrani immediately assumes the disguise of a normal, helpful, caring friend, empathizing in the death of Nora's aunt, and artfully persuading her to stay in her own home, thus enabling her to keep an eye on Nora. Nora pleads that she couldn't accept such an offer of hospitality, but gives in because she is homeless and has no friends in Rome. The villain uses other means of deception. Picking up an article of clothing left on a chair, Laura complains about the maid's untidiness especially if no one is around to supervise so that Nora's being there will be a help. Nora now uses her mother in America as an excuse, not knowing where her daughter would be staying. Laura puts her arm around Nora's shoulder in friendly concern responding that she should call her mother so she will know her new address. This incident is another critical point in Nora's accepting Mrs. Craven-Torrani's invitation, as it allows Nora to tell her mother that she is going to prove that the murder she witnessed was not a figment of her imagination.

6. The victim submits to deception and thereby unwittingly helps her enemy (VII).

Although the villain has not caused the death of Mrs. Ethel, she takes advantage of Nora's impossible position: left in a foreign city with her aunt dead, Nora accepts Laura's offer to stay at her house since to remain at Mrs. Windell's is either impossible, because she doesn't have the right to the deceased woman's apartment, or if able to do so, it would bring unpleasant memories of her aunt's last hours and Nora's inability to save her. Nora is caught between a rock and a hard place, and Laura knows this. At first the meeting between Laura and Nora in the cemetery seems fortuitous so that the viewer is not privy to the deception, but it is soon evident that Nora is in danger by the telephone call she receives as soon as she takes possession of Laura's house. Upon the accidental discovery of the newspaper clippings on the alphabet murders, she gets a threatening phone call as if the caller could see what Nora had uncovered. The caller, in a disguised voice, insinuates that Nora will be the next victim of the alphabet murderer.

7. **The villain causes harm or injury to a member of a family (VIII).**

Propp considers this function "exceptionally important since … the actual movement of the tale is created. [All previous categories] prepare the way for this function."[18] Propp also states that the patterns villainy takes are considerably diverse and lists 18 different forms. The pattern that expressly pertains to this film is subcategory #8: "The villain … entices her victim," usually "the result of a deceitful agreement." The description of this has already been noted in VI above. If Nora didn't accept Laura's invitation to stay at her house, she would never have been placed in an increasingly dangerous situation, her reliance on and romantic involvement with Dr. Marcello Bassi might never come to fruition, and she would be unable to prove that she actually did witness a homicide. There are other forms of villainy that also apply. "The villain commits murder" (subcategory #14): The crime Nora witnesses is the murder of Straccianeve's daughter who attempts to blackmail Laura because she knows Laura has killed her own sister but is subsequently killed by Laura; Professor Torrani running after the daughter to cover his wife's crime, is also an accomplice. Subcategory #18, "The villain torments at night," is also relevant since most of the infamy happens in the evening. Aunt Ethel's death sends Nora out into the streets at night to find Dr. Marcello Bassi where she witnesses the first murder and is mugged; telephone calls to Nora are at night, particularly one which tells her to go to an address where she finds a message on a tape recorder. Nora's discovery of Andrea Landini's body takes place during the day, but it is suggested that this has happened the night before. Finally Nora, at night, opens the room thought to be locked in the Craven-Torrani house, and the deranged Laura, who has just mortally wounded her husband, confesses to the murder of her sister and is about to kill Nora.

8. **The heroine is tested and attacked which prepares the way of her receiving a helper/donor (XII).**

This again has many variants with Propp listing ten. Subcategory #3 states: "A dying person requests the rendering of a service." Just before dying, Mrs. Ethel Windell requests that Nora give her the medicine on the night table. Nora prepares it but at that point the aunt dies and Nora drops the glass of medication. When she attempts to call the hospital the telephone line is filled with static from the storm and she runs into the night to seek Dr. Bassi; this act prepares the way of her receiving the doctor as an assistant, for once outside Ethel's house she witnesses a murder, is mugged, is left unconscious and finally is taken to a hospital and pronounced "delusional," but is befriended by Marcello, the young doctor on the staff.

The second variant (#8) states that "A hostile creature attempts to destroy the heroine." The means used are psychological not physical, that is, until the conclusion. Nora is given threatening messages on the phone, on tape, and by extension newspaper articles dealing with the alphabet murders. Those murdered around her presage her own death: (1) the alphabet victim Nora first encounters on the Spanish Steps; (2) Andrea Landini, the journalist whose body she discovers; (3) Professor Torrani who is mortally wounded in her presence by his wife; and finally (4) Nora herself who is about to be killed by Laura.

Within the broader function of category XII, Propp places "Disputants request a division of property" (#6) as one of the conceivable means of systematizing the folk tale. This subcategory applies to the villain for it constitutes the basic reason for the murders that have been committed—the Craven-Torrani inheritance precipitates all the other murders including Nora's near fatality.

One other subcategory under the "testing" function may also be entertained. "The donor greets and interrogates the heroine" (#2). Dr. Marcello Bassi meets Nora at the home of her aging friend's house and is immediately attracted to her as she is to him. He gives her his number at the hospital in case Mrs. Ethel's condition should change. After Nora's ordeal on the Spanish Steps and when she gets out of the hospital, Dr. Bassi gently interrogates the all too willing heroine about the crime she witnessed which he assumes is imaginary. Only when he follows her to an empty apartment and discovers the intimidating taped voice does he believe her and she is rewarded by his help.

9. **The villain is defeated (XVIII).**

Laura Craven-Torrani is killed without a preliminary fight (subcategory #5) with the heroine. Nora confronts Laura Craven-Torrani in the unlocked study of Professor Torrani who has already been stabbed by his wife. This sequence becomes a one-sided combat since Laura, deranged and armed, holds all the cards. The murderess pleads her case before the young woman and asks Nora to believe her insane story regarding the alphabet murders which, according to Mrs. Craven-Torrani's unhinged reasoning, are quite logical. In the same manner she tells Nora that she must kill her too. The dying professor kills his wife before she is able to harm Nora. Intriguing, neither of the two main characters brings Laura to justice: Marcello is not present at the scene and Nora is powerless to do anything but plead for her life. In fact, the lovers' sleuthing does not uncover the killer's identity and only Nora's curiosity at the unlocked study door brings her face to face with Laura Craven-Torrani.

10. **The heroine is married (XXXI)**.

It would seem that after the death of Laura Craven-Torrani the bridegroom and his "kingdom" are awarded at once (subcategory #1) to Nora as the logical outcome of their adventures together. Marcello lovingly lays down the law to his bride-to-be by announcing their forthcoming marriage as he and Nora look over Rome. The patriarchal order is quickly established: (1) Marcello takes control by reminding Nora to stop brooding over Landini's death, implying that it is enough for her to be his wife, an unpardonable way to comfort her considering all she has been through. (2) Nora, forgetting that she still has marijuana-laced cigarettes, gives one to Marcello and then, realizing her mistake, pulls the cigarette out of his mouth and throws the pack away where it is picked up by a passing priest. Nora still appears the befuddled blond who needs a man to bring meaning into her life. She cannot become the self-reliant heroine of her mystery novels for she cannot tell Marcello the truth about the cigarettes for fear of being laughed at; she even questions her own experiences thinking they might have been a marijuana-induced fantasy. The intimation is that she will live a very proper married existence without the excitement of her novels to brighten up her day. (3) In the English-language version Nora, promising Marcello that she will never mention the subject of murder again, sees a man shoot his unfaithful sweetheart and her lover, but acts as though nothing has happened in order to please him. This ending portrays a submissive Nora, ridiculing her blind obedience to Marcello in order to maintain the relationship and lead a secure life.

2

A Vice in Common

Sergio Martino's
Lo strano vizio della Signora Wardh
[*The Strange Vice of Mrs. Wardh*, 1970]

> I remember reading with a horror ... the way the martyrs ... suffered the most dreadful fates with something like joy. From then on, agony, gruesome torture seemed like a pleasure.
> —Leopold von Sacher-Masoch, *Venus in Furs*

Lo strano vizio della Signora Wardh, coming early in Sergio Martino's career, garnered him a tailor-made reputation in the slasher genre. The film opens with a biologistic quote from Sigmund Freud: "We are descended from an unbroken chain of generations of assassins for whom the love of murder was in their blood, as it is perhaps in ours too," informing the viewer of atavistic transgressive tendencies of which we might not be fully aware. This idea of transgression and taboo, the dual mechanism that complements and strengthens antisocial behavior, is articulated more fully by Cyndy Hendershot in claiming that Georges Bataille's "understanding of taboo and transgression ... does not posit transgression as an act that undermines taboo ... [but] completes and reinforces it." The quote is particularly applicable to *Lo strano vizio*, combining masochistic violence through an arsenal of phallic symbols coercively expressing the killer's desire. Bataille explains the disturbing relationship between sex and violence:

> The lover strips the beloved of her identity.... She is brusquely laid open to the violence of the sexual urges set loose in the organs of reproduction; she is laid open to the impersonal violence that overwhelms her from without.[1]

This conflation of eroticism and violence finds its ideal in Martino's heroine, Mrs. Julie Wardh (Edwige Fenech), an affluent woman in a heady milieu of ennui, seeking diversion from a wearisome marriage and from the guilt of sadomasochistic cravings through parties and new lovers. Correspondingly, the occupation of Martino's males is barely hinted at. Julie's husband, Neil (Alberto de Mendoza), is a prominent man in finance, but one never sees him at work—only his absences from his wife are noted. Jean (Ivan Rassimov), Mrs. Wardh's ex-lover, dallies with photography, but with the exception of a few photographs of models in his mansion, his only tangible employment is tormenting Julie. George Corro (George Hilton), independently wealthy, spends his time in pursuit of Julie. Divorced from the reality of a work-a-day world, Martino's characters lose themselves in acts of deceit and murder: from the outwardly affectionate husband who plots his wife's death; to Julie's newly acquired lover, George, who only feigns love; to her former lover, Jean, who is paid to murder her. In this insulated world, trust is inconceivable, love is an illusion and eroticism leads to violence.

Within the characters resides a bloodlust that, in Freud's quote, references the archetypal slaying of Abel by Cain in Genesis ("we are descended from an unbroken chain of generations of assassins") through a string of murders and attempted murders: Julie's attempted killing by carbon monoxide, Carroll Baxter's (Cristina Airoldi) slaying with a razor in the park, Jean's murder by George, a partygoer's homicide in her shower and an unsuccessful attack against an airline stewardess in her home. At the conclusion we learn that Neil and George have the same motivation in killing the women they purportedly love: Neil wants Julie's money to stave off bankruptcy, and George wants his cousin Carroll's inheritance for himself. Thus, Neil will kill Carroll so that her death will be blamed on the Vienna serial killer, while George will have Jean kill Julie to make her death look like a suicide. Jean's motivation in carrying out Neil's bidding to slay Julie is monetary, but it is also in retribution for Julie's leaving him when their lovemaking became too bizarre. The planned murders of Julie and Carroll hint at the crisscross murders in Hitchcock's *Strangers on a Train*.

The film opens with the "Vienna Slasher" stalking prostitutes and butchering them for sexual gratification, his blade replacing his phallus as an instrument of pleasure/pain, approximating Jean's brutality toward Julie by slashing her body with broken glass to achieve orgasm. Julie's transgressive memories of Jean centering on eros and fatality, used as chronotopic metaphors to organize the film's structure, are four in number and occur during times of stress.

Flashback 1: During a torrential rain, Jean slaps Julie about and then rapes her.

Flashback 2: Jean pours alcohol over Julie's body and breaks the glass around her.

Flashback 3: Images of the "dead" Jean and Carroll appear along with George.

Flashback 4: Images of Jean's bloody body in a bathtub.

Jean's sadistic lovemaking has caused Julie alternately to isolate herself physically from him and seek him out in her fantasies. For instance, flashbacks 1 and 2 pinpoint the impact of Jean's viciousness toward her, but flashbacks 3 and 4, dealing with Jean's "death," illustrate even more Julie's inability to block out memories of his "bloody corpse" that simultaneously frighten and fascinate her.

Concomitant to the four flashbacks are the four notes Julie receives, always accompanied with vivid red roses constituting an alarming trope on obsession and death.

Note 1: Julie, about to take a bath, receives red roses with a note signed by Jean.

Note 2: Julie's gets a bouquet with an unsigned note as Neil is leaving for work.

Note 3: Neil discovers a bouquet in the car's back seat with an unsigned note.

Note 4: Julie in Spain with George is given roses with a note signed by Jean.

The four notes paralleling the four flashbacks comment on the perverse relationship between Jean and Julie. The first note praises this sadomasochistic relationship with "The worst part of you is the best thing you have" and cements their unbounded interdependence. Its ominous sentiments insinuate that Julie will not be allowed to terminate the relationship. The bloodletting, a factor in the flashbacks, is epitomized by the deep red roses that arrive with each note.

The second note references Martino's 1972 film, again with Fenech and Rassimov, *Il tuo vizio è una stanza chiusa e solo lo ne ho la chiave* (*Your Vice Is a Locked Room and I Only Have the Key*). It builds on the first quote with reference to Julie's secret vice as "a locked room." The key and the keyhole are the Freudian symbols for the male and female genitalia and refer specifically to the couple's sexual perversity, for the lover states that he alone has the key, linking the phallus as the tool that can enter "a locked room," the vaginal symbol.

The third note contains a biblical reference to Adam and Eve's disgrace in Eden after coming to the knowledge of good and evil by eating the forbidden fruit. The "Eve" naturally refers to Julie and the "Adam" to Neil. It hints that if Neil digs too deeply into the "murder" of Jean her past will be revealed, her marriage will collapse and a scandal will occur. Their "paradise" will be lost. But as Neil has been supplanted in Julie's affections by George, her current lover becomes the new Adam. In a reversal of the Adam and Eve myth, Julie is seen in a restaurant with George and Carroll. He, representing the serpent in the Genesis story, tempts Eve/Julie with the familiar apple carved with his initial "G." The sexual tension is made manifest in the interplay between George, Carroll and Julie. Carroll likens the apple to the forbidden fruit but adds that Eve should offer it, not George. As Julie eats the apple he has given her, George asks if Julie wants to eat him, intimating sexual intercourse. Yet the expression also has menacing implications of feeding on people and is significantly apt insofar as husband, ex-lover and lover are in a conspiracy to murder her. Taken in a different light, Julie's reply to George that she has already eaten him foreshadows her Pyrrhic victory by returning from the dead and witnessing her husband and lover perish in a car accident, her adulterous "paradise" forever lost.

The fourth note Julie receives with its reference to the resurrected dead harkens back not only to the trick perpetrated on Julie by Jean's return from the dead to torment her, but to Julie's resurrection from the dead from gas poisoning to confront Neil and George with their crimes on a country road.

The film's ubiquitous "Vienna Slasher" is emblematic of the fear within the patriarchal order. According to Freud, due to "the mysterious, strange and therefore apparently hostile" difference a woman represents to a man, "man is afraid of being weakened by the woman, infected with her femininity and then showing himself incapable."[2] This patriarchal hegemony has been misogynistically restated in many *gialli*. Whether it is, as Freud states, that men, petrified by the difference between the sexes, demoralize women through physical abuse, or whether, according to Argento,[3] hegemony is only a plot device to place vulnerable women in dangerous situations so as excite the audience to Aristotle's pity and fear, or whether women's negative portrayal is inherently pathologized due to the genre's fascination with sick women[4] is not that important. The importance lies in these various discourses' methodologies employed by the critic in reading the film. One critic, Laura Mulvey, claims that women stand in our patriarchal culture for the "male other" in which man's fantasies and obsessions are imposed on "the silent image of woman ... as bearer of meaning, not maker of meaning."[5] Mulvey's 1973 essay was originally presented before Italian universities assimilated feminism into the curriculum,[6] and it is likely that her assumptions had little import on the film industry when Martino helmed this picture. In the preponderated male-dominated picture business, *Lo strano vizio* coded the erotic into the ideological language of the dominant patriarchal order so that Julie not only becomes the object of lust and torture but is also presented as the pathologized heroine. The title of the film tells us that Julie's sexual indulgence is depraved. This seemingly emancipated woman of the '70s is, however, tormented by giving in to her libidinal desires. The audience is meant, therefore, to sympathize with her torment but not with her degeneracy, and she is punished for this.

With the same brushstroke, Julie's friend, Carroll, another transgressive female, unapologetically assures us that she is a "whore," relishing her sexually free lifestyle. She comes to the same fate as the prostitute in the film's opening and is mutilated in a park waiting to be picked up by an unknown man. A woman at Carroll's party, who has had her paper dress ripped off while unclothing another female, is also slashed. The only woman who seems respectable, because we know nothing about her, is an airline stewardess who, assaulted by the serial killer, defends herself and murders him. Julie Wardh is alive at the film's conclusion because she has suffered for her previous transgressions, losing both duplicitous husband and lover. But the film is severe with its male characters as well. By assaulting Italian society and culture, *Lo strano vizio* attacks patriarchal bourgeois values and family relations which are presented as avaricious and deceitful. No man in the film can be trusted, not even the police who are basically ineffectual, taking decidedly second place in the investigation.

From 1968 to 1972, Italian feminism was in its infancy and had little to do with the type of women portrayed in *Lo strano vizio*. Feminists at this time numbered about a few thousand in each of the major Italian cities and spoke for "urban women closer to the world of communism than to the world of catholicism." In fact, women's liberation connoted

> freedom from patriarchal and bourgeois ideology in which women were considered sexual objects and objects of consumption of material items. The word *culture* was employed in rejection of patriarchal, bourgeois, and masculinist culture and in affirmation of a "new way to make culture with self-determination and self-management of women."[7]

The Italian feminist movement was not directly concerned with Julie Wardh's world of privileged, pampered, childless, narcissistic bourgeois women whose life was spent in the "consumption of material items" including men. Julie herself is not looking to put an end to patriarchal supremacy. It is obvious from her relationship with Jean that she enjoyed masculine domination. She has abandoned her sadomasochistic practices, and in so doing has turned to Neil, not because she necessarily loves him but because he represents the security she requires and the protection she needs as a woman on the rebound from a bizarre and intimidating relationship. When Julie finds out that Neil is not the "harbor" in which to find a safe mooring for her troubled life, she moves to George who promises to give her the romantic love she craves and the attention she demands. George, after all, works at nothing but the art of seduction; with an inheritance coming his way, he has the time and resources for Julie who requires high maintenance. However, when she discovers that George, at her husband's instigation, attempts to have her murdered, upon their accidental deaths she finds support in Dr. Arbe's arms. This is not the feminists' profile of a woman seeking sexual, cultural and even economic independence in patriarchal Italian society. The child in Julie cannot realize her own individuality and searches for some cohesiveness through identification with men. Julie "remains imprisoned in models of institutionalized behavior and repeats these roles denying [herself] any individual existence."[8] At the conclusion, the hope offered by Julie's new benefactor, Dr. Arbe, again appears to suture her dependency. Thus, the film attacks the glamorous and successful monied class to which Julie and Neil belong.

At the film's opening, the first of the four flashbacks occurs. Arriving in Austria with her husband, Neil, who is immediately called to a financial meeting, Julie is left alone on her first night back in the city. She casually accepts her husband's sudden departure, an occurrence so commonplace that Carroll calls her "the Widow Wardh." Julie's taxi is stopped by the police looking for the ripper who has just slashed a prostitute. The words "sex perverts" are bandied about by the taxi driver arguing for a return of the death penalty. The verbal connection between Julie's sadomasochistic affair with Jean and the words "sex perverts" is one way Martino bridges the gap between present and past, but the second is through the accentuated sound of the taxi's windshield wipers. There is a close-up of Julie's face over the wipers' sound that is then soft focused, followed by a dissolve to rain hitting a different car window in another location in soft focus with the same sound. This shot returns to sharp focus and in close-up, from outside the car, the viewer sees Jean's face behind the wheel of a parked car in a wooded area. Julie is on the passenger side arguing but can't be heard because of the camera position and the tumultuous rain. She opens the car door and runs until she falls on the muddy ground. Jean bends over her, slapping her viciously several times in slow motion as she writhes in pain. The music playing is a synthesized chant-like score for human voice. Jean grabs her shoulders, lifting her so he can kiss her on her bleeding mouth. On top of her, Jean, amidst the rain and mud, rips off her sweater exposing her breasts and pulls it down to her waist as she, with tenderness in her eyes, undulates in sexual frenzy. The taxi's horn brings Julie back to the present as the light changes to green. Julie makes an association between the serial killer, whom the taxi driver calls a "pervert," and Jean with whom, in the violent assault against her, she shares an emotional delight.

The non-verbal sound of the wipers connects dissimilar times and places emphasizing another aspect of the affair: the mud and the rain. Jung employed water as "a living symbol of the dark psyche ... where I experience the other in myself and the other-than-myself experiences me."[9] In *Lo strano vizio*, rain comes to symbolize sexual passion, brutality and humiliation, all of which were relished by the heroine. The link of water with the unconscious is additionally a Christian symbol in the ritual of baptism where one is plunged into water to illustrate emersion into a new spiritual consciousness from a state of unknowingness. Julie, deluged with water, once embraced this new life of masochism. With Jean she confronted her dark side that she now disavows in her tedious life as a financier's wife; Julie has overcome her emotional attachment to Jean but not her memory of him. In dream interpretation water also represents her attempt to overcome emotional issues with Jean; as a bridge between her past and her present it is variously replicated in the other three flashbacks.

In this first flashback of lovemaking, Martino takes a page out of Buñuel's surreal *L'Age d'or* (1930) where Gaston Modot and Lya Lys make love. The script reads,

> A man and a woman are ... lasciviously rolling about in the mud.... Close-up of the lovers. The woman is letting the man do what he likes, an expression of infinite tenderness in her eyes.... The man is biting her ear with a look of insane lust....[10]

In Martino's film we have the *close-up of the lovers* lying on the ground *in the mud* while Julie lets Jean do *what he likes* to her. In place of biting her ear, the *insane lust* on his face is brought about by his physically abusing her before kissing her bloodstained lips. She, although sexually excited by his actions, has a look of *tenderness in her eyes* in the way she embraces Jean's head and shoulders, a connection too precise to be coincidental in increasingly surreal flashbacks.

The second flashback occurs after a party where Julie and Jean recognize each another. Wishing to avoid him, she walks out into the street, but he follows. Neil arrives by car, sees his wife with Jean and slaps the ex-lover's face. Jean laughs and walks away. Julie cautions her husband to let Jean go, adding that he likes hurting people. These words, like those in the previous flashback ("sex perverts"), inaugurate a second one. Like the first analepsis, this syntagma, in the form of a subjective insert, represents Julie's submerged memory. The scene is once again over-cranked. It is shot in a negative space which engulfs Jean and Julie in darkness as if the action were external to a real spatio-temporal world. Julie is on a bed in a white slip covered by dark purple sheets. Jean stands over her with a liquor bottle. Martino employs one aqueous image and its symbolic equivalent as a substitute for the rain in the first flashback. Jean pours the alcohol over Julie's body. When the bottle is emptied, he hits it against a chair, the action being looped three times to negate any real temporality. The minute pieces of the bottle's cascading glass, also looped in triplicate, fall on Julie like glistening rain. As Jean ripped off Julie's sweater in the first flashback, here he rips her slip down the center revealing her

Julie (Edwige Fenech), in flashback, enjoys a sadomasochistic game of love on a bed of glass shards from a bottle that her lover has just broken (Sergio Martino's *Lo strano vizio della Signora Wardh*).

naked breasts. He lacerates her breast with the broken bottle producing a long trace of blood and then makes love as the fallen glass shards cut them both. Not only is the conceit of fluids present anew, as though Julie is reborn through this baptism into an insatiable woman of pleasure, but emphasis is again on pain's pleasures. While the synthesized organ score is similar to the first flashback, it is not as discordant.

Clearly Julie has relished her trysts with Jean but currently feels remorse for the degradation into which she had plunged herself, not for her present adultery with George. Yet George is not so different from Jean in telling Julie that he will make her "feel ecstasy and fear." He enjoys terrifying her, and she savors the fright of the acceleration of his motorcycle. Silvia Finzi elucidates the psychology behind this, saying,

> feminine eroticism remains in the sacred sphere of dominion and of violence ... stretch[ing] out in the imaginary between the psyche and the body. Only in this dimension does the woman feel able to express her fantasies. Social reality constricts her, it continuously disappoints her.

Finzi designates this condition as "Bovaryism" (referring to Flaubert's *Madame Bovary*), an attempt to transport the code of unconscious desire into reality. As Emma Bovary searches for the one true passionate experience, so too does Julie Wardh through fantasies of primal sexuality unconstrained by morality.[11]

In the third flashback, Neil and Julie search Jean's house, finding him "murdered" in his bathtub. Leaving, Neil discovers red roses that Jean has placed for Julie on the backseat of their car. Through subjective inserts we observe the third and longest fantasy capturing the nightmarish quality of

Mrs. Wardh's dream that embraces all those, save Neil, who have evoked her prurient interests. Although the fantasy immediately occurs after they leave Jean's house, the sequence is later revealed to be Julie's dream at home in bed. Jean is observed looking at the camera with water trickling from his hair. The sound of dripping water, audibly recalling previous images and thematically uniting the first and second flashbacks, together with Carroll's distorted laughter, are heard throughout the sequence. The first character in Julie's nightmare is Jean, whose bloodstained body has traumatized her; next in line is a rather stoical George, not giving in to the grim gaiety of tormenting Julie, but gazing on the scene with sad disapproval; then comes Carroll, slashed by Neil, who laughingly smears her bloodied hand over Julie. This terrifies Julie because of guilt she feels since Carroll took her place at a meeting in the park and was subsequently murdered. The director carefully orchestrates the remaining shots so that Julie's fantasy becomes a virtual reality of people interacting with her as she lies in bed, their faces optically contorted. As if in a delirium, Julie's head moves to and fro as though smacked forcefully by Jean, yet eventually her terror disappears and she begins to smile and laugh and finally becomes ecstatic, echoing the first flashback of her brutal beating by Jean in the woods. Carroll's bloody hands now suggest not only Julie's victimization but the brutal consequence of Jean's buffeting her. This fantasy magnifies Julie's sadomasochistic leanings that her prim behavior has concealed. For Mrs. Wardh, brutality + terror = lust.

Julie, to get away from unpleasant memories of Jean's death, has gone with George to Spain. She receives a note ostensibly from Jean, and then is attemptedly shot at with a spear gun on her way back to George's villa. Arriving there, distraught by what she has been through, Julie sees what looks like blood on the carpet coming from behind a drape. This introduces her fourth and final fantasy; the ersatz blood is, in truth, water leaking from a radiator onto rusted metal. The dripping sound of the red water recalls Jean's supposed death in his tub. The shots, in close or extreme close-up, crosscut between Julie's face and memories of Jean's bloody bathtub, his eyes open in death, throat spattered in gore and mouth agape. The accentuation on water and blood influences Julie's emotional state. All her flashbacks have dealt with these two elements, and this one in particular, orchestrated like a *giallocized* version of David's painting, *The Death of Marat*, prefigures Jean's death. The emphasis on blood and water reinstates images from earlier flashbacks of the torrential rainstorm, the liquor poured over Julie's body, and the sound of the dripping water over images of George, Jean and Carroll. At one point during her recollections, the close-up of Julie's face begins to rock back and forth, kinesthetically conveying her unsteadiness while the background swirls in a 360-degree arc. Obviously Julie's love for Jean is deeper than she wants to admit notwithstanding her hostility. As Julie emerges from her hallucination, a hand is suddenly placed on her shoulder; she screams, turns around and faints at the appearance of George.

With regard to the film's brutal set pieces two stand out: Carroll's slaying and the attempted murder of Julie. The Italian-language version of Carroll's homicide includes a TV announcer's voice-over of a motorcycle race that Julie watches at home while Carroll, sexually intrigued by a blackmailer's phone call requesting Julie to meet him at the Palmenhaus Gardens lest he disclose her affair with George, substitutes for her distraught friend. In the gardens, spatial disequilibrium is created through alternately expanded and constricted focal distances; Carroll is either trapped in tightly framed close-ups or is diminished to perilous vulnerability by extreme long shots with a wide-angle lens in an extended space. The initial shots of Carroll in the gardens are ones of tranquility amid the beauty of nature and the baroque 17th-century Austrian architecture. The serenity, however, is broken by two contrivances, one visual and one auditory. Shots of the clock in the gardens reading 5:03 p.m., of Carroll looking at her watch, of Julie in her apartment looking at her watch with an insert of it reading 5:16 p.m., point not only to the passing of time but stimulate viewer anticipation as to the identity of the blackmailer Carroll is to meet. The second disruption in the tranquility occurs with crosscuts between Julie watching motorcycle racing on TV and sounds of the machines inserted over shots of Carroll. A binary contrast established by the stillness of the park is immediately questioned by the tumultuous sound and movement of the cyclists. A *sous rature*, where a concept is both evoked and questioned, is generated. Like the optical contrast in focal distances, a sonic dissonance develops in simultaneous counterpoint to the garden's calm, foreshadowing the attack on Carroll. The TV announcer's opening remarks about the race's start and the competitors' altercations are warnings to us and the distraught Julie about her misgivings in sending Carroll in her place. Before she shuts off the TV, as the cars begin the third lap, the announcer reports that the "final battle" is about to commence. The words anticipate Carroll's death and are heeded by Julie who looks at her watch thinking of her friend.

If one omits the announcer's voice-over presented in the English-language version and simply retains the motorcycle sounds, one is left only with dissonance. Once the voice-over is added, the sound generated by the motorcycles and the threat to Carroll become more ominous, suturing the apartment's space with the park, and marrying the passivity of Carroll with the edginess of Julie, while the announcer's words "fight" and "battle" amalgamate these unlikely spaces. The zeugma yokes rivalry in sports to rivalry over money: Neil's attempt to have Julie killed for insurance money, and George's having Carroll murdered for her inheritance.

As the park's closing time approaches, Carroll takes her leave through the garden's isolated paths. Archetypal stalker shots emerge, and because they are familiar they increase the expectation of inevitable calamity through customary tropes: shots of a man's pant legs following her, a black gloved hand on a tree trunk, leaves rustling as if by an unseen agency, and the tracking camera following her interspersed with shots from her viewpoint devoid of a human presence. A gardener's emergence from behind the bushes alleviates Carroll's growing fears, as it is geared to, but this temporary allayment only signals a false pledge of security. The viewer knows and anticipates the outcome. Regarding this, Noel Carroll bases suspense on earlier narrative elements that pertain to subsequent factors in raising audience anticipation. He maintains "suspense is a subcategory of anticipation, not the whole of it." Suspense arises when alternative outcomes, that is, alternative endings of an answering scene, produce a scenario where evil is the most likely outcome, while the morally correct outcome is the unlikely one.[12] Carroll Baxter's desire to meet the blackmailer in a previous scene is answered by her trip to the Palmenhaus Gardens. The moral outcome to complete her mission and rid Julie of a blackmailer is the more improbable consequence, while the evil outcome, her death, is the more likely result which ensures continued suspense. Once Carroll arrives at the Palmenhaus, the action takes another turn. A razor-wielding man attacks her as she attempts to escape. Carroll, failing, lies on the grass where her hands and neck are slashed. Traditionally, her attacker is never clearly identified. Because of a codified combination of synecdochical close-up shots of body parts, forming the assailant's composite image through montage is denied. Christian Metz metaphorically describes the film viewer as a midwife attending a birth who, by the very presence of watching, assists the woman in labor since, "by watching the film I help it to be born, ... only in me will it live ... to be brought into being by nothing other than the look."[13] But what does it mean "to be brought into being by nothing other than the look"? "The look" involves a process of analysis. The Palmenhaus Gardens sequence necessitates the audience to work at watching, forcing it to reconstruct by ratiocination the story's segments elliptically eliminated through editing. The sequence begs the viewer to ask who this killer is and what his/her relation is to the victim. Does Carroll know her attacker and, therefore, appears shocked, or is she shocked because it is someone unfamiliar? Is the killer one who has not yet been introduced or is he the serial killer? Are there two killers working in conjunction with one another to deflect suspicion? This reasoning structures the requisite cognitive process in helping the film to be born.

The next impressively staged set piece takes place at the underground parking lot in Julie's apartment complex. At twilight she returns from a police interrogation concerning Carroll's death and enters the garage. Synecdochical close-ups of a man's shoes and pant legs are contrasted to the wide-angle long shot of the garage as Julie, in the frame's background, exits her car. The extreme long shot minimizes her height placing her in a disadvantageous light while the exaggerated distance between foreground and background generates a dramatic utilization of space from which anyone can threateningly emerge. Added to this, the degree of ocularization, internal or otherwise, does not belong uniquely to Julie because what it verifies is not what she is seeing but what the viewer is paranoically led to believe is the antagonist's viewpoint. There is another cut to the unknown person's feet, but this time he is walking in Julie's direction from right to left of frame. In two shots the camera tracks her, indicating the other individual's point of view, but leaving enough ambiguity to appear as an objective shot. The next shot of Julie walking from midground to foreground, taken from a low angle, gives us an appreciably self-assured attitude about her strength of character.

The tone becomes more intense when the garage lights are turned off and Mrs. Wardh must make it safely to the elevator. Previous long shots of Julie are now reduced to tight facial close-ups with a pin light detailing her expression encircled by the garage's inky darkness. The viewer is reintroduced to the heroine's internal ocularization so that these shifters[14] in focalization tell us that Julie is cognizant of the elevator's location and the distance to reach it. At this point there is another shift in what she sees. Crosscutting alternates now between her and an auto's intermittently flashing headlights pinning her in its beams like a cornered animal. Julie must pass the car's lights to make it to the elevator, and each time the lights go on she becomes more frightened until she is transfixed by them; the pin light on her face is juxtaposed to the sound of a car rushing toward her. With Julie in the foreground, the car in long shot emerges from the background ready to run her over. She jumps out of the way and falls to the ground. The auto then moves up the garage ramp and out. In long shot she runs from the foreground to the elevator entrance in the background. Due to relentless editing, which fragments the space and extends temporal continuity, the time Julie takes to reach the elevator is inordinately protracted creating substantial unease.

The trajectory of Julie's flight to safety sets up audience expectations in an "internalized calculus of narrative probabilities," and the story's reluctance to satisfy such expectations establishes the norms deemed worthy of narrative representation.[15] Several questions emerge regarding these norms of narration employed in exploiting the spatial-temporal continuum's effects on the *mise-en-scène*: (1) Julie seems trapped by an unknown assailant whose image is mostly concealed. His spatial relation to the heroine is indeterminate. This vagueness is consistent with the *giallo*'s lack of specificity regarding the villain's spatial field which is normally outside the frame where he can instantaneously materialize and summarily dematerialize. The rules regarding space and time are abrogated for him unlike the protagonist who must conform to them. (2) Introduced into the garage space is an auto with its flashing lights, further confusing the audience who expects the antagonist to be walking. Moreover, the attacker at times appears to be walking behind Julie and at other times parallel to her. This is suggested by the tracking camera either ambiguously photographing her subjectively or shooting her from an objective point of view. The audience might even be led to believe that the assailant has moved into a car to more advantageously pursue Julie. On the other hand there might be two attackers either functioning in concert or operating independently. In the moviegoer's mind several possibilities arise: Jean is in pursuit of her, or the serial killer is on the loose with Julie as his next victim. Julie's frozen position rendered by the car's headlights in the subterranean garage recalls Maria in Lang's *Metropolis* (1927) chased by Rotwang in the underground city, pinning her against the wall with a flashlight's beam. Julie's spatial autonomy likewise becomes compromised, circumscribed by the car lights. No matter how Julie is lensed, she is either trapped in tight facial close shots surrounded by darkness, reduced to a small and vulnerable individual in long shot, or observed by a tracking camera hinting at an omnipresent voyeur. (3) One secure space offered is the well-lit area around the elevator, but the intervening space controlled by the villain between her and the lift is charged with danger from outside the frame. The play of the bright car lights contrasted to the garage's darkness also recalls the Manichaean dialectic between good and evil based on the assumption of two preexisting natures: light and darkness. When the menacing car alternately turns its lights on and off, it replicates this duality on a material level while symbolically representing the drama's archetypal battle between good and evil. Once the driver fails to run Julie over, there ensues a momentary caesura. Shifts in ocularization begin afresh, however, alternating between an unidentified attacker on foot and Julie. Reaching the elevator she looks about and sees no one. The sequence continues with objective shots of a petrified Julie and her point of view shots of the elevator indicator signaling that a cab is descending to the basement. When the door opens the camera is positioned from the inside looking out at Julie's astonished face. There is a brief reverse close shot of the murderer wearing sunglasses with a glimmering razor prepared to strike, while around him is only darkness, reminiscent initially of Kate Miller's elevator encounter with the villain in Brian De Palma's *Dressed to Kill* (1980). Intriguingly this theatrical lighting on a tight shot of his lower face draws attention to his appearance by limiting background visibility while shrouding his features in semi-darkness so that they are only partially visible. Julie dodges the razor and flees. For the remainder of the scene only his black leather-clad arm and gloves are visible wielding the blade.

    Eluding the killer, Julie gets into her car, and from her viewpoint the elevator can be seen. Using a wide-angle lens in an extreme long shot, the director visualizes the significant distance between the car and the elevator. Julie drives close to the elevator and rushes into it attempting to close the door before the killer is aware of her maneuver. He places his gloved hand in the closing doors, but she beats them with her fists until he withdraws as the elevator ascends to her apartment. Once on the landing, the crosscutting between the staircase and her apartment door elevates viewer anxiety as Julie pounds on it calling Neil to open. The *point d'écoute* also is increased with the sound of footsteps on the stairway which is assumed to be the killer's. The director escalates the excitement by introducing a man's shadow against the stair wall accompanied by a register of sights and sounds. Suddenly the apartment door opens and Neil grabs her in his arms. As she rushes inside we perceive a mild-mannered man on the staircase, thereby deflating our expectations.

Masterfully, Martino, in four segments, protracts the viewers'/character's anxieties until it is unnerving by segregating individual components from the aggregate: (1) Julie in the underground garage and the killer's feet, (2) the blinking car lights and the attempt to run Julie over, (3) Julie at the elevator door attacked by the killer, and (4) Julie outside her apartment and the approaching footsteps and shadow. Each segment employs synecdoche to obfuscate the identity of an indeterminate presence, setting up a relationship between the familiar and unknown, light and darkness, observing and being observed. Each division calls for the filmgoer to concentrate on a preponderant number of discrete auditory and visual images: feet, car lights, a hand with a blade, shadows, footsteps and supplementary sounds.

This analysis of *Lo strano vizio* points to the film's underlying folk tale themes. Basically the alignment between the slasher film and the fairy tale structure is due to the fuzzy logic of the *giallo*'s plots. The manner of foregrounding style in place of the causal-chronological order of events subordinates the plot's role. The result is a shift in emphasis from "relationships between characters and ... actions as they unfold in chronological order"[16] to a world where logic is detrimental to enjoyment, where appearance masks reality, where chronological order is inimical to *mise-en-scène*. The fairy tale, which denies logic, space, time and factuality, is the perfect vehicle for these films' tenor (the subject) and for Propp's morphological analysis.

1. **A member of the family leaves home (I).**

Lo strano vizio opens with the characters away "on business" arriving from New York. Julie and Neil have taken a trip to Austria, but it is not their only residence since, as international jet-setters, they have been living in the States for some time. Neil calls Austria "home," but he is tied to the business of making money (in the English version, Neil is a diplomat): and although he seems to be comfortable in Austria, Julie reminds her husband that he would like Austria better if it had America's Wall Street. Neil even argues with his wife saying he doesn't have time be a tourist in Austria, thus testifying that they really are not "at home" but simply have an apartment here.

2. **An interdiction is addressed to the heroine (II).**

An inverted form of interdiction is presented by an "order" given to Julie Wardh at a party thrown by Carroll Baxter when she introduces her friend to her Australian cousin, George Corot. Along with Carroll, George has inherited a great deal of money from a deceased uncle. Carroll warns Julie not to steal him, adding that she means it. Its ambiguity is open to several interpretations in the context of the party, but using the emphatic verb construction "don't" and concluding that she means it, Carroll is not simply asking Julie not to monopolize George's time and take him away from the party guests. She recognizes that Julie, in a loveless married relationship with Neil, is promiscuous, knowing of Julie's previous affair with Jean. Carroll's warning implies that she herself is in love with her cousin, which is confirmed when she confesses to Julie that she would date him, "cousin or not."

3. **The interdiction is violated (III).**

Julie's first meeting with George is the beginning of the end for her peace of mind because she violates Carroll's interdiction not to steal her cousin from her. Just as Julie has married Neil on the rebound from her disastrous affair with Jean, so too does she fall into the arms of George as a buffer against her cooling relationship with her absent spouse. She complains to Neil over the phone at Carroll's party that he has been with her only one night in three days. Although George must not be seen as a scoundrel to maintain the deception, he enters Julie's life and eventually seduces her. Simultaneously, the nominal antagonist, Jean, also reappears in Julie's life, which drives the heroine into George's arms more quickly. Since Neil is away from home for days at a time, and since there is a Viennese serial killer stalking women, Julie is even more emboldened to seek out Carroll's handsome cousin. But in succumbing to George's "love," she violates a societal convention by becoming an adulteress with whom the audience is made to sympathize.

4. **The villain receives information about his victim (V).**

Since Carroll is Julie's close friend and confidant, and since Carroll is George's cousin, and since Neil has created an elaborate scheme to kill his wife with George and Jean's aid, it stands to reason that George and the other men know a great deal about Julie. This knowledge, however, is kept from the viewer because (1) Julie initially is the center of vision in this limited third-person narration, restricting the audience's knowledge to what she experiences. As the film progresses the story increasingly departs from Julie's limited viewpoint and moves to an omniscient viewpoint enabling us to see incrementally the other characters' machinations. (2) It must appear that all three men do not know each other lest the underpinnings of the "whodunit" be destroyed. Jean must be perceived as the villainous pervert, George as a compassionate and amorous hero, and Neil as a concerned but sexually unsatisfactory husband. In the *gialli* what develops behind the scenes is as important as what is up front.

5. The villain attempts to deceive the victim in order to take possession of her (VI).
There is not one villain but three. Consequently, all three men play a part in deceiving Julie, but her husband's role is revealed only in the final reel because he has been pictured as the deceived spouse. While the film exploits women, it also is misandristic in its ambiguous premise: on one hand it melodramatically showcases a sexually liberated woman with her psychological hang-ups that amplify her character; on the other hand it objectifies her as a voyeuristic commodity for the heterosexual male audience. But it likewise demonizes most of the male characters so that no major character comes out unscathed.[17] George is the key to Neil's deceiving Julie. Once they are sexually involved, George can carry out Neil's plan to have Jean's killing her look accidental.

Carroll's interdiction forbidding Julie to "steal" George, and his seduction of Julie are inseparably linked. George's premeditated plan to charm Julie, since he and Jean are working with Neil, is fortuitous, considering the presence of a serial killer which drives Julie into George's arms and obfuscates the three men's murderous intentions. She meets Jean at Carroll's party and tells him their relationship is over; he retorts saying that they are united through a common vice. Carroll's suggestion that one man cannot give Julie everything paves the way for George's seduction of Julie.

George's possession of Julie occurs incrementally.

    a. He admits to Julie his specialty is "courting ladies" in their husband's presence.

    b. At lunch Julie and Carroll must sit with George since he has reserved all the tables.

    c. After lunch George takes Julie on a wild motorbike ride that thrills her.

    d. Julie likes George too much to go on seeing him; he kisses her confessing his love.

    e. Julie seeks comfort in sex with George.

6. The victim submits to deception and thereby unwittingly helps her enemy (VII).
Because Julie is neglected by Neil, threatened by Jean, feels insecure

because a serial killer is targeting women and actually spies on her making love to George, she becomes romantically involved with George and unknowingly submits to the fantastic scheme orchestrated by her husband to murder her for her money.

7. The villain causes harm or injury to a member of a family (VIII).

The various subheadings within this function are of specific interest: "The villain orders a murder to be committed" (#13) and "The villain commits murder" (#14). Martino supplies the audience with a triumvirate of villains: one who is suspected, Jean, and two who are not. Ingeniously the red herring is the Vienna Killer whom we are led to believe has finally murdered Carroll and Julie. Neil plays the role of the concerned husband, but is the mastermind who, with George, plans to kill his wife and, therefore, is both villain and a family member. Besides Julie, another family member is harmed: at George's request Neil kills George's cousin, Carroll, but it is attributed to the serial killer. George in turn conspires with Jean to murder Julie, and then kills him when Jean asks for his cut of the money.

8. The heroine is tested and attacked which prepares the way of her receiving a helper/donor (XII).

The heroine is tested in several ways: Julie is blackmailed over the phone by an anonymous voice whom she thinks is Jean but who might be the Vienna Slasher; she is threatened with a razor by the slasher in an underground parking lot; she is menaced by Jean in the street and receives four notes with roses which are veiled threats that she can never be rid of him; she narrowly misses being killed in Spain with a spear gun; and finally she is chloroformed by Jean and then allowed to die from gas poisoning.

There are two ersatz "donors": George who seems to be Julie's protector against Jean and who substitutes for her spouse by gratifying her sexually/emotionally, and Neil, her husband, who evinces deep concerned about her welfare, going to the police with a picture of the serial murderer found in Jean's camera to put Julie's mind at rest. This leads to a subset of the "tested heroine" which is that "Disputants request a division of property" (#6). Eventually we are made aware of the motivation and the antagonists responsible for Carroll's homicide and Julie's attempted murder. Neil needs Julie's money in order to cover financial investments, and George doesn't want to split his inheritance with his cousin, Carroll.

One other subcategory under the "tested heroine" function is "The donor greets and interrogates the heroine" (#2). First, the police constitute "donors" who reopen Carroll's case through the insistence of their forensic expert who has cross-examined everyone who knew her. Since none of the other "donors" are trustworthy, the viewer is left with those who only appear to be: George and Neil. Second, with respect to George, the greeting and questioning functions constitute a seduction. He informs Julie in her apartment that he is waiting for Neil, but then quickly asserts that this is an excuse for seeing her. She disdains his explanation. George rejoins with a remark that is also an invitation: his game is romancing women in their husband's presence. In the restaurant where he obliges Julie and Carroll to sit at a table he reserved, watching Julie eat the apple he carved with his initial on it elicits George's sexually explicit question about eating. Third, with Neil the questioning of Julie takes a different approach in his attempt to prove that he cares for her. Dreaming about Jean she wakes up screaming, and Neil concernedly asks if it is about *that* man? She won't answer. When she receives an anonymous gift of roses with a message she knows is not from Neil, he inquires who her admirer is and she replies that she would like to think it was he, but flowers aren't items on the stock exchange. He asks Julie what is wrong, and if she feels neglected. After the slasher attacks Julie in the underground garage, Neil questions his distraught wife. When she tells him, he inquires if it was Jean. Neil takes a gun to Jean's house demanding of Julie where he lives. Developing the photo found in Jean's camera, he interrogates his wife as to the man's identity, and she remarks that he is the one who threatened her in the garage. He goes to the police with the photo.

Carroll also supports Julie by giving sound, although hedonistic advice about men, and attempts to take Julie's mind off her brooding about pursuing a meaningful existence. She is Julie's uninhibited id, taking her friend's place when the possibility of an unsavory situation arises and losing her life because of it. Finally, the most credible donor is Dr. Arbe who has saved Julie's life, but his greeting and interrogating of her happens off-screen at the finale; presumably through her information to the doctor, Neil and George are cornered by the police. Arbe comforts her at the death of her conniving husband and treacherous lover. The concluding trope of Julie and Arbe going off by car into the distance attests to a possible future with the love of a good man for a woman who has paid dearly for her injudicious choices.

9-10. The villain is defeated (XVIII)/the false hero is exposed (XXVIII).
As reported, there are several villains. Julie's assistance in bringing the false heroes, George and Neil, to justice takes place off-screen with the police and her doctor, although in revealing herself to Neil and George on a roadway after they believe her dead, she places herself in jeopardy once again. Having verified that she is alive, the two men panic as the law peruses them by car. The villains crash into a river and their car topples over. Primarily off-screen, Dr. Arbe plays an active role in bringing the criminals to justice by saving Julie from gas poisoning, thereby enabling her to startle the killers into a panic which costs them their lives.

The police rarely intrude into the story, but it is the police's pathology division that reopens the case, noticing a difference in technique in Carroll's murder. Likewise the police do not bring the serial killer to justice, for he is killed with a letter opener by his intended victim, a flight stewardess. Jean, the only apparent menace to Julie outside of the serial killer, is murdered by George and not apprehended by the law.

3

Wrap Your Troubles in Dreams (and Dream Your Troubles Away)

Lucio Fulci's *Una lucertola con la pelle di donna*
[*A Lizard in a Woman's Skin*, 1971]

> *Dream and give yourself permission to envision a You that you choose to be.—*
> Joy Page

Lucio Fulci's *Una lucertola con la pelle di donna* purportedly deals with a woman's forbidden desires released at night in sleep, forming indispensable chronotopic structures in their representation of time and space.[1] The concept of released repressions through dreams recalls the trance films of Curtis Harrington, Maya Deren and particularly Kenneth Anger's gay cinematic poem, *Fireworks* (1947), which begins with his voice-over: "Inflammable desires dampened by day ... are ignited ... by the libertarian matches of sleep." The trick in *Lizard* is to make the audience believe that Carol Hammond's (Florinda Bolkan) "inflammable desires" are repressed during the day and only in sleep are they brought to life, driving her to the couch of her Freudian psychiatrist, Dr. Kerr (George Rigaud). Fulci misleads us into believing that Carol has a moral sense so that we, due to the exigencies of the *giallo*, will suspect everyone else but her.[2] Carol's real identity and motivation for the crime she commits are filtered through Kerr, the authentication authority, whose analysis of his patient is unreliable because Carol is falsifying her own story. The *giallo*'s woman-in-distress trope is routinely fraught with overwrought heroines in physical danger, and, in certain instances, in need of psychiatric treatment. Barry Keith Grant argues that "the emphasis on the details of female victimization work to present a disturbing picture of a besieged white phallocentrism,"[3] but in *Lizard* the prime danger comes from a woman within the respectable *haute bourgeoisie* world who is both victim and villain. Carol Hammond at first appears to be a passive victim stalked by nightmares. She is married to an ostensibly loving lawyer husband, Frank (Jean Sorel), in her father's employ, who has been having an affair with Deborah (Silvia Monti); Carol's father is a prominent English barrister, Edmond Brighton (Leo Genn), who hypothesizes that Julia Durer (Anita Strindberg), a woman murdered in their swank apartment building, was blackmailing Frank because of his adultery and that he murdered her and blamed the crime on his wife. Joan Hammond (Edy Gall), Frank's daughter from a previous marriage, is concerned for her father when suspicion falls on him. Inspector Corvin (Stanley Baker) is on the case.

In Fulci, the anti-heroine, Carol Hammond, at the start is seen in a dream that she has fabricated for the benefit of Dr. Kerr. In the first of several fantasy set pieces, two arising from dreams, others from Carol's lived experiences that take on the caliber of fantasies, she, in a white fur coat, is on a train, isolated from others, in an empty corridor unable to open the door to compartments filled with travelers completely unresponsive to each other and to her frantic gestures to gain entrance. In a wide-angle long shot, her segregation is pronounced as she now moves forward into an empty space becoming isolated from humanity. Following this, the shots of Carol evolve into tight close-ups and instantaneously the deserted train corridor is so filled with middle-aged individuals that she must push them aside. These spatial extremes suggest a schizophrenic attitude, first causing Carol anxiety at the void she experiences when no one is in sight, and then the perturbation she feels at the conflux of people. Little wonder that the film's U.S. release title was *Schizoid* (1973).

With a direct cut to an over-cranked scene, Carol is now in a corridor, not on a train, packed with naked young adults making love. Some men attempt to fondle her but she pushes them aside and continues forward as the slow motion returns to normal speed. The significance of her aloofness doesn't register straightaway until Carol's lesbian relationship with Julia Durer and her disaffection for her husband are revealed. She screams and, in a tight facial close-up, begins to fall in slow motion. In her downward plunge, the negative space transitions to her next encounter creating a frightening void into which the character floats in free fall. The camera cuts between Carol's distraught face gazing downward and the gorgeous Julia Durer whom she is about to encounter.

As a symbolic sign, the act of falling in a dream signifies a loss of emotional equilibrium or self-control. "Falling" represents Carol's inability to cope with her murdering Julia and its consequences. In Carol's hallucinatory flight through train compartments and corridors, she desires neither social nor sexual intercourse with people, but seeks those segregated from one another as she is by her crime. This movement through several corridors covers various facets of human relations: those socially disengaged, those so engaged, and finally, before falling into Julia's arms, those communicating through effortless, heterosexual couplings. Her flight, by way of a transit metaphor, from solitary individuals who give her no sanctuary, to those she repels engaged in social discourse and finally to those she struggles against who only sexually interrelate, is from Julia whom she, in her initial descent, "falls for," but finally cannot relate to either verbally or physically.

Julia's seduction of Carol occurs on a large red satin bed with numerous pillows set on a red carpet surrounded by darkness. Laughing, Julia wears merely a black shawl, her breasts exposed and her blond hair blowing by an unseen breeze. Carol, looking terrified, stands on the bed wearing only a fur coat. She tries to run away but Julia pulls the fur off Carol's naked body, caressing her while pulling her down. The latter seems shy and looks away from Julia. The languid movements augmented by slow motion impart a decadence to the seduction. The off-centered blocking of the two women produces a framing imbalance signaling a tension in the lovemaking while hinting at their relationship: the dominant, lascivious Julia and a demure, manipulated Carol. The darkened background's space enhances the women's isolation and thrusts their soft, warm flesh tones into prominence against the bed's red fabrics. Red hyperbolizes viewer attention on the women's bodies while carrying connotations associated with blood, its shedding and its expiation that anticipate Carol's ritualistic murder of Julia on love's altar—the bed.

At the end of Carol's first dream there are six facial close-ups of her climaxing to orgasm while Fulci cuts back and forth from her dream to her slowly awakening, striking a contradictory note. While the dream speaks of coercion, the spontaneous orgasm Carol experiences before awakening speaks of collusion. We are led into a problematical situation where the character's veracity is questionable with its *odi et amo* theme. The camera twice zooms back to a wider picture of her bedroom separating Carol's dream-self from her waking-self while revealing her grasping the pillows in orgasmic frenzy. The painting of a large swan on the back wall functions as a feminine symbol, a link to the unknown—from the erotic to the sublime, from the mysteries of life to those of death.[4] These peculiarities are associated with the women's erotic relationship, Julia's murder, the mystery surrounding her death and the person responsible for it. The swan's sensual connotations are found in Greek mythology where Zeus, in the form of a swan, rapes Leda as she sleeps. In this dream Julia supplants Zeus by raping Carol, the new Leda, but it is Carol who has instigated the affair possibly because of strained conjugal relations with Frank who is seeing another woman. Furthermore the swan, a symbol of music, is dedicated to Apollo, who was said to transform into a swan. The film's musical reference is mimicked by Ennio Morricone's melody through female vocals, piano, clarinet and saxophone. The viewer is thus coerced into psychoanalyzing Carol through "the spatial arrangement of scenery ... and the central use of dream as a way to move the narrative along."[5]

Freud divided dreams into three categories within their latent and manifest content—the manifest content being the dream itself, the latent content the material uncovered by the analyst investigating the dream. The problem with analyzing Carol's dreams is that (1) she is the murderer, creating the manifest content, professing no recollection of committing it, but feeling culpable nonetheless, appearing innocent while suffering from an overscrupulous conscience. (2) She writes a diary with a partially fictionalized scenario to prove she has a dual personality and, therefore, is not responsible for her crime. (3) Her analyst, therefore, given a false manifest content, provides the dream's latent content which exonerates Carol from guilt.

Freud's first type of dream is that which is intelligible and easily able to be inserted into the context of Carol's psychological life. Carol dreams that she has killed Julia Durer, and in fact she has because Julia has threatened to expose their relationship. This is the reality, but since the audience is uncertain of Carol's victimization insomuch as the homicide is presented as a surrealistic dream, the manifest content cannot be analyzed accurately.

Freud's second dream category is one that is coherent but has a bewildering effect because the dreamer cannot determine how it pertains to her situation. We have from Carol's dream a murder that she fears she may have committed but admits knowing nothing about even though her fur coat, scarf and letter opener are found at the scene. Depicted in terms of a fantastical dream transcribed in her diary, the murder's manifest content is translated by her analyst as a dramatized wish fulfillment in which her conscience disapproves of Julia's lifestyle, but her "chilly" marital relationship attracts her to Julia's bohemian existence, suturing her loathing and yearning to imitate what she detests. The outcome of which is either to believe in her guilt or innocence.

The third group of dreams, those without intelligibility, seeming disconnected, confused and meaningless,[6] resides in Carol's surreal train ride with its variety of people ending in her plummeting through inky blackness into Julia's arms. Fulci would have us believe that the person who seems to be guilty and who is the story's heroine cannot possibly be the murderer and, second, that with all of the miscellaneous suspects, one must unquestionably be culpable. This clever stratagem creates a mounting ambivalence about various individuals' culpability in Julia's death, while it promotes a vacillating attitude toward Carol.

Carol Hammond and her social class are just as censurable for their

Lucio Fulci's Una lucertola con la pelle di donna (1971)

Carol (Florinda Bolkan) confronted by Inspector Corvin (Stanley Baker) in the cemetery. The strategically placed cross separates the quiet, methodical, impartial lawman from the grasping, self-centered, ruthless society woman (Luciano Fulci's *Una lucertola con la pelle di donna*).

meaningless lives as is the counterculture she is drawn to. For instance, her friend, Mrs. Gordon (Ersi Pond), a matronly woman, is having an affair with her young, handsome chauffeur (Piero Nistri), but when he interrupts her on the phone to Carol, she is quick to call him an "imbecile," and then condescendingly, "sweetie." The brief scene highlights the way the upper class uses its privilege to sexually exploit the working class and, concomitantly, the way the working class is sexually capable of manipulating the idle rich. Consequently, the *haute bourgeoisie* as well as the youthful counterculture become modern examples of moral alienation, targets of Fulci's depiction of societal instability resulting from a breakdown of values. The two groups lack standards, except those which feed their egocentric appetites because, like the Hammonds and Mrs. Gordon, they can get away with it. The counterculture represented by the affluent Julia Durer and the hippies, Jenny (Penny Brown) and Hubert (Mike Kennedy), live in a drug-induced utopia that, while divesting themselves of establishment standards, prey upon the rich. Behind their posture of peace and free love lurks murder and blackmail. But if both groups are morally bankrupt, where lies the principled values to anchor modern life? The answer for Fulci resides in the inexorable process of the law that sees justice is done through the reestablishment of the patriarchal status quo. It is a justice that is impartial to class and rather impassive in its carrying out of the law. Inspector Corvin is patient, not given over to arrogance; does not delight in his victory over Carol; and is not provoked to anger by the corruption around him. Perhaps these are virtues stereotypically attributed to British reticence, but indirectly the inspector echoes the ideal of love stated in Paul's first letter to the Corinthians (chapter 13). At the film's conclusion, in a small cemetery where Carol has gone to pay her last respects to her father, Inspector Corvin, without emotion, quietly confronts her. Corvin's final statement that she is without a conscience alone suggests his disgust for the crime and his regret that justice is only legally satisfied by Carol's incarceration. In this sense the detective acts as a guarantor of the transformation of lawlessness into a stable universe through the reestablishment of normality,[7] requiring an inviolable impartiality through the law. To mirror the inspector's own sangfroid, Fulci presents us with Carol, a self-possessed, clever, cold-blooded killer who has destroyed several people so that she might go undetected while enlisting an unsuspecting doctor's support. In these last few moments, the anti-heroine's true nature comes to the fore and audience sympathy is ingeniously turned against her. Up until now we have seen a confused, sympathetic and withdrawn woman who has few friends and lives in the rarefied atmosphere of a privileged class. Compassion for Carol stems from her psychiatric conversations with Kerr who assures us of her normality and the deviance of her neighbor. But Fulci decimates the very establishment he has painstakingly set up not only by introducing a murderous society woman as tormented heroine, but an adulterous husband with a veneer of respectability that suits his career, and a father who, out of an erroneous sense of honor, futilely commits suicide to save his daughter's reputation by avowing his own guilt.

Carol's first psychiatric session ends as the quiet of Dr. Kerr's office is juxtaposed to Julia Durer's wild, psychedelic party. As the doctor tells Carol that she is attracted to Julia's open lifestyle, there are repeated close-ups of Julia's face followed by swish pans to the activity at her party. The reiterated panning to Julia's features is analogous to the repeated zoom in to Carol's face after her dream of Julia linking the two women through these signifiers. With Julia as focalizer, the swish pans blur objects within space while extreme close-ups destroy the depth of field explaining her unfocused and apathetic mental state with the surfeit of noise and plethora of semi-naked bodies in motion, a hedonistic lifestyle already producing in her its counter-passion. With a split screen, Fulci briefly juxtaposes Julia's Dionysian revelry with the staid propriety of the Hammonds' formal dinner recalling the film's opening between the stasis of older people and the sexual exuberance of youth. Although the sounds from Julia's gathering can be heard, the only sound that first breaks the icy stillness at the Hammonds' dinner is a close-up of Frank cracking a nut. It is a reminder of the characters' impenetrability, each living isolated in his/her own shell with secrets that lie just below the surface of their respectability. Frank's reflected image on the dinner table surface creates a doppelganger effect and notifies us of another self than the one he projects for his family. The effect is further enhanced by a close-up of Carol eating nuts followed by a similar cut to her image mirrored on the tabletop. This replicated imaging is reiterated again when the camera cuts to the family patriarch, Mr. Brighton, who comes to believe his son-in-law wants his wife out of the way. As the camera zooms in on self-absorbed Carol, the irritating clamor emerging from Julia's party increases as though it has become internal diegetic sound from Carol's viewpoint. The cut to nude young party people is again spatially subverted by the camera's panning once more across soft-focused images to Julia's impassive face. As Julia's party progresses, Dutch-angled shots of hippies together with a handheld camera, compounded by extreme close-ups of them in soft focus substantiating their drugged gyrations, attest not only to their vitality as they dance or make love, but also to their lack of equilibrium in life. Close-ups of semi-nude female bodies that Patricia MacCormack terms "phantasmagoric vistas and viscous configurations of flesh"[8] are juxtaposed to Julia's soft-focused face. Cutting to Carol, the camera dollies out from her perturbed features to the others at the dinner table.

Both Carol and Julia, wearing similar expressions, seem unconnected to their surroundings. Carol's passivity, however, signals her withdrawal from social intercourse on a broader scale than Julia's, but both bear the consequences of jouissance. Lacan in "The Ethics of Psychoanalysis" explains the polarities at work within the terms *jouissance* and *pleasure*. For him pleasure, as a controlled state that occurs within cultural norms, operates as a limitation, the repressiveness of the law commanding the individual to "enjoy as little as possible." Similarly, the subject invariably endeavors to contravene this proscription imposed on his enjoyment to go beyond the pleasure principle in an over-the-top attempt to indulge in polymorphous sensual activities. The consequence of violating the pleasure principle is, nevertheless, not more enjoyment but anguish, since the subject can bear only a certain amount of pleasure beyond which pleasure turns to pain. It is this pain that Lacan calls *jouissance*[9] which ultimately becomes suffering. In the pursuit of pleasure there occurs within the individual a mechanism, call it the superego or conscience or societal taboos, which recognizes the excess of the polymorphous perverse self and tries to counterbalance it with its opposite. So it is not only the repression of our passion that can produce self-destruction, as Norman O. Brown observes, but the pursuit of our passion can lead us down a comparable ruinous path because the pleasure principle is indestructible.[10] Similarly, Charles Fourier, the socialist philosopher, remarks that "every passion ... suffocated produces its counter-passion, ... malignant as the natural passion would have been benign."[11] This is one reason contributing to Carol's edginess and uncommunicativeness within her own family: a lack of balance in life. Neither as the spouse of Frank nor as a lover of Julia can she bring herself to engage in meaningful relations with others. Carol's withdrawn state generated by her lesbianism and societal taboos, coupled with Frank's infidelity, galvanizes her despondency, eroding her chance at happiness. In *Lizard*, both women have reached a point where sexual promiscuity has been satiated and has turned venomous; pleasure is now predicated on masochism. Having a notorious reputation with little to lose, Julia resorts to blackmail while Carol wants back her bourgeois respectability and murders Julia for it. Neither woman can hope to possess the other and call it love since love implies acceptance of the other's freedom which their self-centered possessiveness cannot brook.

Because of Fulci's Marxist leanings and the film's societal class dichotomies, Carol's murder of Julia might be viewed through a Marxist-Freudian perspective. Robin Wood succinctly underscores this by announcing that the social and sexual revolutions are inseparably linked and necessary to each other. Marx exposes the manner in which bourgeois capitalist ideology is capable of concealment behind various guises, while Freud's psychoanalytic theory examines ways in which this ideology is perpetuated through the institutionalization of the patriarchal family taking the model of "repression" as the contributing behavioral factor. Wood perceives "basic repression" as necessary in accepting postponement of gratification and making us distinctly human in order to co-exist with each other. However, "surplus repression" is for Wood a culture-specific process whereby people are conditioned from childhood to take on predetermined cultural roles as monogamous, heterosexual, bourgeois, patriarchal capitalists but Wood has doubts that such a model works, and if it doesn't he finds the individual turning to neurotic behavior. In *Lizard*, Carol is conscious of the ways in which she is oppressed by the patriarchy and employs, as a counter-mechanism, her manipulative personality under the mask of feminine passivity. Her repressed personality stems from her bisexuality and, a priori, the capitalist model of normality. Carol has cloaked her desires through role-playing as a self-restrained, irreproachable wife. Yet she has had to deal with this repression by the subtle oppression of others. Carol is barely civil to Joan, her stepdaughter; is unloving toward her husband, Frank, likely realizing his infidelity; exhibits little filial concern for her father; and uses Julia Durer to fulfill her sexual fantasies. When her affair is in danger of discovery, she is capable of committing murder.

Carol is assumed to be sufficiently fulfilled by her marriage to Frank, although the lack of children offers another hint of their estrangement. We have likewise observed that her sublimated sexuality, which Wood translates as "creativity," is not fulfilled because, being part of the idle rich, Carol seems to have nothing satisfactory to occupy her time. She goes out with no one except Joan; we don't see her reading, engaging in cultural activity or being part of a social group. Carol assumes a bifurcated role of being the oppressed and the oppressor, the heroine and the villain. Her lesbianism is an insult to capitalist monogamy and the myth of finding the "right person" to share one's life. It is also a threat to reproductive sexuality and a transgression of bourgeois social criteria of manliness and womanliness constructed on the basis of biological difference leading to specific, predetermined social roles.[12] While Maslow believed that the emancipation of one's inner drives was a precondition for the reorganization of the exterior social order,[13] Fulci, instead, offers little hope for the social prerogatives of class, or for psychiatric sessions as a replacement for sacramental confession, or for uninhibited sexual license to achieve self-fulfillment. Rather, Fulci affirms the presence of "The Law" as the author of meaning and interpreter of social and moral order since it is above class consciousness, meeting out justice without fear or favor. If anything, Fulci, as a Catholic traditionalist with Marxist propensities, condemns both the privileged classes and the counterculture.

Once the Hammonds' meal has concluded and Carol, in a close-up, now sits in an armchair looking screen right, a split screen takes us back to Julia's raucous party as a black male's hands are seen caressing a white woman's naked body. This fleeting metonymic reference of miscegenation is employed as one sexual metaphor for '70s Italian countercultural decadence. Carol, the representative of establishment mores, seems to be vicariously indulging in this orgy. Her voyeuristic gaze to the right of the split screen is so intense it is as if *her* body were being fondled. As Carol lies back on the chair smoking a cigarette, and the progressive diegeticization of the music becomes subjectively louder, there is a cut from her to the naked Julia. The increase in sound coming from the other apartment implies that Carol's thoughts are preoccupied with the party. Furthermore, the cut to Julia's nakedness connotes Carol's fantasizing about her state of undress. Julia approaches a young man and kisses him, her head moving toward the camera in a close-up that blurs her image, not only indicating it is taken from the man's viewpoint but also implying that she is kissing the moviegoer and insinuating that Carol envisions Julia kissing her.

Carol's murder of Julia with a letter opener is brought to light in her second session with Dr. Kerr; it's her elaborate scheme to feign insanity while ridding herself of her blackmailer and her guilt incurred by her affair. Here both the cognitive and emotional focus of the dream resides with her circumscribing her sensory range[14] and lulling the viewer into the fallacious conviction of her victimization. In Carol's second dream she is again wrapped in fur forcing her way down a train corridor crammed with nude young people in conversation, indifferent to her. This image segregates her in several ways: first she is wearing a warm coat while the other people are comfortably naked; second, corridors, as Freudian signifiers, connote vaginal symbols and her traveling down them suggests a pathway to Julia's sexual orifice. In the first dream, the "hallway" of the train carriage is morphed into the psychiatrist's conversation about the hallway of Julia's apartment, described as being unnaturally long, and unites it with the sexual signifiers of the train's passageway. This erotic association is further confirmed by her sighs which sound like an orgasmic reaction to her intercourse with Julia, but in effect relate to her effort to push her way through the crowd. While there are constants in this second fantasy, namely, her fur coat and the nude youngsters, there are also divergences: the scene of Julia forcing her way through the crammed train is succeeded by ghoulish shots of decaying corpses of Carol's family and friends replacing her slowmo descent into Julia's welcoming arms. Then, too, an enormous swan chases Carol followed by her stabbing Julia's breasts with the ornate letter opener as two nude, sightless hippies watch on a balcony in Durer's apartment. When Carol realizes this, the camera cuts several times to her face to accentuate the horror she experiences in having witnesses. The culminating long shot of Julia's corpse, segued by Dr. Kerr's voice-over intoning that she has killed Julia Durer, places us back in the psychiatrist's office, but unlike the first session, where her dream ended in lovemaking, this one ends in death. At the conclusion of the first nightmare, Carol stares at the letter opener Joan had plunged into a flower vase, while this new dream ends with Carol thrusting the same letter opener into Julia's body.

The second fantasy has become more sinister: the dead and disemboweled relatives, the monstrous and menacing swan winging its way over Carol as she bolts from it, the murder and the dead-eyed hippies all presenting a grotesquery that at once makes the audience commiserate with the heroine while doubting her innocence. In the first dream Carol declares that she has never been in Julia Durer's apartment, while in the second she not only is in her apartment but is brutally stabbing her. The one constant in these discrepancies is the train ride to nowhere. Besides the obvious sexual signification of the train compartment's vaginal association, the act of traveling itself implies movement toward some destination as well as its opposite, the movement away from something else since traveling per se is not a goal but a means. So why do Carol's dreams begin with travel? Where is she going and from what is she fleeing? The representations of fatality in her second dream at once signify that she is running from her murderous deed and subconsciously retreating from a morally decaying social class. Grotesquely, Fulci is deriding the upper classes and their ersatz sense of entitlement and rectitude. Ironically Carol, who appears to be detaching herself from all of this, finds death in it all, and at the end of it all. Yet the naked youths in both dreams coupled with the elderly of the first dream also are journeying to their death. Both the young unknowingly and unheedingly traveling through life's sensual pleasures as well as the aged, sullen passengers, whose life is half over, are all comparable victims, journeying to an unknown destination where death is the great leveler. One might also believe that traveling connotes Carol's leaving a man who doesn't love her for Julia's more attractive bohemian lifestyle that scuttles moral and social conventions. Yet her murder of Julia argues that she is torn between her comfortable, privileged existence and its antithetical hedonistic non-conformity.

What about the dead and eviscerated individuals of Carol's second dream? As she begins to turn her head to look about, there are four percussive close shots of her frightened face visually foregrounding Carol's shock. The room is filled with corpses in various states of decomposition seated on dining room chairs seen previously at the Hammonds' dinner table. The first corpse Carol notices is Deborah, Frank's lover. This is followed by the camera tracking/panning and cutting to other male guests in the same decomposed state both in dizzying close and extreme close shots, punctuated by an extreme Dutch angle of Carol causing her head to be nearly inverted before returning to a conventional close-up. These are accompanied by soft-focused close shots of other grotesque males with spotlights on their white faces simulating overexposed film. The camera employs double exposures to give this expressionistic scene a sense of Carol's growing unsteadiness. There is an overexposed fade to a long shot of Frank's corpse, the camera zooming in to him three times in different seated positions. These and other shots appear to be Carol's wish fulfillment in seeing family and friends dead and the hypocrisy she and they typify. The seated corpses recall Francis Bacon's portraits. In fact, in Carol's living room, there is a reproduction of Bacon's 1953 *Study after Velázquez's Portrait of Pope Innocent X*. It is no coincidence that Bacon's misshapen images of people as well as Carol's picture of a swan find their way into her nightmare, arguing that Carol might be a cunning criminal transposing these works into monstrous signs of her neurosis while beguiling family and therapist alike.

Looking further about the room in her dream, Carol screams, as if to stifle the horror. Crosscutting now occurs between Carol and her dead white-faced stepdaughter, then a zoom in to Carol framing her face in a tight off-centered close-up to signify her disorientation. When cutting back to Joan's face, the camera tilts down to her ruptured abdomen as she holds her bleeding entrails. Once her intestines are seen, the camera mercilessly zooms with a jump cut to an even closer shot of them. This jump cut registers Carol's trauma through its percussive editing as though we and the heroine are being punched repeatedly in the solar plexus. This incessant revisiting of Carol's horrified features through the camera's fidgety maneuvering coupled with the swift tempo of the cutting speed becomes part of Fulci's rhythmic development of the event. These two components generate a dichotomy within Carol: a simultaneous desire to turn away and a concomitant desire to return her gaze to that horrific spectacle. Concurrent with the dream's visuals, dissonant but empathetic music conspires, through electronic synthesized instrumentation, to disarm the viewer into accepting Carol's distraught state. Commenting on the film's hallucinatory effects, Patricia MacCormack remarks, "[These] ... unintelligible dreamlike sequences ... express meaning through subtle and disorienting situations rather than through characterization or narrative."[15] To partially compensate for this unintelligibility, Fulci employs the duped psychiatrist as dream interpreter.

In this second dream, a gigantic swan with the identical markings as those in the painting above Carol's bed flies through a crimson haze toward the camera until its face is in close-up, a strident screech emanating from its open beak. The swan, as already stated, symbolically links the dreamer to the unknown, to the erotic and transcendental elements of life and death. In essence it expresses the yin and yang of existence, ostensibly opposing forces interconnected and interdependent in the world of nature. The "unknown" figures prominently in Carol's life as the consequences of murdering Julia spin out of control, while the erotic underpinnings associating sex and death, fetishistic paraphernalia and lesbian love are transfigured through Carol's imagination into a fantasy of riotous settings and color to underscore the spectacle. As the head of the bird approaches the camera, there is a cut to a long overhead shot with the bird's shadow on the intersecting walkways of a lawn. The camera's height makes Carol seem insignificant compared to the swan who is transmuted into a bird of prey and whose shadow hovers over the fleeing woman. As the swan approaches the camera, a triangular mark is pictured right below the bird's neck. The dissolve which follows is to Julia's lower torso with her black trilateral-shaped panties intimating that she is that predatory bird, a symbol of Julia's pursuance of Carol engendering fright, not love. The triangle on the bird indicates a series of endless triadic groupings with Carol as the invariable factor: (1) Carol as wife of Frank and lover of Julia, (2) Frank as husband of Carol and lover of Deborah, etc.

Finally, the murder of Julia is introduced into this last segment of the second dream. As in the first dream, the camera is situated in Julia's apartment with the background in velvety darkness. There is a tilt up from her black silk-booted legs to her black panties and naked breasts with her streaming hair blowing in slow motion. Carol is in her fur coat while Julia attempts to caress her. Carol pulls out the letter opener and with a resolute look she repeatedly stabs Julia. Fulci jump cuts to several slow-motion shots of Julia's face, her audially distorted screams paralleling the jump cuts on Carol's face earlier when she discovers the corpses around the table. As Julia falls to the bed in slow motion, Carol's coat comes off revealing her naked body. She bends over her victim stabbing Julia multiple times in her breasts. With the phallic knife there is an underlying eroticism that belies the graphic visuals of penetration; the withdrawn, aristocratic-looking Carol becomes the aggressive male thrusting, almost blindly, the weapon into living flesh. Fulci then capitalizes on more jump cuts to Carol's face as though the impact of what she has done has finally made an impression. There is a whine of electric instruments to amplify the emotional intensity presaging the initiation of a woman actively forging her own predetermined fate. In horror, Carol looks to the room's balcony where two nude hippies, Jenny and Hubert, dangle their legs through the intricate lattice work of the balustrade looking down at Carol. Fulci crosscuts between Carol and the pair constantly zooming in to the duo. There is another cut and Carol runs naked down an endless, brightly lit narrow corridor, a sign of her enmeshment within a Freudian sexual orifice and her fixation on Julia. The camera quickly zooms out and then dissolves to her in the same corridor hastening toward the camera and an unseen fissure in the floor continually hurrying from the crime only to return to it. Even with the woman's death, Carol is under her dominance and will become increasingly involved in it. Over the final shot of Julia's bloodstained body is heard the doctor's voice comforting Carol saying her "symbolic" killing of Julia represented that part of her attracted by vice, and that the decomposed bodies were a liberating dream.

Freud believes that the convenient way to bring together two distinct dreams is to alter the verbal form of one of them so that it will meet the other which, in turn, "may be similarly clothed in a new form of words."[16] Kerr has altered the verbal form of Carol's dream by interpreting the act of murder as something morally righteous, no longer ethically reprehensible but a metaphor for Carol's sense of decency and struggle for balance in life. She has conquered her attraction to vice and sin by figuratively killing the person who exemplifies such behavior. The doctor implies a further liberating act of Carol by theorizing that the decomposed bodies of relatives and friends are what Carol wishes to be dissociated from, that is, the restricting elements in her life. For Kerr, these individuals are a portion of the problem in her psychic struggle between two worlds of existence spoken of by Nietzsche in *The Birth of Tragedy*: the Apollonian and Dionysian, between her orderly structured life and the hedonism of Julia Durer's. Dr. Kerr continues this line of thought when Carol mentions the two hippies watching her. The psychiatrist translates this as ego-invented spectators whom she wants as witnesses to her crime. The hippies now become a positive symbol of Carol's ego, her conscious mind that controls her thoughts and behavior. The fact that Carol leaves her coat and letter opener at the scene is interpreted also as a positive sign, the removal of a mental block that has enabled Carol to open up to him in the first session. Over this scene is played on an electric keyboard an ostinato-like phrase of a sensuously soothing melody from the opening dream recalling Carol's seduction by Julia. The music intimates a still lingering fascination with the debauchee by the woman who killed her. Once absolved from the crime by her psychiatrist, Carol, even if discovered, can resort to an insanity plea exculpating her of the murder. However, over her final remarks to Kerr, a siren is heard segueing into a shot of a police car's radio report about Julia's body. Paradoxically, the sound becomes a sign of the law which will destroy her insanity plea.

At one point Sergeant Brandon (Alberto de Mendoza) announces to Inspector Corvin that he will investigate the apartment building's residents where the Hammonds live. As he gets up to leave to the left of frame there is a cut to him in the Hammond apartment in the same spatial location asking each family member to look at the suspect's photo. This is a subterfuge to procure their fingerprints and match them with those on the letter opener. As Brandon gives the photo to Frank, he looks down at it. There is a segue to police headquarters and to the magnified slides of the same suspect with the Hammond family's fingerprints clearly defined on each slide. These scenes have been yoked together by ellipsis first through the figure of Brandon, second by the suspect's photograph and finally by the photos containing the family's fingerprints. The final scene in this triad now takes place in the presence of Brandon, Corvin, and Beth (Ursel Eberz), a police officer, while Lowell (Ezio Marano), a forensics expert, projects and explains the results from evidence on the slides. The zeugma marries these three visuals into one concept: exposing the murderer. The fingerprints that fill the entire screen (reminiscent of Lang's *M*, 1930) are identified, through Beth's voice-over, as Carol Hammond's. As the sound of her name echoes over the image of the huge fingerprint there is a cut to the pupil of Carol's eye with the reflection of an officer on it saying, in the same echoing tone, that anything she says may be used against her.

Brighton's daughter is released from jail on bail, although Sgt. Brandon argues with Corvin that setting a high bail is a clear indication of Carol's guilt. Corvin is doubtful; there is evidence but no motive. If Carol is playing a game with her family, Fulci is wagering a similar one with the audience by advancing well-calculated contradictory sentiments about her that, even with Carol's dream of murdering Julia, the moviegoer is left in a quandary as to whom to believe. It is an audacious stratagem on Fulci's part that comes off deftly since Carol isn't particularly a sympathetic individual.

While we have witnessed two wordless dreams of Carol as she recounts them to Dr. Kerr, her present terror at St. Paul's Clinic, where she is undergoing tests, unfolds like one of her dreams as Hubert spies on her. Fleeing, Carol is pursued through the clinic's maze of corridors accompanied on the sound track only by the cadence of her footsteps and heavy breathing. The lack of clearly defined spaces within the clinic creates its own oneiric atmosphere. In her headlong rush through the clinic she enters several darkened areas. Fulci situates her in the room's background with backlighting coming from the open hallway door so that the foreground and midground spaces appear threatening in their shadowed emptiness, while she is physically diminished by her positioning within a deep space. In one room Carol, through an opaque screen partition, sees a man's shadow coming toward her with a knife only for the audience to observe, in a reverse shot, that he is a doctor preparing surgical instruments on a cart. She opens another door to behold vivisected animals stretched out on racks, the magnified sound of their hearts and tubes circulating blood from one specimen to another in extreme close-ups draws her to near madness echoing Carol's second dream of the dead family members arranged around a room. Fulci exploits the zoom here to convey Carol's traumatization as she faints. There is a dissolve to her in bed, as though awakening once again from a dream. Her husband is at her side and the clinic's director (Jean Degrave) apologizes for her experiences, but, unctuously warns her not to be so curious, attributing the hippie chasing her to hallucinations. For pathologized women like Carol, even doctors can't be trusted.

In the final shot at the clinic, Frank is positioned to the right of the frame looking left. There is a cut to close-ups of photographs of Frank and Deborah in bed as though Frank in the clinic were gazing at them, but now he is seen in Edmond's office. The operative word connecting the character's sight lines to two locations is "spying." Carol's report of a hippy spying on her is dismissed as delusional, while Frank's being spied upon cannot be denied, with photographic evidence which could terminate his business relationship with Edmond. Edmond suggests that Frank, blackmailed by Julia, has killed her, placing the blame on Carol. Frank reminds him of Carol's belongings at the crime scene and that if someone else had committed the crime, he must have had a remarkably detailed telepathic dream. Edmond counters that Carol kept a diary of her dreams and anyone could have read it and committed the murder. As Edmond pronounces the words "real crime" there is a cut to the crime scene with Julia's silhouetted image. This external rhyming continues by juxtaposing Edmond's accusing Frank of reading her diary so as to place his wife's belongings at the crime scene with a cut to Frank reading Carol's journal. This type of editing has positive features. The rhyming, acting to unify the linear narration of a complex story, leads the viewer further afield by multiplying the number of linkages between characters creating even more suspects and hypotheses as to the killer's identity. The rhymed articulations reject the illusion of zero-degree editing by foregrounding it so that the continuous-discontinuous potential for an editing rupture is, therefore, eliminated and in its place is a pronounced conjunctive zeugma. These slick transitions to unite divergent clues mimic Fulci's story line which centers on contrivance.

Carol, riding a horse on her father's estate, encounters Jenny whose enigmatic message functions like a directive from a folk tale adventure-quest that the heroine must carry out to reach a goal. Jenny instructs Carol to go with 50 pounds to Alexandra Palace's basement at 4 p.m. if she wants to know who murdered Julia; a lit candle will indicate the exact location. Carol once again seems absolved because Jenny was an "eyewitness" to the murder. The viewer is unaware of two truths: Carol's intricate motivations for implicating herself in Julia's death through the invention of a convoluted dream and that the drugged hippies, while present, are not reliable witnesses. Carol drives to the appointed meeting while her step-daughter proceeds by motorcycle to prove her father's innocence in Julia's death. In Alexandra Palace's basement a lighted candle awaits Carol. As she hears footsteps and sees the light from an electric torch, she fearfully runs through the underbelly of the building's Romanesque archways and debris-laden floors. A motorcyclist with a helmet and pulled-down visor flashes a knife raising the question whether the motorcyclist is Joan or one of the hippies. Dreamlike, doors mysteriously open for Carol as her pursuer follows. As in dream states, the editing allows for no analogous spatial connection between a silo-like room she now finds herself in and the basement where she came from. Carol runs up a huge metallic circular staircase as the camera, shooting from above, makes her appear inconsequential and assailable while her attacker quickly follows. She enters the lofty great hall with its skylights and immense Henry Willis pipe organ. Shooting Carol in an extreme long shot encircles her in an intimidating expanse of emptiness. Although these scenes constitute an established reality, they take on a nightmarish quality that mimics Carol's dreams in the first half of the film. Suddenly a low-angled close-up on Carol's face represents "a phase to be reached" in the film's temporal development.[17] The audience, after seeing her in extreme long shots, anticipates a facial close-up to reveal her accumulated stress.

Carol surveys her escape options, the camera imitating her anxiety by moving about frantically as in her dream of decaying corpses. The scene recalls that faced by the heroine in *Alice's Adventures in Wonderland*, toying with logic. Carol crawls into a peculiar little door in the pipe-organ housing barely large enough for her to fit, climbing through a maze of rafters. Her leather-clad aggressor, Hubert, hears Carol when she accidently hits the organ's starter button, and he follows her. The handheld camera's dizzying display of organ pipes produces a synesthetic equivalent of the intense sound leveled at Carol who covers her ears against the noise. Pursued, Carol races up another stairwell through more corridors, finally locking herself in a storage room where she is assailed by bats, recalling Melanie's attack in Hitchcock's *The Birds* (1963). It might also be noted that both Marnie Edgar and Carol Hammond serve as the films' heroines and villains, both are calculating, dangerous and use men to further their goals. Hitchcock, mindful of America's love of upbeat endings, has Marnie tamed by the patriarchal representation of manliness, Mark Rutland. Fulci instead uses Stanley Baker as the patriarchy's means of punishing this transgressive woman for committing murder, causing her father to sacrifice himself, and preferring same-sex love. Carol is stabbed by Hubert who gets through another small door to the roof, but before Hubert has a chance to kill her, the police arrive and he escapes on a motorcycle.

Joan, in a similar black leather outfit to Hubert's, enters a seemingly abandoned building. A knife, recalling Hubert's, is thrown near her head which drips red paint. So similar is Joan's red hair and outfit to Hubert's that the viewer is momentarily confused by the ostensible coupling of identical characters. Once the knife is thrown, however, the audience reconstructs another scenario where the assassin is now out to murder Joan as he attempted to kill her stepmother. Startlingly, the knife thrower is Jenny, painting by submerging the blade in paint and then throwing it onto the blank canvass and calling it *Putrefaction*, suggesting the film's attitude toward countercultural art. The knife's red paint embedded in the canvass also recalls Carol's plunging a knife into Julia's breasts in what first appeared to be an amorous encounter. In Fulci's universe, oneiric phallocentricity becomes perceptibly manifest in omnipresent knives brandished by Jenny, Hubert, Carol and even Joan. Joan, friendly with Hubert, is hoping to see him there and to uncover the real murderer in order to place blame on Carol. As Jenny, taking Joan's hand and putting it inside her pants, attempts to seduce her (paralleling Julia's seduction of Carol), the latter agrees to give her money for the painting if the hippie will tell her where Hubert is. The scene nonchalantly links abstract painting to perversity and perversity to lesbianism in a film where "the other" is either killed, grilled by the police or carted off to jail and pigeonholed as villain, seducer, debauchee and double-crosser.

Joan phones her father, not knowing Edmond is listening, that Hubert may be able to vindicate Frank in Julia's death, and goes to meet the hippy at Woburn Abbey. This phone conversation causes Edmond to commit suicide believing that Carol killed Julia. A jump cut to the abbey discloses Joan's severed throat. Hubert confesses to the murder and the attempt on Carol, but not to killing Julia Durer. Corvin theorizes that the murderer was the person Julia was blackmailing but rules out Frank. In corralling the two hippies for an interrogation at Julia's apartment, the inspector discovers that they were so wasted that they saw nothing, although Hubert admits that he might have killed Julia unknowingly, but can only recall seeing a lizard in a woman's skin, referring to the fur coat which Carol shed. Since Carol and Joan knew he was in the apartment, he tried to kill them both. When news is brought that Edmond, in a suicide note, has confessed to Julia's murder, there is a jump cut to Carol at her father's grave site where Corvin unravels the mystery. No one told Carol about the blackmailing phone call to Edmond from a "Mrs. Smith," providing the motive in Julia's slaying.

Lizard in a Woman's Skin, conflating the protagonist with the antagonist, leaves no probability for a happy ending other than justice being served. The villain's defeat corresponds to the heroine's capture in a uncharacteristically subdued scene at the cemetery.

1. **A member of the family leaves home (I).**

    Carol Hammond is first seen on a train; it is a metaphor for the trip through her psyche. This form of absentation is a momentous journey although it doesn't cover an immense physical distance as it does an emotional and psychic one. She has gone to see her psychiatrist, and this more prosaically constitutes the trip away from home.

2. **An interdiction is addressed to the heroine (II).**

    The interdictions against societal and civil taboos given to Carol are in the attenuated form of "suggestions" by her psychiatrist to remove the mental block causing her conflict. His affirmative attitude toward Carol's dreams serves to exonerate Carol from guilt and persuade her to think and act positively. The dreams indicate her conscience's disapproval of Julia Durer's lifestyle, although her sexual openness attracts Carol. Dr. Kerr tells her that killing Durer is only symbolic, a liberating act, killing that part of Carol drawn to sin and vice. He argues that Carol must not think the hippies that saw her are real, but witnesses invented by Carol's ego to attest to the crime.

3. **The interdictions are violated (III).**

    Although the interdictions are "suggestions" that Carol should follow, they are affirmatively spoken because Kerr regards them as a wish fulfillment expressed through a dream. Nonetheless, within that dream are taboo subjects that must be presented solely as symbolic signifiers for a patriarchal society to accept, forcing Carol to hide her vices and ignore Kerr's advice. Her lived reality, however, includes lesbianism, adultery, murder and its concomitant vice, blackmail, violating not only social and moral conventions but civil as well. So while there is no verbal, forthright interdiction, except for her not to think negatively, there is an implied one which prohibits murder and adultery. At this point Propp states that the antagonist enters the story. This film is unique in that the principal protagonist is also the preeminent antagonist. In effect, Carol is the anti-heroine, and her lover, Julia Durer is the catalyst, a malicious woman whose attempted blackmail of Carol results in her death.

Without Julia's death, Hubert (a minor antagonist) would not have tried to murder Carol and kill Joan, believing they saw him go into Julia's apartment the night of the murder.

4. The villain receives information about her victim (V).

Since the villain may be bifurcated into at least two people, Carol Hammond and Julia Durer, with Hubert in a subsidiary role, the choices are plentiful. The viewer learns, through Inspector Corvin, that Julia was blackmailing Carol because she could use her to threaten the Hammond family and prevent Edmond Brighton from running for political office. The real nature of the Carol-Julia relationship naturally cannot immediately be revealed, but because it is a sexually intimate one, Carol has full knowledge about her victim and the victim's lifestyle, while Julia has enough information about the Hammonds to blackmail her lover. Hubert's knowledge, however, is flawed, proceeding on the erroneous assumption that he might have killed Julia under the influence of drugs and that Carol and Joan can link him to Julia's death knowing he was with her the night she died.

5. The villain attempts to deceive the victim in order to take possession of her (VI).

Obviously, sexual intimacy doesn't necessarily reveal everything about your partner's motivation, especially when real love is not the foundation. Carol, who appears to be the more submissive one in the lesbian relationship, becomes the aggressor when threatened with blackmail which, if known, will ruin her socially and her father politically and serve as an excuse for her husband to divorce her. Carol deceives her family and psychiatrist to manipulate them toward her ends. Julia who first appears simply to be a bisexual hedonist utilizes her knowledge about Carol to blackmail her, turning out to be a ruthless, mercenary woman who uses sex for pecuniary advantage. Hubert, who is drugged much of the time, oblivious of the world around him and living in a hippie enclave, becomes a killer when he believes his life is on the line and lures Joan and Carol into thinking that he knows who murdered Julia.

6. The victim submits to deception and thereby unwittingly helps her enemy (VII).

Carol submits to Julia's deception because her relationship with her husband has grown cold. He has a mistress and Carol takes on a lesbian lover. Julia deceives Carol, interested in taking advantage of her wealth and privileged position. In all probability Carol is aware of this, but submits to Julia's subterfuge because she is attracted to the woman's lifestyle. Joan is so desperate to clear her father and involve her stepmother that she agrees to meet Hubert who pretends to have information for her only to kill her.

7. The villain causes harm or injury to a member of a family (VIII).

Propp considers this function immensely significant since by it the actual movement of the story is created. Carol's manufacturing of a story for her therapist to cover her adulterous liaison and murder is responsible for her father's suicide and Joan's death and possibly her husband's taking on a mistress. Julia's attempted blackmail has repercussions not only for Carol's social footing but her father's bid for public office. Julia's lifestyle and her death also have reverberations for the hippy community in the person of Hubert and Jenny. The story's complication is inaugurated by the villainous acts of Carol and Julia which manifest themselves within Propp's subcategories: Carol murders Julia, the benefactress of the hippy community (#14); Julia torments Carol by attempting to tell her father that his daughter is a lesbian with the purpose of blackmailing him (#18); and Hubert, a minor villain, causes bodily injury to Carol by stabbing her in the arm (#6) and murders Joan by slitting her throat (#14).

8. The heroine is tested and attacked which prepares the way of her receiving a helper/donor (XII).

We have considered Carol as a protagonist/antagonist as opposed to a traditional *giallo* heroine. Usually the films posit a villain, unknown but singled out to the audience by his/her attire or peculiar voice patterns whose motives and features remain unidentifiable until the very end. The villains who imperil these women bring about a donor to rescue them, usually in the form of a potential love interest. In such films, the law, in most cases, is ineffectual in solving the crimes, and it is the donor/male romantic lead who helps resolve the case and rescues the heroine. *Lizard in a Woman's Skin* has as a traditional donor, Inspector Corvin, and nominally, in the figure of a psychiatrist, Dr. Kerr, despite its non-traditional anti-heroine. Neither of these two are romantic leads, although both initially are there to help the heroine: the inspector attempts to save her from legal prosecution, the doctor from mental anxiety.

Several of category XII's ten variants apply directly to Fulci's story: (#2) "The donor greets and interrogates the hero," (#7) "Other requests" and (#8) "A hostile creature tries to destroy the heroine." Inspector Corvin does interrogate the heroine/villain in an attempt to find out the murderer of Julia Durer and the motive for the killing. He is on Carol's side seeking to aid a woman who appears to have been framed. The police are also there for her when she is about to be stabbed by another secondary villain, Hubert. Dr. Kerr is present to assist Carol through her supposed psychological problems and thus cope with life. Although the audience does not witness Dr. Kerr directly interrogate Carol, we can presume professionally that he has, since the responses he makes to her in their sessions, and the dreams she recounts to him are the results of his questioning her. As far as "requests" are concerned,

Julia, also a secondary antagonist, doesn't voice her request to Carol directly for money, but indirectly attempts to destroy Carol through blackmail. In this fashion Julia becomes a "hostile creature" endeavoring to make Carol submissive to her will.

9. **The villain is defeated (XVIII).**

The several villains of the narrative are defeated in diverse ways. Julia is murdered by Carol "Without a preliminary fight," believing that the latter is there to make love to her (subcategory #5). Carol is defeated by Corvin in a "Contest of wits" (subcategory #2), the inspector's deductive reasoning leads to her arrest in the cemetery, and finally Hubert is "Beaten in open combat" (subcategory #1) with the police and is arrested.

10. **The task is resolved (XXVI).**

The resolution finds most of the principal characters getting what they deserve. After the fact, the film's hero is Inspector Corvin who painstakingly sees that justice is done in a professional, objective and unobtrusive manner. Carol, under Italian law, would not receive the death penalty which was abolished in 1948. Julia and the strong-willed Joan received the harshest treatment, and one might surmise that the film's handling of them is more than a little misogynistic. The police have brought Hubert to justice who would be imprisoned for murder, attempted murder and possession and use of cocaine. Corvin is able to see through Edmond Brighton's suicide as a noble but foolhardy gesture to protect his daughter whom he knew was a murderer. One feels sorrow at Joan's death in attempting to clear her father from possible murder charges. The only person allowed to go free is Frank Hammond. With the death of his father-in-law and the incarceration of his wife, Frank would inherit the estate, continue his position in the law firm and be free to marry his mistress.

4

Murder According to the Good Book

Umberto Lenzi's *Sette orchidee macchiate di rosso* [*Seven Blood-Stained Orchids*, 1972]

> *That practis'd falsehood under saintly shew,*
> *Deep malice to conceal, couch'd with revenge.*
> —John Milton, *Paradise Lost*

Cornell Woolrich's novel *Rendezvous in Black* (1948) concerns the senseless death of a woman killed before her wedding day by an empty liquor bottle thrown from a charter plane by a businessman. She and her fiancé, Johnny Marr, met at the same time, in the same place every day. When he arrives late, he finds a crowd surrounding her body. Marr then methodically takes jobs at all the charter plane companies to discover which one flew over the spot where his fiancée died. He finds a list of the five men involved and gets revenge by killing females closely associated with them. After each death, the men find notes asking, "How does it feel?" The police eventually catch Johnny but only after all the women are killed.

Based on the Woolrich novel, the seeds of Umberto Lenzi's *Seven Blood-Stained Orchids* are here. Silver half-moon crescents have been substituted for the prosaic notes, but in *Seven Orchids*, unlike the novel, the police don't apprehend the murderer. Yet both the film and novel's driving force is the revenge motif: in the novel, Marr seeks revenge for his fiancée's senseless death; in the film, a brother seeks revenge for his sibling's senseless death. In *Seven Orchids* it is the hero, Mario Gerosan (Antonio Sabato), a fashion designer, together with his wife, Giulia Torresi (Uschi Glass), who solves the mystery of the murdered women, not the police. In Woolrich's novel, the antihero is driven to act as judge and jury, dispatching his victims methodically;

in the film a minister, attired like a Roman Catholic clergyman and only identified as "The Priest" (Renato Romano), is the unredeemable villain planning to murder a number of women, one of which he believes is responsible for his brother's death. The catalytic agent is Anna Satori (Marisa Mell) who has been having an affair with the priest's brother, Frank Saunders, leaving him to die in a car accident rigged by his jealous homosexual lover, Barrett (Bruno Corazzari), because, being married, she doesn't want a scandal. The priest, only aware that the guilty woman worked or stayed at a hotel nearby run by Giulia and her family, manages to kill six innocent women, but Anna goes unscathed. Giulia, one of the priest's potential victims, is attacked by him on a train and left for dead. Soon after, she and her husband set out in search of the murderer.

Lenzi was not entirely gratified with the finished product, commenting that the well-photographed story was sententious. He agreed with Argento that a logical story line in a *giallo* is a matter of opinion because an audience prefers "spectacular events to a turgid screenplay ... with ... pedestrian explanations to events which distract the audience's attention."[1] The director's comment about Argento is shrewd. Argento creates spectacular set pieces, as does Lenzi to a lesser extent, but Argento's are in the form of nightmare fantasies that eschew logic in their hallucinatory quality. Argento's complex internal logic in his stylistic murder scenes is connotative rather than denotative, suggesting rather than indicating; his images proceed from one to another, not linearly but poetically.[2] Lenzi's set pieces are usually denotative rather than connotative, akin more to realism than surrealism, more to a docudrama than a lyrical style. The disparity between the two directors might be further analogized. Lenzi's *Seven Orchids* is shot well but it is formulaic, and what subordinates it to Argento's *Opera* or *Tenebrae* is that Lenzi follows all too closely the well-defined structures of the classic whodunit without any of Argento's daring that ruptures the mold of orthodox detection films. Argento considers his films "like a dream. Or like a séance. Or like psychoanalysis." For him solving the crime isn't as crucial as it is in Lenzi, since "motivation doesn't matter ... very much.... I'm interested in seeing what goes on in people's minds."[3] This then is the problem with Lenzi's film. The viewer gets to watch the conventional point-of-view shots, but never gets into the characters' minds. Lenzi's story sticks to a surface reality found in ratiocinative fiction, but the outcome is to make *Seven Orchids* quite talky.

One tradition Lenzi has maintained is to imitate the husband and wife celluloid sleuths like Nick and Nora Charles of *The Thin Man* series (1934), the difference being the mundane manner in which Mario and Giulia go about their criminal investigations. Gone is the banter that made Nick and Nora human, giving them some depth and credibility even as Hollywood escapist fare. While Argento captured this joie de vivre between the sleuthing couple, Marcus Daly and Gianna Brezzi in *Profondo rosso* (*Deep Red*, 1975), which created an unlikely chemistry between them, there is little chemistry between Sabato and Glass; their characters are more functional than relational in moving the plot forward. With this as a limitation, Lenzi, nevertheless, has some genuinely splendid set pieces that this chapter will investigate.

An insouciant Ritz Ortolani score opens the film, eschewing the conventional ominous music heralding many *gialli*, with a predominant percussion by unpitched wood blocks, bongo drums and electric guitar. The tune's smooth, mellow beat acts contrapuntally to the scene which initiates the activities of a killer. Most of the opening credit roll is over a subjective shot from a car interior at night on a busy highway and concludes with a reverse exterior shot as the car comes toward the camera, its lights virtually blinding our eyes and ending in an extreme close-up of a Mercedes grill. Lenzi flawlessly sets up the next sequence through judicious editing. A figure in black emerges from the car surrounded by darkness; a streetlight sheds little illumination on the killer's features or attire, and when taken from an extraordinarily low angle his black clothing blends into the shadowed landscape while a Dutch angle destabilizes the space. The camera begins its brief probe of the area outside an apartment building, the antagonist's destination. There is a cut inside to a brightly lit stairwell where a black gloved hand releases a switchblade. Much of this sequence is taken from the killer's viewpoint leaving the perceptual and psychological facet of the discourse greatly constricted through his perspective. Once inside the darkened apartment, the killer turns on a flashlight which shines into the camera, purposely obscuring his features on several occasions and thus compromising the shot's intended objectivity. The camera then moves further into the apartment. As is the wont of the *giallo*, the individual is represented through synecdoche. The camera slowly scrutinizes the space through subjective and objective viewpoints, quickly progressing, however, to mainly subjective shots, thereby forcing the viewer to be complicit in the culminating act of murder of an old woman by positioning him in the assailant's place. In the victim's bedroom, the probing subjective camera eventually rests on a photograph of a young woman emphasized by a quick pan to it on a night table followed by a tighter shot on her face. Scant attention is given to the stabbing of the old lady in bed to concentrate on the picture, implying that the murderer has mistaken the sleeping woman for her daughter, a prostitute, and the object of his search. Lenzi[4] denied that he had copied the killer's traditional black costume from other directors inasmuch as the murderer is a priest. It was natural for Lenzi's antagonist, therefore, to be dressed as such, unlike other directors who canonically used black clothing as a generic symbolic signifier.

The murder of the old woman's daughter begins with establishing shots of a group of prostitutes plying their trade, but concentrates on the woman identified in the photo as Inez Tamborini (Gabriella Giorgelli), but known as "La Toscana." In long shot the villain sounds his car's horn, and she gets into his black Mercedes. Although "La Toscana's" slaughter, comprising 15 shots, is photographed with traditional crosscuts from the victim to killer, there are subtle touches. A long shot of the prostitute getting into the Mercedes jump cuts to another long shot of the now empty car parked in a wooded area preparing the viewer for the next shot of the woman undressing in the bushes by including foliage that appeared in the preceding shot; the car also acts as a metonymic referent closely associated with the villain. Amid tall leafy branches, the prostitute, stripped to her panties, her back to the viewer, turns toward the camera informing the john to begin. The camera dollies in to a close-up of her anxious face. She backs away moving to and fro, the camera panning to follow her movements. Finally the camera dollies in to her in close-up as she, in fright, backs onto a walkway pleading with the killer. The alternating shots begin first from the murderer's point of view followed by the synecdochical references to the killer from the prostitute's viewpoint, that is, shots of his black gloved hand and machete. Although "La Toscana" views the villain's entirety, we only see a glove and a weapon. This strategy serves two purposes: one is to show her psychological fixation on the instrument of death to the exclusion of the murderer himself, and second, to conceal the serial killer's identity through synecdoche that eschews realism for filmic convention. These alternating shots must culminate where both victim and victimizer are within the same space. The prostitute's arm is raised to ward off the blow as the camera pulls back from her to reveal blood dripping down her naked breasts. With the man's arm and blade soft focused in right foreground, he slashes the woman in sharp focus on the ground. She lifts her head and falls back. Then there is a subjective shot of a close-up of the killer's hand holding a gory blade. In medium-close shot the woman lies on the ground; the hand and blade are in the right bottom corner of the frame. The camera zooms to her bloodied face and open mouth as she dies. The aftermath shows only the killer's legs and feet walking through the underbrush while the final shot of swaying foliage is all that is needed to authenticate his departure. Although the prostitute has been viciously slashed with a machete, Lenzi has learned from Hitchcock's bathtub scene in *Psycho*. Never once can the machete be seen piercing the woman's skin; the movement of the blade from either the killer's or victim's viewpoint is highlighted only in its downward circular arc.

The film's prologue, now concluded, establishes the killer and his technique; no immediate reason is supplied for the murders. The film proper begins with the police investigation and introduction of the romantic leads, Giulia and Mario. At the crime scene Inspector Vismara (Pier Paolo Capponi) finds the silver crescent left by the murderer in the prostitute's hand. There is a cut to Giulia in a boutique trying on a wedding dress when she receives a call from someone who hangs up as she picks up the receiver and fashion designer and husband-to-be, Mario, walks in. We are made to realize that someone on the opposite side of the street is watching the heroine at "La Petite Jolie." At the shop, Giulia confides to Wanda (Linda Sini), the owner, that she wants the traditional white dress with orange blossoms while Wanda refuses to follow Mario's designs for the dress. Mario informs Wanda that if she removes the scarf from Giulia's outfit, she would look like a whore, linking her with the murdered prostitute previously seen and implying that Giulia's unknown caller might be that prostitute's assassin.

At an art gallery the killer calls to see if Kathy Adams (Marina Malfatti), a painter, is there. There is a cut to the killer's black leather gloves, pants and shoes; the rest of his body is blocked from view by the opened phone booth door. As with Giulia, he positions himself across the street from the gallery and walks over to see Kathy pick up the phone. There is a justification for dramatizing these two seemingly unessential scenes because the murderer's approach reveals something personal about him. Why call the women when he is so near? One answer is that he doesn't know them by sight and must confirm who they are by calling, hanging up, and then noting who picks up the receiver. The question then would be, why does he want to kill women he doesn't know? This leads to a labyrinthian mystery only answered when Mario forces a confession from Anna Sartori, an intended victim whose twin sister is mistakenly killed in her place.

Seven Orchids, among others, pushes femicide to an extreme. Since the villain doesn't know which of seven women have left his brother to die, he is willing to slay them all. Toying with these females' lives becomes the film's set pieces illustrating Dario Argento's belief that women make the best victims because they appear more vulnerable than men, unlike the "Final Girl" in today's films who is capable of defending herself. This phenomenon is due in part to the feminist movement, the decline of the archetypal passive fictive heroine, and concomitantly the need to have women as role models since they are now asserting their independence through control of their own bodies, freeing themselves from traditional domestic duties through labor-saving devices, as well as occupying executive positions in industry and government. Feminism *a l'Italiano* was belatedly introduced in the early 1970s when such *gialli* were popular and reached its culmination between 1974 and 1978 toward the end of these thrillers' heyday. The earlier objectives of the movement included combating violence against women, but as slowly as feminism arrived in Italy it swiftly departed, being turned over to less militant and more traditional women's organizations and those in lay political parties.[5] Yet this initial empowerment can fleetingly be observed in Giulia, although when placed in difficult situations she is apt to faint, the male arriving just in time to save her. All the same, Giulia can be viewed as an amalgamation of the new feminine assertiveness taking hold in Italy, while embodying characteristics of an older mythos associated with the defenseless heroine. On the one hand she longs for the traditional bridal gown with orange blossoms but wears, to please her fiancé, a '70s mod outfit designed by him. On the other hand she risks her life as a decoy to aid her husband in trapping the murderer, puts up a feisty battle with the villain on the train, ventures to outmaneuver the killer in her home and attempts to attack him with a spade at poolside.

But female empowerment is in short demand when Lenzi exploits variegated weapons used to dispatch the other females. The old woman at the film's opening is knifed, her daughter is butchered with a machete, an artist is strangled by a phone cord, a senior is drowned in her bathtub, a teacher is strangled in a confessional while another is murdered with a power drill. Lenzi is able structurally to justify the exclusive killing of females, but this does not mitigate the fact that women's bodies are on display in all their beauty for the sole purpose of being degraded. The biblical injunction, "An eye for an eye," or what is known as "equitable retribution" found in Leviticus (24:19–21), Exodus (21:22–25), and Deuteronomy (19:21) ironically dovetails with the priestly killer's vocation as minister. He is simply killing by the "Good Book."

Kathy Adams goes home that night from the art gallery and ominous chords set the tone and warn of impending danger. Her apartment has been turned into an art studio with canvases, easels, frames, wall paintings and objets d'art. As she gives her three cats their milk, noise from an open patio door is heard in another room. Next, one is aware of the chirping of birds off-screen. Kathy becomes aware of the cats' yowls, then discovers that their milk has been poisoned and sees them dying. She walks into the living room, hears footsteps, and, gasping, stares at something off-screen. A swish pan unites her gaze to her drawing of a woman's face; blood-red watercolor dripping from the figure's eyes and head confirms an intruder's presence. The camera zooms to Kathy's eyes and then to those in the painting when, in a wide shot of the studio-living room, the lights go out. Kathy runs to a red phone and dials. Immediately a black gloved figure grabs her, strangling her with the telephone cord as she struggles. From her point of view the camera moves dizzily about the room indicating her distress, cuts back to a close-up of her face with the wire around her throat, zooms in to an extreme close shot of her eyes as the cord is pulled tighter, then cuts to an extreme close-up subjective shot of the eyes in the painting streaming with red pigment, finally cutting back to an extreme close-up of Kathy's eyes as though art is mirroring life. The armored figure decorating her living room sways back and forth on ropes as if also to mimic her distress. There is a cut to a close-up of her exposed breasts and a zoom out from her half-naked body to a long shot as black and red paints drip onto her chest from cans on a shelf above. The association between the vandalized painting and the victimized Kelly conflates into one as paint continues to trickle onto her body. From frame left the black-clad killer bends over her as the camera zooms in to a close-up of her face with eyes staring out blindly.

The murder sequence is stunning in its execution while employing traditional tropes to effectuate its suspense. Dialogue is inessential, sound being more vital to the dramatized conflict. Changes in focal distances between extreme close-ups and long shots alternately limit Kathy to a confined space or broaden it through deep focus and wide-angle shots making her appear open for an off-screen attack. Ambient sound, without its visualized source, is paramount as it employs the apartment's off-screen area to psychologically suggest danger from an impalpable presence. The first important sound comes from a patio door which, from the kitchen, cannot immediately be identified. Here sound is progressively diegeticized and first operates as a signaling device to raise expectations of an imminent crisis only to reveal that the noise emanates from an unexceptional source of an unlocked door. That the door is ajar insinuates, however, that someone has gained access to the apartment. So, while the discovery of the noise's origin is designed to allay Kathy's fright, it adds to our developing fear. From this point on, Lenzi continues to unite each of the incidents leading to Kathy's homicide through sounds occurring in a steady sequential progression. The sound of her chirping birds appears immediately after the closing of the patio door. Kathy's unconcerned look and the birds' tranquil pitch add to the flat's normality. Yet immediately following this comforting sound, we hear the cats mewling in distress. From Kathy's viewpoint we observe their milk bowls, then a close-up of her face followed by another shot from her perspective as the camera pans over the prostrate bodies of the three cats. A direct overhead shot now minimizes her figure to appear more inadequate to the situation as she tastes the milk. She stands up quickly while over the wailing of the dying animals, a sonority of footsteps walking on a wooden floor is detected, but when she moves into the living room no one is present although the sound persists. Kathy calls out. The chirping from the aviary is heard a second time seeming to indicate normalcy, but as she moves through the living room their sounds are appropriated by a cacophonous tympani to alert the audience of the murderer's appearance. When the lights go out, Kathy screams, and for a third time the only sound is that of the chirping birds. Picking up the phone, an over-amplified dial tone signals her call. The pitch of the dial tone, like that of the birds, is also palliating in that it is a connection to outside assistance. Yet the phone, as a means of communication, is employed as an instrument to dispatch Kathy, its cord suddenly wrapped around her throat. As she struggles, there is a cut to the birds that now mimic her distress while their escalated cadence simulates an empathetic sound effect. The clangor made by a suit of armor adds a hollow dissonance to the homicide, intimating the struggle transpiring just outside the frame.

As the killer starts to deliver his second silver crescent, there is a match cut to Inspector Vismara, the crescent in his hand, appearing as though the killer had placed it in the officer's own palm from the previous shot. The brief talk between Vismara and Lieutenant Palumbo (Aldo Barberito), his aide, concerning the murdered women and the killer's motivation is at pains to inform us that the police are faithful in carrying out their job, but they, at the film's conclusion, are not even present to apprehend the assassin. Although quite ineffectual at bringing the killer to justice, the police are no mere decoration. There is an incongruity here and even a social message that police cannot always protect society: laymen must take the law into their own hands. This idea feeds into the sociopolitical climate of the times. 1968 was the year in which socially heterogeneous groups in Italy created a mass movement to topple the government and its political systems to effect a radical transformation of society. The result was that the country's swift growth and economic expansion during the '60s ended in a recession in the early '70s. During this decade in which films like *Seven Blood-Stained Orchids* were produced, the political tensions gave birth to terrorist movements that unsettled Italy. Right and left-wing extremists took arms to try to transform the Italian state according to their own visions, and the *anni di piombo* ("years of lead"), leaving many dead, was launched. With this shift in the sociopolitical environment, cities became unsafe places in which to live. Criminal developments unsettled the public's feeling of security, and political terrorism, both by the neo-fascists supported by rogue components of the CIA and extreme leftists, became daily features on television and in the newspapers.[6] This turmoil spurred on a slew of police pictures as if to take cinematic control of the cities. Steno's *La polizia ringrazia* (*Execution Squad*, 1972) and Fernando Di Leo's *Milano Calibro 9* (*Caliber 9*) and *La mala ordina* (*Manhunt*, 1972) are a few of the many police films made before and during the years of unrest in Italy. These *poliziottesco* led, within the *gialli*, to alternative crime-solving films; Italians took a page from American pictures which in previous decades had featured amateur sleuths unraveling mysteries that police weren't capable of handling. This convention enabled audiences to identify with the "average person" in the story, becoming more absorbed in the investigation as armchair detectives while matching wits with the killer.

As Vismara tells Palumbo (a pun on the U.S. TV detective, *Columbo* [released March 1, 1971], and possibly on the word *piombo*) that Kathy was murdered as she was about to go to bed, the remark signals a parallel edit to the train on which Mario and Giulia are preparing to go to bed. Consequently, the first time we see them as husband and wife is the night Giulia is attacked in her train compartment combing her hair after Mario leaves to tell the conductor that the blinds will not close. The lights go out and the killer attacks.

The manner in which characters are accorded filmic space in the train compartment allows the audience to be drawn to either both of them or individually in several ways. Since the killer is costumed in black in the dark, Giulia's pale blue blouse automatically draws the viewer to her first, but, that aside, the cutting rhythm also directs the viewer's gaze. Periodically both the killer and Giulia receive equal time, but in most shots one or the other predominates. Since the heroine is the more important of the two and since the killer is meant to remain the shadowy figure, Giulia receives more film time. The assassin predominates only in one shot and then through the synecdochical black-gloved hand and arm. Punctuating the action, like rhetorical breaks in the unfolding drama, are exterior shots of the speeding train in blurring close-ups similar to swish pans, creating an episodic sequence of the attack in mini-episodes through an implied chronological development so that the audience only sees its highlights. Several shots begin with the same rhythmic movement of the upraised dagger poised to strike Giulia, the action playing out like a dance of death with the partners holding on to each other as they move around the compartment's small space. The killer's phallic knife becomes a misogynistic sign of loathing for the opposite sex and for its annihilation. Most of the prevailing shots are close-ups that confine the figures in a tight space leaving little room for Giulia's escape. The one long overhead shot of the struggle attenuates the couple while still allowing the attacker to loom over the heroine. A single shot takes us outside Giulia's compartment to focus momentarily on the conductor who saves her life. The scene's coda begins by bringing three participants in the drama together, summarizing the results of the previous ones: Giulia, wounded in the shoulder and neck, has been spared further injury; the conductor has saved her by his presence; and the assassin has escaped without knowing if she is dead. While the first shot of the sequence deals with Giulia standing before the mirror combing her hair, the final shot deals with Giulia prone before the mirror. The ambiguity of Giulia's condition is exacerbated by the next scene in the cemetery with Mario and a host of friends seeming to confirm his wife's death, but this counterfeited funeral is a stratagem to prevent her from being assaulted again. Later, to bring the killer into the open, news is released that Giulia is alive. At the funeral, police photograph the mourners for Mario to identify. Vismara, in a telling statement, confesses to Mario that without inside information the police are useless, forewarning us that amateur sleuthing is a necessary alternative to the law's inadequacy.

Leaving the private clinic after her attack, Giulia asserts that the silver crescent Vismara had given Mario was the same one the killer had sent to

Umberto Lenzi's Sette orchidee macchiate di rosso (1972)

A common trope, borrowing from the American films of the '30s and '40s, presents a husband and wife team who search for the killer: Mario (Antonio Sabato) and Giulia (Uschi Glas). (Umberto Lenzi's *Sette orchidee macchiate di rosso*).

their home as a sign that she was dead. Shown in flashback, Giulia reports that two years ago an American had a key chain crescent, but he wasn't a hotel client but only came to eat. This scene is pivotal, for less than half an hour into the film both spouses become a team to track down the man in black. After examining the hotel register, the page they are searching for, dated September 29, 1969, has been ripped out. They find that the murdered painter, Kathy Adams, was at the hotel during this time. Mario compiles a list of the people that were there a day before the 29th and the day after. Giulia remembers three names on the list, Elena Marchi (Rosella Falk), Concetta di Rosa (Petra Schurmann) and Anna Satori (Marisa Mell), while counting the murdered prostitute, Inez Tamborini, who worked for Giulia as a hotel maid; Giulia herself, who was thought to be murdered; and Inez's mother, the total is seven. Mario and Giulia conclude that the American might have a grudge against the women and set out to call on those remaining. Lenzi cuts to a mental institution where Elena Marchi resides convinced someone is out to kill her.

Once the lights are out in Elena's hospital room, the audience is treated to a barrage of simple diegetic sounds that have become familiar tropes. The murder sequence's textural system fittingly intensifies the suspense through a strategically implemented alternating syntagma between the victim and the newlyweds attempting to reach her in time. The visualization of the tension engineered through editing is thus:

Shot	Number of Shots	Content
#1	1	Elena fearful in bed
#2–#4	3	Mario and Giulia searching for hospital

4. Murder According to the Good Book

Shot	Number of Shots	Content
#5–#9	5	Elena more alarmed
#10–#12	3	Mario arguing with woman at door
#13–#14	2	Elena crying for help
#15–#17	3	Nurse Franca averse to answer call
#18–#22	5	Elena and killer's attack
#23–#25	3	Mario and Giulia searching for hospital
#26	1	Elena dragged to tub by killer
#27	1	Mario arguing with nurse Franca
#28–#37	10	Elena murdered in tub

The sequence opens with a single shot of Elena Marchi to set up the *mise-en-scène* where the significant action occurs. The shot (#1) of her mounting fear and subsequent death (#37) frame the sequence. Thunder and lightning cause Elena, in the dark, to cower in her bed. Most of the shots privilege the mental patient, although, as the sequence progresses, a systematic alternation in the number of shots is launched: there is a continuous accumulation of shots of the mental patient (#5–#9) accompanied by a diminution (#13–#14), then an increase (#18–#22) followed by second reduction (#27), finally reaching a considerable proliferation devoted to Elena and her killer (#28–#37). The cross-cutting between Elena (#1) and the newlyweds' search for her (#2–#4) is calculated to increase audience expectations of her plight by expanding the time it takes for the killer's attack. The final shots (#28–#37) of Elena are consequently the longest, the sequence building up to these concluding ten which synopsize the emotional and psychological consequence of the preceding 27. Because of their repetitive quality, scenes relating to the couple's search for Elena's address (#2–#4, #10–#12, #23–#25) are stable with no alternation in the number of shots until #27. They illustrate Mario's growing frustration (#10–#12) as he asks an uncooperative woman to use her phone to call the sanatorium. This parallels his argument in the hospital's lobby with an uncooperative nurse as he seeks to speak to Signora Marchi (#27), thus continuing to prolong the time Mario can reach the intended victim. The pattern of shots of the thwarted couple's search correlates to the pattern of shots of Elena's escalating alarm seen first in shot clusters of five and culminating in a cluster of ten. The first five (#5–#9) begin when she is awakened by the sound of thunder and lightning as Elena futilely attempts to switch on the lights, and conclude with an indication of the killer's presence by light streaming from her partially open bathroom door. The second cluster of shots (#18–#22) begins with her rushing to the door of her room screaming for help but unable to open it because nurse Franca has locked it from the outside, and ends with the killer's initial attack on Signora Marchi who faints at his approach. The third and culminating cluster is naturally the longest comprising 10 shots (#28–#37) of Elena's death as the killer drowns her in the bathtub and concludes with the black-gloved hand ready to place a silver crescent on the body.

Umberto Lenzi's Sette orchidee macchiate di rosso (1972)

The police, thanks to Mario and Giulia's investigation, proceed to the next woman on the list, Concetta di Rosa, a schoolteacher in Spoleto who remembers the victims, but not a tall American who ate at the hotel where the victims stayed. Mario discovers that the American was a Protestant who went to Catholic mass on Sundays for the Gregorian chant and that he is a friend of the hippy, Barrett. Barrett remembers the American as "Frank Saunders" who possessed a crescent key ring and had been dating a woman, but Barrett hasn't seen him since 1969.

Two police follow Concetta into church but leave when she goes into the confessional. The sequence's structural pattern illustrates its aesthetics:

Rhyme	Scene/No. of Shots	Content
a b	**Scene 1**: 1 shot inside church	ELS[7] Concetta kneels on the side of the confessional; the priest enters the curtained booth.
	Scene 2: 1 shot outside on church steps	Two policemen; one reports Concetta is in the confessional.
c b	**Scene 3**: 3 shots at police headquarters	Vismara and Palumbo listen to recording of the call made to Concetta by the parish priest [accomplished by two shots of them and an insert of the tape recorder].
	Scene 4: 1 shot of police on church steps	Police silent.
c d	**Scene 5**: 3 shots at police headquarters	Two police listening to tape. Cut to the parish priest who enters their office saying he was falsely called away to attend a dying man.
	Scene 6: 4 shots of police car	Police car rushing through streets to the church.
b a	**Scene 7**: 2 shots of police on church steps	Officers hear police car sirens while one goes into the church as others follow.
	Scene 8: 5 shots inside church	Tracking shot of police to confessional. Vismara pulls away curtain discovering Concetta's body inside priest's confessional, camera zooms in to her face sitting in the chair; cut to his face staring at body (off-screen), (his POV shot) camera zooms in to extreme close-up of her neck; cut to his face staring at body (off-screen), cut to CU (his POV) of Concetta's hand holding a crescent.

78   4. Murder According to the Good Book

The sequence constitutes 20 shots with eight scenes (only four discounting repeated scenes). Of the 20, the first scene and shot and the eighth scene and first, third, and fifth shots directly pertain to Concetta, for a total of four shots. The police procedurals take 17 shots counting the insert of the tape recorder in scene 3, highlighting the police's growing incapacity to protect the civilian. If one were to create a rhyme scheme of the scenes by using the content in each of them as an indication of the rhyme, beginning with the letter *a*, it would look thus: *ab*, *cb*, *cd*, **ba**. The content's repetitive design is varied enough to be intriguing without being perfunctory, familiar without being predictable. The sequence is divided into two parts: *ab*, *cb* (police in ascendency) followed by *cd*, *ba* (police in defeat), all alternating interior with exterior scenes. In each of the two scenes within the eight, a pattern and variation is established. Each scene is yoked to an unfamiliar one. The first two launch the pattern: *a*, an interior shot inside the church of the victim at the confessional, is linked to *b*, an exterior shot of the officers in front of the church. Not only are the two connected spatially but they also are yoked thematically by the person the law is protecting with those who do the protection. This is followed by *cb*, *c* being the new scene, *b* the repetitive scene: here the narrative tension has been increased; the interior of police headquarters is united with the exterior of the church, enforcing concurrent images of protection: the superiors masterminding the security and those who carry out their orders. This is succeeded by *cd*, *c* being the repetitive scene at police headquarters and *d* the new scene of their race to protect the woman under surveillance, linking not only interior with exterior but causally linking the information obtained in *c* with the resultant action in *d*. Observing that most of the shots are rather static, these four action shots in scene *d* of the law coming to the woman's rescue, while not rhyming with any anterior or posterior shots, break up the static quality of the sequence midway. In order for the concluding scenes [*ba*] to provide a ligature for the entire sequence, it is essential that they end with familiar scenes repeating the two opening scenes but in a reverse order so that the main action, "to protect Concetta," ironically concludes the sequence with external shots of the church and officers still standing guard followed by five shots of the church interior with the inspector examining the murdered woman they were to safeguard.

Within this sequence is an alternating syntagma to create a "coming to the rescue" trope. It has already been established that the sequence begins (scene 1) and ends (scene 8) in a church. While the first scene employs a static camera, the eighth scene uses a long tracking shot and zoom. While scene 1 consists of only one shot to establish that the woman is going to the confessional, scene 8 comprises five shots, the largest in the sequence, to stress the corpse's condition, the swift reaction of Vismara as he strides into the church, and his adroit observation in examining the body of the strangled woman with a crescent in her hand. The extreme long shot of scene 1 has been attentively planned so that the facial features of the priest cannot be identified, and since the killer is a priest, the shot is not meant to mislead us into believing that the man in a black cassock and biretta is anyone other than a priest. Since the European confessionals are so constructed that the penitent kneels outside the box rather than inside, it is reasonable that the officers are outside the church to grant the woman privacy. Scenes 3 and 5 are parallel in establishing police procedure through an investigation of the phone call, but act antithetically, presenting the evil priest's disembodied voice (scene 3) contrasted to the benevolent priest's physical presence at headquarters (scene 5). Likewise scene 3 seems to confirm the parish priest's call to Concetta while scene 5 denies that the parish priest made the call. In short, the caller had to be the killer who telephoned the schoolteacher impersonating the parish priest. Scene 4 parallels scene 2, taking place outside the church, substantiating that the police are on duty which, like scenes 3 and 5, implies that Concetta is safe while denying the reality within. Scene 6 acts as a transition between the cerebral investigation at police headquarters and the crime site. The accelerated editing of the shots of the car traveling through city streets conveys Vismara's concern. The second half of the sequence consists of scenes 7 and 8. Once more we are faced with two antithetical scenes: scene 7 proclaims the signs of police protection but is belied by Concetta's corpse in scene 8. Consequently the sequence is replete with contradictions that lull the police into a false sense of security through their own investigative methods. For Lenzi nothing is predictable, neither the detailed police investigation to guard a potential victim nor the apprehension of the murderer even when he is in plain sight.

Mario's continued search for Frank Saunders leads him to the "Protestant Cemetery." Since Saunders was Protestant and, as we later learn, the killer, his brother, is a Protestant minister, all of this makes sense. Mario finds on Saunders' grave seven red-stained orchids and makes the connection between the number and the seven women being hunted down. He also discovers that Saunders was left to die in the car accident with Anna Sartori at the wheel; her emotional fragility, tied to the possibility of being discovered in an adulterous relationship, prompts her to leave the scene. Giulia informs Mario that there is a link between the killer and Saunders. Mario connects the informer who told him where to look for Saunders with Barrett, but the hippie has taken heroin and is "on the nod." Barrett couldn't forgive Frank for falling in love with Anna and not with him and engineered the auto accident.

The next murder begins when Anna Sartori, under police protection, is refused permission to pick up her son from school; she calls on her identical twin, Maria (the same actress). The killer unknowingly stalks Maria and when she tries to resist cuts her face with a metal crescent and drags her into the apartment basement tool room, killing her with a power drill. The first striking fact about the 20-shot scene is its circumscribed space employing only close-ups or extreme close-ups. Within this constrained area, the editing, enunciated by a fusillade of shots, methodically directs our attention to the most important objects: the woman's face, eyes, mouth and finally chest together with the killer's hand and the power drill he wields. These shots, however, contain a considerable bit of panning, tilting, and zooming. The percussive editing of the shots' repetitive content gives the impression of a notable expenditure of physical activity while temporally prolonging the murder to an unbearable length of emotional intensity. With a pan, the opening shot of three water valves and pipes is joined to black-gloved hands placing Maria on the floor followed by shots of the killer searching for a power drill. The proceeding shots (second half of #2 through #16), dealing with the killer's menacing movement toward the woman with the power tool, are crosscut with the victim in a quickening succession of shorter edits. The remaining four (#17–#20), as a climax to the deed, focus on the drill steadily penetrating the victim's flesh and wielded with sadistic delight. The act implies a sexual assault through symbolic penile empowerment. Unknowingly, the killer in murdering the women's twin sister, doesn't realize the car "accident" was a result of Barrett's jealousy over Frank Saunders's leaving him for a female. Both Barrett and the priest are united in their vindictiveness through their perceived notion of the power exercised by the female as "other."

Giulia and her husband arrive at a risky stratagem to capture the killer. As planned, Mario is hauled off by the police with reporters on the site. Giulia runs out of the house as they snap countless pictures of the "deceased" while that night broadcast news confirms that she is alive. Mario's wife now becomes the murderer's target once more. What follows is a superb trompe l'oeil of staging, the *mise-en-scène* placed strategically at the end of the film to mislead the viewers into believing that they are about to watch the killer's arrest. Giulia is alone in the house, but in this spurious finale where the audience expects closure, it is not the assassin who breaks in frightening Giulia to the point of unconsciousness, but Mario, who, with the law, has been keeping watch. Since she is the focalizer of the sequence, the audience derives its cues exclusively from an overwrought and therefore unreliable witness. *Seven Blood-Stained Orchids* mines the melodramatic tropes initiated by Gothic novels. One salient characteristic of such fiction involves both the psychological and physical terror flawlessly exhibited here. The mansion's Gothic architecture has been replaced by a modern house, but it is nonetheless threatening. Darkness and death, staples of such novels, are also present as well as the eventual revelation of family secrets uncovered in the final chapter, while the villainous priest in Lenzi's film is a counterpart to the prototypic cleric of Matthew Gregory Lewis's *The Monk* (1796). Giulia likewise embodies the archetypal Gothic heroine, a virtuous but emotionally distressed young woman, while Mario incarnates the typically strong, resolute fictional hero there to protect her.

The sequence begins with Giulia alone in the house. Nondiegetic music is kept to a minimum, the film relying more on diegetic sound to build suspense. Electronic instrumentation, with a hornlike pulsating beat, is abutted by reverberations of deep chords once the unsettled Giulia turns off a lamp and proceeds to light a cigarette pacing back and forth. There are no establishing shots of police presence in the vicinity so that Giulia seems quite unprotected even though we have been informed of her strategy as a decoy to expose the killer. Sound again plays a major role as in the former set pieces. The heroine's footsteps on the wooden floors form a repetitive resonance that testifies to her restlessness; her pacing suggests she is incarcerated awaiting execution, and in a manner of speaking she is. Accompanying this image is the amplified ticking of the clock which subjectively distends the temporal duration of the shot. But these sounds produce something else. Once the viewer is accustomed to hearing the scene's environmental acoustics, he is taught through this mechanism to become conscious of additional noises in the sonic register that might supply more information to produce what Jacques Lacan calls the "invocatory drive," that is, the desire to hear. The audience takes the sounds as cues to indicate emotional states of characters, the presence of another outside the *mise-en-scène*, the passing of time, and "secure" and "insecure" noises (those familiar versus those unfamiliar). For example, the ticking of a clock is a familiar sonancy and might be considered a "secure" noise, but for Giulia it also indicates time is passing slowly as she becomes on edge. The ringing of the telephone, usually associated with communication from the outside world, presages the presence of the killer. The heroine is further isolated because she cannot make an outgoing call since, once the killer has phoned, he has purposely left his receiver off the hook. That the assassin might be determining if she is at home suggests itself to Giulia, increasing her distress. The opening music now ceases and a succession of diegetic resonances replaces it. The sound of the electric shutters being closed is a "secure" sound, but it creates a feeling of entrapment. Likewise, the sound of bolting the door produces a feeling of security, but traces of this ubiquitous murderer's presence are evident since Giulia has heard a noise, discovered a wine bottle on the floor and found a lit cigarette. Here the moaning of the wind is a typical trope used as a correlative to indicate the woman's overwrought emotions. The fluttering of drapes next to an open window recalls the old dark house ambiance in numerous cinematic prototypes from Paul Leni's *The Cat and the Cannery* (1927) to Argento's *Suspiria* (1977). Giulia's screaming and sighing, terminating in her fainting, are likewise Gothic conceits signaling the heroine's perturbation and defenselessness as well as a fancied safeguard from sexual violation.

Cinematographically, the most conspicuous editing is not between the intended victim and victimizer (the threat is non-existent), but between Giulia and a baroque clock on her bedroom desk. There are three shots of the heroine interspersed with three shots of the clock ending in a tilt up to the clock's face. If Lenzi zooms in to the clock's face or simply shoots it with a static camera, he matches this with identical shots to the woman's face. The clock is there to visualize, in an existential fashion, how the systematic distension of time and space is affecting not only the character but the audience. Ironically at work is the counterpointing of slowly passing time with a percussive editing style that quickens the pace of the story's linear development generating conflicting emotions in a brief amount of film time.

Consider also the standard ploy of the *giallo* regarding confined dramatic space and its lighting: Giulia, positioned in the background and lit from behind, walks to the foreground through a space of some distance that, because of its low key lighting, enhances the room's intimidating quality and represents a movement from the light, typifying security and the known, to darkness epitomizing insecurity and the unknown. Her figure in the open door of a room furthermore, because of backlighting, becomes two-dimensional, physically less corporeal and ostensibly more exposed. Long shots of empty rooms and corridors add to the dramatization of space becoming ominous avenues that the killer can access from any point of the frame. These long shots are juxtaposed to confining close shots hemming Giulia in, and by lowering the angle, Giulia's confinement is exaggerated, seemingly pushing the ceiling nearer to her head. Again synecdoche is engaged to describe the unknown intruder by fragmenting his image to reveal only his hands, breaking a corridor window with a gun butt, his feet and black pant legs. Mario's break-in to the house is also staged in a fragmented fashion to mimic an assassin's forced entrance. Augmenting this, expressionistic devices of Mario's shadowy figure reflected on house walls give him a specter-like appearance able to access Giulia's private space. The director toys with his audience through this character bifurcation while the real intruder has escaped the police.

Vismara traces the open phone line on the killer's side because Mario's telephone has been tapped revealing Barrett's name, address and number, but they find that the hippy has hanged himself. Barrett had been to Giulia's hotel and discovered evidence that a woman there left Frank Saunders to die in his car. The police come to the conclusion that Barrett, out of jealousy, has tampered with his former lover's car, and believing that he had been found out, committed suicide, the half moons considered nothing more than a fetish. Mario disagrees with the police's verdict, and although they assure

Anna Sartori's husband, Mr. Palmieri (Andrea Bosic), that the affair is over, Mario gets Anna to confess that she was at the wheel of Saunders's car. Anna believes the crescent was a gift from Barrett's brother, and her physical description of him causes a flicker of recognition on Mario's face.

From Anna's home there is a cut to Giulia packing while a male voice on a phonograph record croons. The record suddenly stops. Giulia finds a silver crescent on it and the telephone wire cut. She opens one of the room's doors to see the wide-eyed priest looking at her. She screams, jumping out the window with the priest pursuing her, which is crosscut to one shot of Mario's car heading home. The limited space of the house is now opened with tracking shots of the priest running after Giulia though the extensive grounds. The crosscutting between the killer and his victim ends when both occupy the same frame at the pool where Giulia, about to pick up a spade for defense, is prevented by the priest. Just as he places a cord around her neck, Mario arrives and a fight ensues, both of them falling into the pool. Giulia, like a classic heroine, stands by helplessly as the two men fight. Lenzi cuts back no less than 12 times to Giulia's frightened face or to long shots of her isolated in space watching the struggle. Both individuals go under the water and as the priest rises from the pool, Giulia begins to run away, but he sinks back and Mario surfaces. That the director prolongs the excitement by the uncertainty of who will emerge victorious is a clever, if standard device, to make us hesitate in believing that the hero has been killed. As music rises, the two embrace and walk away from the camera to the house, while the priest's body remains underwater. The couple's movement away from the camera, heralded by a full orchestral accompaniment, constitutes a classic trope to signify the conclusion, and their movement toward a brighter future, substantiated by the well-lit white plaster house in the background, signals a return to normalcy and the resumption of an interrupted honeymoon.

Seven Blood-Stained Orchids conforms to Propp's fundamental folkloric categories.

1. **A member of the family leaves home (I).**

Giulia Torresi has taken a trip to a fashion boutique to be fitted for a non-traditional bridal dress that tells of her impending marriage and takes her away from her own residence. But the trip in another way is significant because: (a) it is the heroine's first fleeting contact with the killer who has already murdered two women, and (b) it introduces her fiancé, Mario, a fashion designer.

2. **An interdiction is addressed to the heroine (II).**

The interdiction here is an inverted form of a "request" that Giulia come to the phone at "La Petite Jolie" to answer unknowingly a call from the killer (subcategory #1). The initial situation describes a couple's "particular prosperity" which serves as "a contrasting background for the misfortune to follow." The very act of Giulia coming to the phone serves as her death sentence and acts as a prelude to that misfortune "hovering invisibly above the happy family"[8] following the deaths of a prostitute, her mother and Kathy Adams. The call serves as an oblique interdiction that Giulia does not immediately grasp, but that the audience realizes: the murderer will kill her, believing she might be responsible for his brother's death. So it is within this phallocentric situation, where the male dominates female desire, that the killer makes his first contact with Giulia via the telephone.

3. The interdiction is violated (III).

The violation of the interdiction can exist without the interdiction being addressed as with the aborted phone call she receives. The heroine, knowing that she is a target of the villain when attacked in the train compartment on her honeymoon, nevertheless takes on the task with her husband to track down the serial killer because all the women on the murderer's list stayed at the hotel she ran, and she feels a responsibility to bring him to justice.

4. The villain receives information about his victim (V).

In *Seven Orchids* the information the villain receives about the seven women is not dramatized because the incident is part of the backstory, but it comes to the fore through the couple's sleuthing. The malevolent cleric knows little about the seven women but has gotten information from Barrett who has been told by Frank Saunders, the priest's brother, in a letter before he died in a car accident, that he, Saunders, has left Barrett for a woman. Barrett knows that she was one of the females living/working at the hotel run by Giulia and has conveyed this intelligence to the priest. The priest murders Barrett so that the authorities won't trace the crimes to the clergyman, making it look like the suicide of a man burdened with a guilty conscience. The gift of a silver crescent given by the priest to his brother, Frank, now becomes the padre's calling card left on the females' bodies, their names having been obtained from the hotel registry, the dates determined by the day before to the day after the accident occurred. That is all the information the priest is able to procure about the woman in the car with Frank. It becomes his excuse for killing most of the women associated with the hotel between those specific days.

5. The villain attempts to deceive the victim in order to take possession of her (VI).

According to Propp, the villain first of all "assumes a disguise." Per se, the villain does not have to disguise himself as a priest since he is one, but as a man of the cloth he poses as an honorable representative of Christian religion in order more easily to get close to those whom he wants to kill. This is the reason he is so adept at strangling Concetta di Rosa with the police guarding the church door while the victim is in a confessional. The clergyman is also able to persuade Mario of his good intentions to locate a priest, now in Australia, who had known Frank Saunders (subcategory #1, "The villain uses persuasion."). We might assume that the priest has used his clerical position to get near to Giulia and to get close to the other women by becoming invisible to those in authority.

6. The victim submits to deception and thereby unwittingly helps her/his enemy (VII).

The major victim in this case is Giulia, although Mario as a co-protagonist has been deceived by the unctuous priest in two interviews with him, seeming to want to be of assistance. There are also six other victims of the clergyman. Wearing a clerical garb makes the priest inconspicuous and at the same time approachable. We may assume that many of the women he approaches are caught unawares, lulled into a false sense of security by his ecclesiastical clothing.

7. The villain causes harm or injury to a member of a family (VIII).

"Family" in this case is to be understood not only in terms of Mr. and Mrs. Mario Gerosan but more generally of the women in Giulia's hotel. Of the 18 subcategories listed by Propp pertaining to the patterns villainy takes, subfunction #6 is most applicable, "The villain causes bodily injury" as is the case with knifing Giulia in the train and stabbing Mario at the sanatorium. Regarding the other women, subfunction #14 is more appropriate, "The villain commits murder," since he murders five women who are connected to Giulia's hotel. The final applicable subfunction is #18, "The villain torments at night." With the exception of Maria Satori, Anna's sister, all the murders are committed at night when a villain can physically conceal himself more easily and exploit his day job as parish priest to cloak his more despicable activities at night.

8. The hero/heroine are tested and attacked which prepares the way of their receiving a helper/donor (XII).

The hero and his wife are knifed but not mortally wounded as they attempt to solve the mystery (subcategory #8, "A hostile creature attempts to destroy the hero/heroine"): The priest fails twice in his attempt to murder the heroine, once on the train and again on Giulia's own property, and twice in his attempt to murder the hero, once in the sanatorium and again at the pool in a climactic fight. The traditional donor is nominally the law. Although they are ineffectual in solving the mystery and protecting the couple, they must also be included as an essential part of the story for several reasons. The subcategory of this primary function is #2: "The donor greets and interrogates the hero/heroine." According to Propp, this "interrogation assumes the character of an indirect test." The law interrogates both Mario regarding the mourners who attended Giulia's sham funeral and interviews Giulia in her hospital bed about the pictures of the murdered women.

9. **The villain is defeated (XVIII).**

This takes place at the rented home of Mario and Giulia where her husband comes to her rescue and wrestles with the villain-priest both at poolside and in the pool (subcategory #1, "The villain is defeated in open combat"). We can observe what Mario has done to him when the priest's inert body is seen at the bottom of the pool. This battle is carried out with much cross-cutting between the heroine and the two men fighting, signifying her role in attempting to initially engage the villain when Mario takes over.

10. **The task is resolved (XXVI).**

Mario and Giulia set out to find the person murdering a number of women associated with the hotel she ran. It is through a joint strategy that the priest is defeated, although the couple's honeymoon is in abeyance until he is disposed of. At the conclusion, Giulia's packing her belongings at the rented house may be interpreted as her returning to her original home with her husband to begin a new life, or it may be construed as a beginning of their interrupted honeymoon.

5

His Blindness Is His Sight

Sergio Pastore's *Sette scialli di seta gialla* [*Seven Shawls of Yellow Silk*, 1972]

> Purring ... That same hideous nightmare thing,
> ...as he lapped my blood,
> ...Saying for ever, "Cat! ... Cat! ... Cat!..."
> —Robert Graves, *A Child's Nightmare*

Seven Shawls of Yellow Silk is set in Copenhagen and concerns a blind music composer for films, Peter Oliver (Anthony Steffen), who investigates a series of grotesque murders, the weapon being the claws of a black cat steeped in curare. Unfortunately, the film's English title, *Crimes of the Black Cat*, dissipates some of the initial mystery. Peter is determined to find the murderer of his ex-girlfriend, Paola Whitney (Isabelle Marchall), inexplicably killed at the fashion house where she works. He teams up with Margot Thornhill (Shirley Corrigan), a friend and co-worker of Paola's at the fashion house, and his butler, Burton (Umberto Raho), to find the killer. Before long they discover that Paola has had a liaison with Victor Ballais (Giacomo-Rossi Stuart), the husband of Françoise (Silvia Koscina) who manages the *maison couture*. Harry (Romano Malaspina), a photographer and cousin of Paola, has pictures of Victor and her in bed and is blackmailing him, but he also ends up murdered. All this occurs in the first 30 minutes.

The film's homage to various motion pictures is in no way a slavish imitation. To begin with, Pastore's *giallo* takes place in the fashion industry which had become a trope initiated in Mario Bava's *Sei donne per l'assassino* (*Blood and Black Lace*, 1962) and continued in Emilio Miraglia's *La dama rossa uccide sette volte* (*The Red Queen Kills Seven Times*, 1972). The most obvious homage, however, occurs in a scene where Peter is sitting by a moviola in his apartment watching a murder from Fulci's *Lizard in a Woman's Skin* in which Carol

Hammond slashes the breast of Julia Durer with a letter opener. Pastore exploits this selfsame act at the conclusion of *Seven Shawls* where Margot Thornhill's breast is likewise sliced open by the killer while taking a shower in Peter's apartment. The scene becomes a meta-reference to Fulci's film, but also mimics the shower scene in Hitchcock's *Psycho*.

References to other motion pictures imbedded in Pastore's are only tangential but use similar situations. In Jean Yarbrough's 1940 *The Devil Bat*, Bela Lugosi kills those responsible for denying him his share of a perfume company's profits by giving each of his employers' family members a cologne whose scent attracts a genetically engineered bat to attack any who wear it. In *Seven Shawls*, a cat with curare-tipped claws attacks those models wearing shawls embedded with an undetectable scent and whom Françoise wants to kill, abetted by an old friend, Susan Leclerc (Giovanna Lenzi), to cover up her murder of Paola. *Seven Shawls* also recalls Fred Zinnemann's *Eyes in the Night* (1942) where a blind detective is aided by his assistant and a butler similar to Peter Oliver's girl pal, Margot, and his butler, Burton, in Pastore's film. In Henry Hathaway's *23 Paces to Baker Street* (1956) a blind playwright walks into a bar and overhears a muffled conversation between a man and a whimpering woman whom he browbeats to perform a kidnaping. A similar incident initiates the action in *Seven Shawls*. Paolo Cavara's *La tarantola dal ventre nero* (*The Black Belly of the Tarantula*, 1971) concerns the blackmailing of drug addicts like Pastore's Susan Leclerc and a venom-tipped needle used to paralyze victims before killing them akin to the curare tipped cat's claws in *Seven Shawls*. In Dario Argento's *Il gatto a nove code* (*Cat O'Nine Tails*, 1971), a blind man, Franco Arno, also solves a murder mystery like Pastore's Peter Oliver which, concluding on a freeze-frame of Françoise Ballais's death, suggests another homage to Argento's *4 mosche di velluto grigio* (*Four Flies on Grey Velvet*, 1971) where a freeze-frame on the villain Nina Tobias's decapitated head terminates the story. In addition to this, Susan Leclerc, the white-capped drug addict, finds her counterpart in the mysterious capped murderer of *The Red Queen Kills Seven Times*. Such a homology among these films becomes self-conscious fiction calling attention to the film's status as artifact. The *gialli*, viewed in this light, are akin to metafiction which comments on its own linguistic identity, comparable to narcissistic narratives "designating this textual self-awareness."[1] John Barth calls this the "art of exhaustion" premised on the impossibility of novelty in today's literature.[2]

Seven Shawls introduces its protagonist, Peter Oliver, in a restaurant-pub. His ex-girlfriend, Paola Whitney, sexually involved with Victor Ballais, has previously gone there to give him a "Dear John" letter, not willing to face Peter. When the composer enters the pub, he overhears snatches of a conversation coming from the other side of a glass-beaded partition where the words "blackmail" and "supply" are brought up in whispered tones.

Unfortunately, a woman dancing to a jukebox melody prevents Peter from hearing much of the conversation. As the mysterious woman behind the beaded curtain leaves the pub, a shot of her chest reveals her white-hooded cape and pendant with an enormous eye. The unseen "man" she is talking to does not walk out with her. A waiter suggests to Oliver that the other party might have left through the back door, initiating a misleading supposition. As Peter walks out of the pub, a man lurks in the shadows, perhaps the one spoken of by the waiter, out to do the composer bodily harm. This frequent dissembling of the *giallo* sensitizes viewer into paranoia where every nuanced gesture from a character and every chord from Manuel De Sica's score become clues to any of the cast's imaginably vile intentions providing as many false leads as can be entertained without surrendering to the preposterous.

The shot of Peter walking down a lonely, dark street is followed by that of a sinister-looking individual in black with his face clearly visible, observing the composer off-screen. The unidentified man moves toward the camera in Peter's direction. Given the series of shots, the cutting and the *mise-en-scène* establish the trope of the stalker and his victim. Crosscuts to the men's feet predominate as synecdoche, but quite contrary to the *giallo*, the audience has seen the stranger's face, heightening the dubiousness of his function. Since the enigmatic individual walks from right to left of frame and Peter walks from left to right, the suspense will reach its climax when the two meet in a confrontation. In an overhead shot the two do meet, but it is not what has been anticipated as the intruder calls the pianist "Mr. Peter" and Peter answers with "Burton." This introduces a motif elaborated throughout *Seven Shawls*: ocular testimony is a misleading representation of reality. As the film's enunciator, the blind composer is competent to relate the story because he is able to "see" better than those with sight, but his "seeing" comes through his olfactory and auditory senses and from these his deductive reasoning, not from deceptive appearances.

At night Susan Leclerc comes out of the pet store she owns carrying a basket, the camera emphasizing in close-up her amulet with an eye as its focal point. In Egyptian myth, the eye was an agent of action or wrath, and in *Seven Shawls* it serves these two purposes. Susan is both an agent of action, delivering a cat with poisoned claws to a variety of victims, and an agent of wrath representing the embitteredly jealous Françoise Ballais. Susan arrives at the fashion studio and looks about a room filled with undraped mannequins. Mirroring Susan's drugged-addicted state through an expressionistic device, multiple swirling exposures of frightening mannequins fixate upon her with dead eyes. Maintaining the expressionistic ambiance through a Dutch-angled shot, the camera follows Susan as she walks upon the seemingly pitched floor, the canted photography capturing the supports of a balustrade in soft focus that break up the space's stability with diagonal lines engulfing her in their prison-like confines. She opens dressing room door number 3 with her cloak, leaving no fingerprints, and deposits a basket.

The following day, Paola Whitney, one of the models and Peter Oliver's former girlfriend, goes to dressing room number 3 to change and finding a yellow shawl places it over her shoulders. Noticing the basket, she opens it. There is a cut to a close-up of her face as her head is propelled backwards, her screams conflated with the electronic twang of percussion instruments while the visuals are looped three times to emphasize the woman's shock. Margot enters room 3 and is confronted by her friend's dead body. To illustrate her reaction, subjective shots of the corpse are looped repeatedly by four identical zooms to Paola's wide-eyed face on the floor with Margot's scream echoing over the image. The final zoom on Paola is held a bit longer. Pastore follows this image with a left swish pan to close-ups of two models' faces turning their heads frame left at the outcry. This shot is succeeded by a close-up to another woman's face, framed by a mannequin, who likewise turns to screen left in amazement, followed by another cut to an older woman by a clothes rack turning her face left. In turn this shot is supplanted by close-ups of three women who turn their faces to the camera, joined by another swish pan to the left of a woman in medium shot rushing left to the door of dressing room 3. This is accompanied by still another long shot of six women at a cutting table leaving the room quickly. Cutting back to dressing room 3 in long shot, horror-struck Margot stands over Paola's body (off frame) while other shocked women congregate by the door. This is followed by a medium shot of the six women "cutters" outside the dressing room door, pushing to get a look inside as the camera pans to the left with them. Finally there's a close shot of Paola on the floor as Victor, grabbing her hand, pronounces her dead.

While Pastori maintains a repetition of zooms in the first half of the sequence, the second half, dealing with the results of Margot's screams on the fashion house, contains reiterative shots of characters' gazes directed to frame left as though the sound is coming from that location. The introduction to the first character is bracketed by a right swish pan and concludes with a left swish pan from the final character to guide us back to the door of room 3. Since the eye is accustomed to read left to right, the movements right to left are subtly discordant and accentuate the commotion. The director likewise breaks up the direction of the gaze by having three women look directly *out of* the frame at the audience as if to coerce them into participation, while, in another shot, six women run to the back door of a cutting room forcing the viewers to direct their attention *into* the frame. These two shots further complement each other by containing multiples of three women.

The affinity among the shots in the murder sequence evidences a Russian montage theorized by Eisenstein in the 1920s. First, there is a "metric" montage where segments of film are joined together according to their lengths. In the death of Paola three quickly edited looped shots of extremely short but similar length constitute the murder. This repetition may be compared to three "measures" of music as though some percussion instrument beat out the hammering rhythm of the woman's startling end. This is followed by another set of zooms to the dead woman. Dividing the first set of three looped shots, with an identically repeated quaternary of zooms in to a close-up of the dead model's face, is a shot of Margot coming upon Paola's body, which acts like a musical interval in the action. While the impression made by the first triad of zooms is unmediated through any character's viewpoint, and is therefore being directed solely toward the viewer, this second group of four zooms is mediated through Margot and represents her emotional distress. That the final zoom is held a bit longer than the rest attests to the way one lingers over a tragic scene once the initial impact has been absorbed. Although the overused technique of zooming during the '60s and '70s had become hackneyed, if thought of as a narratorial gesture, an emotional equivalent of registering sudden stupefaction, its presence is eminently cinematic as opposed to its mimetic counterpart which is primarily theatrical. In this instance the zoom is an extension of the characters' motor responses or, in the case of the extradiegetic narrator, it foregrounds the image that he wants us to see. Second, a "rhythmic"[3] montage, now utilized after Paola's murder, is made contingent on the dynamism within the frame. Each of the women's reaction in various parts of the store to Margot's outcry is edited on their turning their heads left or walking to left of frame, but there is no spatial connection between them or their whereabouts regarding room 3. Additionally, these shots are united through nondiegetic, electronic, quasi-atonal music.

Police Inspector Jansen (Renato De Carmine), questioning those in the fashion house, believes Paola was murdered despite claims that she died of a heart attack. Margot informs Jansen that Peter Oliver cared too much about her to have harmed her. A swish pan to Peter's apartment connects the investigation to the blind composer where a sound mixer and a tape recording his piano playing are observed. The pan continues frame right moving halfway around the apartment until it stops at Peter by the keyboard. The joining of the two scenes momentarily insinuates Peter's complicity in the proceedings, especially since Paola has left him for Victor. Margot and Inspector Jansen arrive there to inform Peter about Paola's death, the inspector counting on their collaboration. At this point, Act 1 of the film's three acts comes to a close with Peter's twofold statement that (1) he can't resign himself to Paola's death even though he had no illusions about her infidelity, and (2) that he has to find the killer. This is the major plot point ending the act. Margot's willingness to help him is intercut with Burton in close-up listening in on the conversation, thereby joining all three amateur detectives in the investigation.

When Margot speaks to Peter about Paola's cousin, Harry, aiding them, there is a rhymed cut to the red light in the photographer's developing room. Harry, bathed in that light, is aiding Paola in blackmailing Victor with bedroom photographs of the couple. Paola has threatened to show them to Victor's wife, Françoise, because she wants to become Victor's spouse and inherit the fashion house. It is ironic, for this reason, that Harry's studio is named after the goddess of love, the "Venus Agency," but it brings to the fore the equivocality of appearances in the *giallo*. To add to this irony, when Harry's girlfriend (Imelde Marani) knocks at his darkroom he won't let her in, and in exasperation she taunts him about his impotency, hinting that he's in the perfect place to hide from his shortcomings. If, as Gary Needham conjectures, some *gialli* pathologize femininity and are fascinated with "sick" women,[4] Pastore portrays a number of repugnant women: the unfaithful Paola Whitney, more interested in blackmail than love to advance her career; drug-addicted Susan Leclerc, blackmailed into complicity by the homicidal Françoise; Harry's girlfriend taunting him about his sexual performance; and the real murderer, Françoise Ballais, manager of the haute couture establishment, whose murder spree is primarily driven by her initial crime against Paola. What profession could better portray this narcissistic world than the fashion industry?

In Pastore's film beastly women and decent women are butchered equally with no "Final Girl" left to tell the story. The pseudo "Final Girl," Margot Thornhill, is fatally mutilated in the shower by the female antagonist. A cruel irony is at work here for the director to leave the one woman who has been Peter's sleuthing partner and with whom he is expected to become romantically involved, to be murdered at the conclusion. It is as electrifying a concept as having Marion Crane knifed to death in the shower before *Psycho* was truly underway. While the female villain has been masculinized to the point of dominating her husband and dressing in male attire while committing crimes, Peter Oliver has been feminized. He is portrayed as a sensitive, caring, artistic individual who doesn't fight for Paola when she abandons him for a man who can further her career; he even takes her infidelity with a stoical detachment. He is doggedly attached to Paola's memory and finds himself compelled to investigate her death.

The murder of Harry takes place in his studio, which is awash in primary colors of red, green and blue. The director has orchestrated his shots to present death in a formalized manner to underlie the aesthetical pleasure involved in its staging. Rather than the pronounced floridness of an Argento, Pastore utilizes subtler methods of comparison and contrast between the shots. Although Argento's audaciousness bears little resemblance to Pastore, there are two intriguing stylistic flourishes in Pastore that mirror Argento's. For instance, Harry's murder was echoed ten years later in Argento's *Tenebrae*

(1982) where a beautiful journalist has her throat slashed. Her white blouse, as she pulls it over her head, is lacerated by the killer to get at her throat, acting like the scrim in *Seven Shawls* which the killer lacerates to get at Harry's throat. Harry's death is not particularly elaborate but what the sequence lacks in showmanship it gains in a subtle play of shots. The camera zooms in twice on the killer's silhouetted figure, first behind a glass-partitioned doorway and then behind a white screen relegating it to an incorporeal two-dimensional image. Close-ups predominate. From the killer's viewpoint Harry's head is silhouetted behind the screen while the assassin's gloved hand quickly plunges a knife into the photographer's outlined image; the next shot depicts the results of the attack on the other side of the screen: Harry's throat is slashed and he falls to the floor. This is followed by a close-up of the killer's hand withdrawing the dagger from the slashed scrim succeeded by the hand removing Harry's corpse. The set design's colors also evoke Argento's theatrical lighting in *Suspiria* (1977), *Inferno* (1980) and *Opera* (1987) with saturated reds and greens to indicate the characters' emotional states or to create a scene's overwrought ambiance. In *Seven Shawls*, the primary colors of red, green and blue are pragmatically placed within the set as photographic studio props. In Argento, these trichromatic arrangements are introduced through a theatrical use of lighting, frequently emanating from undefined sources. In this sequence, the lighting is naturally suited to the photographer's studio. The first four shots present an alternating similarity of images rhyming *abab*; the final four shots behave more like rhyming couplets, *ccdd*, where their homogeneity is replicated in pairs in each succeeding shot. The first four shots are joined primarily through technical means, whereas the next four are tied into story continuity.

Shots 1[a] and 3[a]—both zooming in to a close-up of the killer	Shots 5[c] and 6[c]—cause/effect: killer's blade slashing/its effect—Harry's bleeding throat
Shots 2[b] and 4[b]—panning from R to L with Harry/Harry's movement within the frame R to L	Shots 7[d] and 8[d]—gloved hand withdraws knife from the hole made in the scrim/gloved hand pulling Harry's body away by his legs

Seven Shawls is a typical *giallo* with Janus-faced individuals who reflect a fashion industry where artifice dominates over reality, where predatory people pose at being superficially beautiful, and where avarice, addiction, and vindictiveness galvanize the desires and ambitions of many characters. For example, Victor Ballais attempts to get rid of evidence in Harry's studio that places him in bed with Paola. The situation suggests, however erroneously, that Victor has killed the photographer since he has a motive. He presumably is happily married to Françoise but Jansen, the police inspector, calls him a "gigolo." Victor bluntly acknowledges to Jansen that he only stays with Françoise to exploit her, while Jansen lets Victor know that the police have his criminal record with two convictions for exploiting other women. Other characters are no exception: Françoise uses her business as a cover for murder; Susan, the pet store owner, is an accomplice to manslaughter; and Helga Schurn (Annabella Incontrera), the elegant lesbian model at Françoise's fashion center, is a cheap blackmailer threatening to expose Susan. Even the director dissembles: Margot, the "Final Girl," never makes it to the film's conclusion.

The scene of Helga's death contains an imposing buildup of 31 shots in the apartment she shares with her lover, Wendy Marshall (Lilana Pavlo). Dividing the sequence into four parts, it takes two shots to introduce Helga walking into her apartment in Part 1. Part 2 commences with the villain's black-gloved hands on the circuit breaker and mysterioso music of high-pitched string instruments together with the amplified dissonance of drums, and concludes with Helga's discovery of the shawl. Part 3, the heart of the sequence, introduces the cat that signals Helga's death, employing more close and extreme close shots of Helga and the cat that betoken the character's spatial entrapment. Part 4 is the finale: Wendy's discovery of Helga's body and her flight into the street. Interspersed with this action is a shot of the villain's gloved hands picking up the cat.

Each of the four parts contains a predominant sound/s associated with it. The first begins with Helga's heels on the floor; the second introduces three distinct noises: the circuit breaker being shut off, the blowing wind and the squeaking door; the predominating sound in the third is the meowing/screeching of the cat while the final portion consists of the clatter of Wendy's heels on the stairs and her screams.

Helga's entrance into her apartment is devoid of suspense except that her blackmailing someone by phone suggests something untoward will occur. A woman alone in an empty apartment in any *giallo* becomes a trope to signal vulnerability. Although *Seven Shawls* doesn't isolate Helga in a traditional remote setting, any locale in a *giallo* possesses potential danger in a world inhabited by a ubiquitous serial killer who preys on the vulnerability of women. But even with this knowledge, the director assuages expectations through eye-level shots of Helga signaling normalcy. Her turning on the lights immediately dispels some fear of assault, revealing a cozy, brightly colored, femininely appointed flat. Once the lights go out, the opening two flat-angled shots of Helga give way on separate occasions to two overhead shots reversing the normal spatial dimensions signifying her precariousness by attenuating her size. The angle, requiring the viewer to interpret the shot's perspective, also insinuates the presence of a virtual transcendent focalizer controlling the proceedings and able to watch Helga without her being able to return the gaze (a scopophile whose aloofness is represented by the camera's domineering height).

The amplified sound of Helga's heels on the wooden floor of her flat is consequential because its hollowness indicates a lack of human presence. While danger at first appears remote, this changes early on with a close-up of the iconic black-gloved hand. The slasher's ensemble, which negates gender and physiognomy through synecdoche, and whose ubiquitous presence annihilates space, functions with the single-minded purpose of generating absolute, nameless evil. Darkness is the realm in which the killer operates but he/she must emerge from darkness into light, from the virtual world of off-screen space into the concrete reality of on-screen space. The close-up of the gloved hand turning off the circuit breaker posits the perpetrator as one of the "children of the night" (1 Thessalonians 5:5), and the gloom provides the portal through which evil can enter. The sound of that circuit breaker connotes, with classic finality, darkness overtaking the light.

In the second part, sounds distinctly sharpen with the squeaking of an off-screen door signifying an intruder whom Helga mistakenly believes to be Wendy, followed by the whistling wind and billowing curtains recalling classic Gothic techniques of Paul Leni's *The Cat and the Canary* (1927) which prompt Helga to put the shawl on.

Diegetic sonority on and off-screen is consistently important in the sequence's third part where the sound of the black cat announces Helga's death. It begins with four alternating shots first of the animal and then of Helga. The accentuation on close-ups of Helga's face foreshadows where the cat will strike once the shawl is introduced. The alternation of the feline and Helga augments the excitement until the two are spatially joined, but even here they are a distance apart: Helga in the foreground, the animal in the background. The pattern of four alternating shots is repeated but now reversed, first of Helga and then of the cat. When the two are again within the frame, the distance between them has been abrogated, and the animal attacks the woman's face. To increase audience anticipation, Pastore utilizes Helga's viewpoint as the cat springs toward her. This action is looped four times in extreme close-ups so that the animal is springing toward us creating an empathetic bond between audience and victim. The final shot of the cat's attack begins as an extreme close-up of Helga's face but ends in a long shot as her body falls to the floor, opening up the claustrophobic space that underlined the attack. Employing a cat as murder weapon has its antecedent in the Egyptian god, Bast, pictured as a woman with the head of a cat. Bast was one of Ra's avenging deities and became known as "the god of evil sendings." The cat is so linked to Susan that she becomes the goddess's counterpart. Peter Oliver even tells Inspector Jansen that Susan smells feline.

A finale, comprising six shots, repeats some images from the opening two shots of Helga: Wendy's entering the apartment, the sound of her shoes, and the overhead angle to exaggerate her vulnerability. There are other parallels to Helga that are directly repeated: Wendy calls out Helga's name as Helga called out Wendy's. The panning that has taken place through the first 25 shots now becomes more intense with a swish pan to mirror Wendy's sudden shock on discovering Helga's body. Finally, to mimic the disoriented woman, a Dutch angle provides spatial destabilization when Wendy leaves the building and is attemptedly run over with the killer's yellow Volkswagen.

The tension created in the previous sequence is again amplified on the street through 16 shots. To begin with, there are six point-of-view shots between Wendy and the anonymous killer (#2, #4, #5, #8, #14, and #15) to place the audience in the complicitous vantage point of both the killer in the driver's seat and the targeted victim in the street. The first group of shots involves the premeditated homicide of Wendy. In an objective shot (#1) the parked Volkswagen is sighted outside the apartment followed by a reverse subjective shot (#2) from inside the vehicle framing Wendy in the background through the car's window conjoining the two spaces. This is now coupled with a close-up of Wendy's first reaction to the car off-screen (#3). Since she has been seen from the killer's viewpoint, this is complemented with Wendy's view of the car coming toward her (#4) culminating in another subjective shot from the car's interior as it hits her (#5) pushing her aside by its force, to Wendy still reeling from being hit by the car (#6), to a reverse angle with the victim in the foreground and the car hammering into her in the midground to emphasize the auto's impact as she is thrown on the cobblestones (#7). A total of seven shots comprises the sequence's first half. Just as the first shot began with the car heading toward the camera, now the Volks, taken from the fallen victim's viewpoint, speeds away (#8). There is a brief pause in action with the auto coming to a standstill (#9) giving a respite from the previous shots' frenetic movement. Now commences a variation of the first nine shots by reversing the order. Whereas the very first shot began with the Volks moving forward followed by a shot of the woman, now there is the woman's image (#10) followed by a shot of the auto's tires moving backward to finish the job (#11). Shots also parallel one another but again in reverse order: in one shot the car backs into Wendy (#12); then in the next she looks off-screen at the car seen in the previous shot (#13); earlier on Wendy looks off-screen at the approaching Volkswagen (#3), while in next shot we see the car she is looking at (#4). Likewise shots alternate between Wendy's viewpoint and the assailant's reiterating but transposing previous shots which alternate between the killer's viewpoint and Wendy's reeling from the car's impact. In the last shot the car speeds away once more (#16) restating a previous shot (#8), but reversing the image of the Volkswagen speeding toward the woman in the opening shot (#1). Whether or not we see the hit and run from the killer's viewpoint, Wendy occupies most of the 16 shots through her on-screen presence while only three shots rightfully can be said to be objective, dealing exclusively with the killer's car where Wendy does not initiate the gaze. The final bit of off-screen dialogue between Peter and Margot who rescue Wendy gives the sequence closure, informs us what has happened to Wendy, and prepares for a later scene where she is hospitalized.

One of the more complex characters in *Seven Shawls* is Susan Leclerc, a villain who is also a victim. Pastore elicits sympathy for her in a wordless passage of recollections. In the small anteroom of the pet store where she sleeps, Susan's eyes look over a poster of the "Dansk Cirkus." The camera quickly zooms in to a clown whose superimposed laughter, over his image, is employed as internal diegetic sound followed by an extreme tight shot of Susan's face. It is as if the clown were laughing at what she has become. An orchestral composition now plays over two other posters of Susan as a beautifully young and smiling circus performer. As Susan looks in the mirror, one sees that she has passed her prime and the camera, from her viewpoint, tilts down at her youthful poster pictures cruelly emphasizing the change. She gazes at the costume in the closet she once wore while applause is nondiegetically superimposed over her image. A smile crosses Susan's lips as if in recognition of the audience's appreciation. This lamination of mimetic and non-mimetic events, coalescing in present time but having taken place years past, is heartbreaking.[5] As Susan shuts the closet door the music ceases and the camera zooms in to the face of a purring black cat in close-up. She, being around big circus "cats," has now devolved into using domestic cats not for entertainment but for murder. She admits her loneliness while stroking the animal saying that it is her only friend, her career having ended when her husband, a circus owner and lion tamer, was killed by a lion. Susan, no doubt, recognizes the irony of using a cat to kill people and her own spouse's death, easing his loss with drugs.

Susan now experiences the pain of drug withdrawal while the pets in the store simultaneously respond to her suffering as through some psychic connection. The camera cuts to all the animals in rapid succession in an agitated state. To stress this symbiosis between her and the animals, termed "anthrozoology," once she injects herself and lies in bed, they become quiet except for the chirping of birds, which attests to her at-oneness with them. At the doorway, covered by semi-transparent linen curtains, a silhouetted figure in a man's fedora watches the sleeping addict. From a subjective point of view the curtains part to reveal a table with various wigs on it. As the camera continues to dolly into the room, it pans to the right to see Susan asleep on the bed. The figure's shadow approaches the bed as the camera persists in dollying to the woman. Hands come out of the right corner of the frame and grab the black cat asleep beside her.

The edit from the pet store's interior to Wendy Marshall sleeping in her hospital bed evokes Susan's slumbering in the previous scene. The hospital sequence sets up expectations of danger only to shatter them, lulling the viewer into a temporary complacency that remains effective despite the number of times the trope is exploited. Later a similar trope will be echoed when, in Hamburg, Françoise receives a call from Victor, for Pastore takes pleasure in paralleling one scene with another. As suspense is built with the slowly turning doorknob on Françoise's hotel room only to reveal a waiter with a coffeepot and cut flowers, so too does the eight-shot scene in Wendy's hospital room rely on similar tropes that exploit sound and visuals for a comparable effect. Pastore treats these shots like a mini-set-piece to murder. The context for such murders is frequently an isolated spot. Yet this scene is placed in a hospital which, even at night, should have some activity, but no establishing shot of the hospital, its reception desk or even a hallway is presented. Instead the scene begins in Wendy's darkened room which appears sequestered from normal hospital activities. The suspense functions well. Previously the killer has removed the black cat from Susan's bed, we remember Wendy's fear about a renewed attack in the hospital, and we now have a woman, defenseless in bed and alone in the dark. All this works because the traditional tropes consistently mislead us to a predictable but, nonetheless, horrific setup: first, a shot of the isolated woman asleep, then a slowly opening door which, unusual for a hospital, creaks, back to the alerted woman, a restricted view of the intruder from the ankles downward, back to the woman, to the intruder's viewpoint coming upon the woman, and finally, to extend the anticipation before the concluding reverse shot to reveal the individual's identity, a disembodied voice with a man's hands holding a mysterious package. *Seven Shawls*' set pieces employ crosscutting to extend the temporality of the action between the known and the unknown. There are four shots of the woman intercut with four abstracted shots of the orderly's shoes, legs, hands and shadow on a wall, but at some point there has to be a culmination in the build-up of tension. The presence of the intruder is made known not only through shots that exclusively deal with his body parts, but by extension through signifiers such as an opening door or a subjective viewpoint. Even the furtive manner of opening the door can be read as a covert action rather than caution in disturbing a patient. Three-quarters of the way through the scene we are treated to the intruder's subjective viewpoint and hear his footsteps as the camera dollies to Wendy's bed. A protruding wall hides Wendy from view until the camera comes around the corner. In a medium shot she cowers in bed and gasps. At this stage, the intruder's subjective point of view coalesces with that of the presumed victim. The subjective camera tyrannizes us through the focalizer's perspective (presumably the killer's), who cannot be seen and, therefore, cannot be trusted by privileging a single viewpoint as hierarchically superior to any other. The scene begins with Wendy as focalizer, but it is transferred to an unknown's viewpoint and becomes suddenly disquieting. Unlike objective shots that convey a pleasurable voyeuristic sensation where the viewer believes he is in control, watching but not being watched, subjective shots disallow viewer control, taking him where he may not wish to go. Pastore has other ruses to dupe the viewer. Since Wendy is basically voiceless, we look for non-verbal clues to determine what she is experiencing. Her body language, before and during the camera's dollying in to her sitting up in bed, insinuates that malevolent events await her through gestures she makes like cocking her ears to listen, positioning her arms defensively and effecting a rigid pose to fend off an attack. She also belies her feelings of dread through gasps at the approaching figure, and her eyes widen in consternation with an unblinking stare. Pastore doesn't have to do much to augment the danger posed by the intruder; the genre conventions, already known and even anticipated, do this automatically to assist in misreading the visual/auditory indicators so that only with the reverse shot of the orderly departing her room do we recognize it as an elaborate directorial hoax.

Upon opening the package Wendy discovers a yellow shawl. Her telephone rings as a canonic disguised voice asks her if she received the gift and tells her that the caller will be there to see how it looks on her. Wendy leaves the hospital in panic and heads to the train station where we are again treated to a wordless sequence. Over the soundtrack, drums coalesce with electronic music producing a dissonance that underlines the disquiet of the visuals. Her solitariness is emphasized by positioning her in the station's mammoth deep space that diminishes her image while the lack of people borders on the surreal. Several times a fixed camera, which does not pan to accommodate Wendy's movement across the frame because of its extreme distance from her, simply records her running through the station, significantly underscoring her helplessness. Nondiegetic piano music now "Mickey Mouses" Wendy's footsteps over the station's tile floors accentuating the place's isolation.

The attack on Wendy at the station platform begins by her looking about in expectation. The open spaces initially seen in the terminal lobby give way to confining close-ups as Wendy is bereft of places to turn. The reiteration of Wendy standing on the platform and turning her head around nervously in three different shots with two zooms out from her face underscores the situation's hyperbolized emotional intensity. The triple edited images evoke oneiric states where the dreamer is confronted with a traumatic situation whose components continually replicate themselves, a Freudian psychological concept known as "repetition compulsion."[6] A single pan then links Wendy to the killer holding the cat, and shooting now alternates between Wendy and the feline, the inevitable instrument of death. Only the killer's cape and hood are seen which at first erroneously suggest Susan's presence, but the viewer realizes that the cat had been stolen from her while in a drug-induced sleep. In extreme close-up, three shots of the animal's eyes are looped as the cat relentlessly leaps forward to Wendy off-screen. From her subjective viewpoint the incident becomes a traumatic event so that the cat's fatal clawing is repeatedly obfuscated in the victim's mind by the animal's eyes. The final four shots of Wendy bear on another privileged moment from the director's interpretative point of view akin to the recurrent shots of the cat's attack. The moviegoer experiences this "repetition compulsion" by viewing Wendy's falling to her death not in one complete action but fragmented into three separate shots as a rhythmic montage: falling backward toward the tracks, an extreme close-up of the passing train, another shot of Wendy falling left of frame as the train is passing, and yet another of her falling backward as the train finally passes. Pastore exploits editing based on time and visual composition inducing a dreamlike fantasy of a moment slipping away from a dying woman fighting to restore control over the situation. Once she is out of frame, the tight shot of the passing train functions as an elliptical wipe to the next shot of Jansen, Peter Oliver and Burton on the scene with Wendy's body on a stretcher wrapped in white cloth. The police discover the head of the cat on the tracks and the bloodstained shawl. This is followed by a cut to an indignant Susan reading Peter's notice in the newspaper about collecting a premium on the mutilated animal.

Susan, afraid for her life, phones Peter and, as she speaks, there is a cut to men's shoes behind the curtain in her room. A gloved hand disconnects the phone line before Susan gives her address. Peter, however, has recorded her conversation, and he and the inspector are able to hear animal noises on the tape. The inspector is puzzled, but Peter quotes a line from Mark 8:18: "You have eyes but do not see. You have ears, but you do not hear." Thus the musician biblically reprimands Jansen, saying that the most misled individuals are those who choose to ignore what they already know. The irony is that Peter "sees" what those with sight cannot through his acute sense of hearing and smelling. But smelling something out has the connotation not only of perception through "examining" or "inspecting," but also of "meddling" and "snooping." While Peter looks upon his role in the case as "examining" and "inspecting," remarking that the investigation has made him forget he is blind, Jansen, up till now, has viewed it as "meddling" and "snooping." So numerous are these interactions between the two men that the film is just as unified around their five confrontations as it is around the set pieces, progressively illustrating Peter's growing competence in the case and the policeman's growing respect for the composer. At this point Peter and the inspector work together to find the pet store's location. This is the plot point ending act 2 which will now lead to the third act's resolution.

When Jansen arrives at Susan's pet shop, he is greeted by her body hanging by a yellow shawl. The emotional impact on the inspector is registered through the zoom to describe his traumatization, first the zoom to his face as he enters the room and then through four repeated zooms to the murdered woman's face. In the last of these, the camera lingers on the victim's countenance a bit longer to suggest that this phase of Jansen's scrutiny has come to an end. The second half again commences with a close-up of Jansen still looking up, but here variations on the first set of shots begin. In one continuous downward tilt the camera (from the inspector's viewpoint) focuses first on the scarf. Comparable to four zoomed shots, this one tilt is subdivided into three segments as Jansen ruminates about the seven shawls, the five victims and the two remaining ones while the camera tilts downward first from the strangled woman's face, then to her chest and finally to her feet. The inspector's verbal response is antiphonally answered by these three prominent segments of Susan's body emphasized through his discourse. The lengthy tilt provides time to meditate on the arresting image which both editing and sound unremittingly accentuate.

The final third of the film, divided into three parts, concerns the revelation of the villains and their retribution: the first part involves the death of Victor and his attempt on Peter's life, the second relates to Margot Thornhill's ghastly killing, and the third part concerns the final attempt on the composer's life by Françoise Ballais and her death.

Peter is lured by Victor to the Berstorf Glassworks and is attemptedly killed, but he is rescued by the police who arrive with Burton. They chase Victor through the mazelike passages of the huge building until, cornered by numerous officers, he falls accidently into a lime pit. Next Burton takes Margot back to the composer's apartment. As she walks into the darkened room there is a cut to the butler sinisterly observing her, the director still seeming to pursue Burton as a red herring now that Victor Ballais is dead. After all, several British and American mysteries stereotypically used a domestic as the culprit since Avram Davidson (1923–1993) first introduced a fictional crime writer who used the phrase "The butler did it," making a great deal of money off of murderous butler stories. To further enhance suspicions about Burton, the director, after the butler leaves to put the car away, employs fragmented shots of the killer's shoes and black gloves as Françoise walks up the stairs and enters the apartment, to suggest Burton's return. Once there, the proceedings are observed through her viewpoint.

The first two subjective shots are somewhat lengthy, positioning the move-goer in the assassin's place. In the first shot the camera leisurely investigates the space from the killer's viewpoint through panning, zooming and dollying to keep the *mise-en-scène* in flux mirroring the killer's/our search for Margot. But this measured pace creates more uneasiness by anticipating the killer's coming in contact with Margot. The second shot, again with its tilting and zooming, takes up the synecdoche of the first shot's image of a black-gloved hand and continues with that hand opening a straight razor. It also introduces the victim. Hers are the only words uttered since she expects Burton's imminent return. There follows a series of rapid, reiterative, basically staccato shots that succeed the languorous first two. These shots, juxtaposed to one another, employ soft focus on the killer's arm making repeated slashing movements on Margot's body lensed in sharp focus.

After the opening two shots, the proceeding 39 come at a furious pace in this homage to Hitchcock's shower scene in *Psycho*. Only on analyzing individual shots does there appear to be a lack of continuity as parts of Margot's body, slashed in one shot, seem intact in another. Shots within the murder sequence are repeated verbatim so that although their joining together is made to seem continuous and contiguous, the effect of analyzing them on digital playback retards the impact of the slashing by harkening back to a previously utilized shot seconds before. These are not similar shots repeatedly used, but the same shots relentlessly exploited. Viewed this way, the attack on Margot turns out briefly to retard the climactic moment of her death. Recollect that film manipulates rhythm through a repetition of images, motion and sound in a regular pattern, yet once the actual stabbing takes place, camera movement and action are limited to the confines of the shower stall. The dissonant string music played mimics the unremitting cries of the victim.

With its meta-references to *Psycho* and *Una lucertola con la pelle di donna*, Margot (Shirley Corrigan) is brutally stabbed in the shower. The iconic close-up from the killer's viewpoint of a terrorized woman is a staple of the *giallo*'s misogynistic stance (Sergio Pastore's *Sette scialli di seta giallo*).

The film's tempo, that is, the number of cuts and the duration of the shots, mirrors another instance of homage to Hitchcock. According to some conservative estimates, Hitchcock employed 50 edits in his shower scene with 77 different camera angles that ran three minutes.[7] While Pastore's film is not as technically elaborate, it makes up in viciousness what it lacks in editing. The flamboyant editing in Hitchcock masks the violence that Pastore makes explicit with fewer shots. Howbeit, the repellent subject matter does not deprecate the artistry. Routinely, the movie public is concerned with a scene's content and action and is not conscious of the way that content and action are constructed, for if they were, the depiction of such an event could turn into an aesthetic experience. Take for instance those shots of the killer's arm brandishing the knife which, brutal in themselves as far as content is concerned, are nevertheless pivotal points that suture the scene together with their bewildering rapidity forming a *ballet mécanique* of carnage. There are at least ten shots dedicated to the assailant's arm. This figure does not include those more numerable shots where the fragmented portions of the assassin's body and Margot's occupy the same space as in the notorious breast slashing which is accomplished in three shots. Pastore employs extremely rapid cutting to give an impression of the sadist's knife-wielding swiftness and the victim's and audience's powerlessness.

The story's final sequence shot in low-key lighting is the cat-and-mouse game played out between the killer, Françoise Ballais, and Peter in his apartment. In fact the murderer wears the traditional hat and trench coat not only associated with the private eye in film noir, but also part of the villain's attention-getting attire in the *giallo*. Instead of the canonic gun, the killer sports a straight razor. Peter Oliver is able to take a cord in the darkened apartment and string it across the floor to trip the assassin while playing taped music to disguise his whereabouts, a stratagem employed by Betty in Argento's *Opera*. The killer falls to the ground and Oliver turns on the moviola, as a distraction, with the scene from *Lizard in a Woman's Skin* where Julia Durer's breast is slit by Carol Hammond. The similarity between the two films hints that the killer in *Seven Shawls* is likewise female. Furthermore, with no visible source, the apartment is bathed in either lurid red or green lighting as was the case in *Opera*. The color red appropriately conjures up a range of contradictory emotions from passionate love to violence while green, a conflicting primary color with red, symbolizes life, growth and harmony. Although these color combinations do not have to mean anything necessarily, they are chosen by Pastore, and their choice can be open to interpretation. For one, they come to characterize the killer (red) and the composer (green).

Françoise corners Peter, attempting to slash him, and reveals herself. The blind man surmises that she is the killer when Margot found some circus photos of Françoise and Susan. Françoise's body was disfigured in an auto accident and she desperately wanted to keep Victor for herself who alone knew her secret. The police arrive and Françoise jumps out the window. From a rear shot she breaks the window, while from a frontal view outside the window her attempted leap to her death as she shatters the glass is repeated four times, saved cinematically from the downward plunge by freeze-framing the action. While Peter ultimately traps the killers, the police, uncharacteristically, bring closure. It is Peter who solves both the "first story," that is, the past mystery behind the crimes (Françoise's killing of Paola after Victor's affair with her necessitates her murdering the others to cover up the first killing) which is missing from the narrative, and the "second story," the present investigation, "whose only justification is to acquaint us with the first story."[8]

The manner in which the film conforms to Propp's morphology is as follows:

1. **A member of the family leaves home (I).**

The journey indicated in *Seven Shawls of Yellow Silk* concerns the hero of the film, Peter Oliver, whose former girlfriend, Paola Whitney is one of the killer's first victims. It is Paola's bizarre death, seemingly from a heart attack, that compels Peter to leave home and do his own investigation, setting out on a quest to find her murderer with Burton, his manservant, and Margot Thornhill, Paola's roommate.

2. **An interdiction is addressed to the hero (II).**

Propp also mentions that interdictions can be in the form of "requests," "advice," an "order/command" or even a "suggestion" given to the protagonist. In one sense the interdiction by Inspector Jansen takes on all of these not only by his tone of voice, but because he is concerned with Peter's safety. The first interdiction comes at the death of Harry, a photographer whom Paola was involved with and whom Margot knows. Inspector Jansen enjoins Peter not to do his own private investigation lest Peter becomes the third victim, warning him that he will handle it himself.

3. **The interdiction is violated (III).**

Peter Oliver is not deterred by Jansen's warning not to interfere in police business. The composer's reason is that his former girlfriend, Paola, was the first victim and that he feels an obligation to unearth her killer. That Paola was also involved with the deceased photographer, Harry, gives Peter an impetus in looking for a causal connection in the murders. He becomes increasingly involved with the case, tracking down Susan Leclerc, the pet store owner whose cat's poisonous paws become the bizarre murder weapon. On a more personal level, Peter declares to Jansen that by sleuthing, with a disability, he doesn't feel blind.

4. **The villain attempts to deceive the victim in order to take possession of him/her (VI).**

The villain seems above reproach as a murderer of the women she employs in the fashion house. Her taking possession of the victim suggests the victim's death: "The villain employs other means of deception" (subcategory #3) through the example Propp gives, "Evil sisters place knives and spikes around the window through which [the hero] is supposed to fly." The basic means of deception are the shawls given to each of the victims which prove as deadly as the "knives and spikes." The scarves are given to the women as a gift from an unknown admirer and either placed in the rooms of the fashion house or the victim's dwelling. They are attractive so that the duped victims will wear them. The cat, brought onto the premises, is also an animal of deception, inciting curiosity and beguiling the victim into a state of complacency until it strikes.

5. **The victim submits to deception and thereby unwittingly helps her enemy (VII).**

In the case of *Seven Shawls*, the victims "mechanically react to the employment of magical or other means" (subcategories #2–#3). Each of the women killed takes the shawl and appears to be pleased by its texture and color, although mystified by its appearance, and tries it on. Even the cat's presence, at times, pleasantly disarms the victim, thereby unwittingly aiding the killer since the chemical on the shawl impregnates the model's skin before the cat claws her. Those victims who are not a prey to the black cat and who are murdered are lulled into a false sense of security by the veritable safety of the location they are in: Harry is slain by Françoise in his studio as he is developing photos to blackmail Victor. Margot is lulled into a false sense of security before being slashed to death, believing she is safe in Peter's apartment, expecting Burton to return to the flat after he has put the car away. The hero, Peter Oliver, is lured to a glass factory by Victor over the phone with the promise of discovering who the murderer is; likewise he is attacked in his home by Françoise because he has found out that she has murdered his former girlfriend, Paola.

6. **The villain causes harm or injury to a member of a family (VIII).**

As previously stated, Propp considers this function significant because by means of it the real trajectory of the tale is crafted. The story's complication is begun by an act of villainy against Paola. While the "family" here is not that of blood relatives, the couturier house is a species of family whose members are under the head of the matriarch and owner, Françoise, and the father, Victor, who appears to be the focal point of the models' sexual fantasies.

Under this function Propp lists "The villain causes bodily injury" (#6) which certainly is the case regarding the hero, Peter Oliver, who is attemptedly murdered in a glass factory by Victor and in his apartment by Françoise. Before killing Wendy, Françoise attempts to run her over with a car putting her in the hospital. Unquestionably Françoise orders the murder of a number of females in her employ with the aid of Susan as her surrogate (subcategory #13, "The villain orders a murder to be committed") so that she will be above suspicion. It is Françoise, however, who is directly responsible in the murder (subcategory #14, "The villain commits murder") of Harry by slashing his throat and by killing Margot in her shower. Not all, but several of the murders or attempted murders against the hero, Wendy, Harry and Margot occur at night, fulfilling Propp's subcategory #18, "The villain torments at night."

7. One member of a family either lacks something or desires to have something (VIIIa)

Françoise Ballais, head of a fashion house "family" and the preeminent villain, along with Victor, has immediate access to all the models. Françoise primarily kills to cover up the murder of Paola whom she knew had an affair with her husband and who wants to marry Victor and take over the *maison couture*; the disfigurement of Françoise's entire body, except for her face, in a car accident is a secondary cause for lashing out at the attractive Paola because Françoise desires to keep Victor's love, the one person who knows of her disfigurement. Françoise must also kill others like Margot who jeopardize her security and whose beauty she envies.

Françoise has Susan murdered because she is about to tell the police the whole story behind the murders. Harry is killed because he threatens Françoise's security in his blackmailing partnership with Paola who expects money from Victor so that his wife will not know of his affair. Peter Oliver is attemptedly killed in discovering that Françoise is paying off Susan in drugs to carry out the assassinations. Since Françoise has known Susan previously, and since the latter has a drug habit, the head of the fashion house bribes her to kill the models, knowing their whereabouts and even who they are seeing.

8. The hero is tested and attacked which prepares the way of his receiving a helper/donor (XII).

This type of attack may be called "indirect." The blind composer is "attacked" through his former girlfriend's murder. It is Paola's death that hits Peter hard and is the catalyst for him to begin the search for her killer, therefore placing his life in jeopardy. He forewarns Jansen that he *won't* resign himself to her death, using the emphatic form of the verb to designate his determination. The inspector, as donor, concerned for the blind man after Paola's death, "greets and interrogates the hero" (subcategory #2) about his presence at the crime scene in Harry's studio since it was his murdered girlfriend who was Harry's cousin. Jansen even asks Peter and Margot for their collaboration in the investigation. From this point on the composer is aided by the police so that law enforcement and the amateur sleuth work together despite the confrontational attitude they sometimes exhibit. But also donors come in the form of Burton, always ready to do Peter's bidding, and Margot Thornhill, who roomed with Paola and discovered her body at the fashion house and who appears to be in love with Peter.

Another type of attack may be termed "direct" as Peter Oliver is assaulted toward the conclusion first by Victor when the police come to his aid and then by his wife Françoise when the police enter to arrest her in Peter's apartment.

9. **The villain is defeated (XVIII).**

In the case of *Seven Shawls* we have two villains and their accomplice: Françoise, Victor and Susan. Victor is killed accidently at the glass factory by falling into a vat of lye as the police corner him in his attempt to murder the hero, and Françoise commits suicide when the police corner her in Peter's apartment by jumping through a window, but not before revealing all those she murdered.

10. **The task is resolved (XXVI).**

Peter Oliver's stated task to discover who killed his girlfriend comes to an end with the villains' deaths and with the aid of the police who finish the job Peter has initiated.

6

No Irises for Miss Landsbury

Giuliano Carnimeo's *Perche quelle strane gocce di sangue sul corpo di Jennifer?*
[*The Case of the Bloody Iris*, 1972]

> White Iris was a princess
> In a kingdom long ago.
> —Bliss Carman, *White Iris*

The working title of *Perche quelle strane gocce di sangue sul corpo di Jennifer?* was *Una strana orchidea con cinque gocce di sangue* (*A Strange Orchid with Five Drops of Blood*), and the film was released under the present title on August 4 of 1972. Its shooting title is reminiscent of Umberto Lenzi's *Sette orchidee macchiate di rosso* released six months earlier on February 24. The title change implies that the director or Luciano Martino, the producer, did not want it to resemble Lenzi's. Giuliano Carnimeo's film, one of the director's best, nevertheless has a misleading Italian title. There are drops of blood on the heroine Jennifer Landsbury's (Edwige Fenech) finger when opening up a food can, but there is nothing strange about this except the reaction of the architect, Andrea Barto (George Hilton), who becomes nauseous at the smallest drop of blood. The film's English title, *The Case of the Bloody Iris*, has symbolic ramifications while approximating an actual film event not particularly crucial to the narrative. Jennifer's past catches up to her when she is stalked by her insanely jealous ex-husband, Adam (Ben Carre), from a hippy commune whose sadistic impulses lead him to submit his wife, while drugged, to group sex and beating. Adam, when spying on Jennifer, has a habit of tearing irises to shreds in his rage at her refusal to return to the cult. One night, a bloodstained iris is found in Jennifer's apartment after she is attacked by a masked killer. In the presence of her roommate, Marilyn Ricci (Paola Quattrini), and her next-door neighbor, Sheila Heindricks/Isaacs (Annabella

Incontrera), Jennifer finds Adam in her closet knifed in the stomach. Flowers, according to Freud, are emblematic of female genitalia so that the violence Adam inflicts on the irises is a symbol of Jennifer's repeated defloration with masochistic undertones. The defloration symbolism of the iris recalls Adam's initiation of Jennifer into group sex with cult members and the subsequent loss of her virginity despite her wish to be loved only by him. In Adam's kingdom, Jennifer is that white iris and princess spoken of in the Bliss Carman poem, who, like Julie Wardh, wants to leave her sadomasochistic yesterdays behind but is constantly reminded of them by a former lover.

Bloody Iris is another misogynistic exercise of men exploiting women: Adam treats Jennifer as an object belonging to him; Andrea, the architect, regards Jennifer as an easy lay; Fanelli (Luciano Pigozzi), the nightclub owner, sees his star, Mizar (Carla Brait), exclusively in terms of the money she brings in; the gay photographer, Arthur (Oreste Lionello), views women as commodities to sell products; and finally the murderer, Professor Isaacs (George Rigaud), Sheila's father, sees them as so much putrescence to be disposed of. The women are perceived as property, assets to be exchanged for money, or objects to be punished for their seductive qualities. These sensibilities inform us about the period in which the film was made, about the Italian male psyche regarding women, and about young, unmarried ladies' positions in society.[1]

The patriarchal perspective taken by men's appropriation of female dependency can be seen in the fetishistic objectification of women targeted for torture and death. The Romantic idea that the death of a beautiful woman is a fitting subject for art has been voiced by Poe in *The Philosophy of Composition* (1846), and later debased in Argento's now infamous quote, "I would much prefer to watch [beautiful women] … being murdered than an ugly girl." In *gialli* analyzed here the death of beautiful women becomes the source of the directors' aesthetics. This fascination of objectifying females through death is what the 19th-century American poet and the 20th-century Italian director share as a basis of their art but with greatly different results.

For Poe, "beauty … invariably excites the sensitive soul to tears. Melancholy is thus the most legitimate of all the poetical tones." Of all melancholy topics, Poe used "death" as the one that was universally understood. Poe believed the death of a beautiful woman was the most poetical because death was allied with beauty.[2] Argento, among other *giallo* directors, does not view a beautiful woman's death as a melancholy subject, at least not in a Romantic sense. Romantic "melancholy" implies a reflective attitude; scenes of carnage in *gialli* are not meant to be reflective moments for the contemplation of death and the evanescent nature of beauty even though both elements are present. At most, Poe's melancholy at the death of a beautiful woman is basically shifted in the *giallo* to sympathy. Taken to another extreme, since the *giallo* focuses on female objectification, certain spectators might experience an aberrant voyeuristic pleasure at the sight of a helpless woman. Plainly, in *The Case of the Bloody Iris*, we are expected to sympathize with the principal victim, Jennifer, but for the minor characters the "thrill" of seeing them die through ingenious means is both a visceral and aesthetic pleasure essentially devoid of sympathy because we reach a point where their personalities cease to affect us[3] similar to the periodically depicted counterculture whose unwillingness to acclimatize to reality alienates them from the economic, political and cultural modernity of contemporary traditional society.[4] Although these films appear to revel in the countercultural lifestyle's excess, glamorizing the hippies' distinctive clothing, home decor, sexual freedom and drug use, it is the same counterculture these films denounce, making it easier to marginalize characters like Adam.

Bloody Iris opens with a bookended gimmick of an attractive young woman, Lona (Evi Farinelli), on a public phone calling a lone, unseen woman at her apartment and receiving the answer to come up. This will be repeated at the film's conclusion with a different young woman on a city street calling a different female who responds similarly. It isn't clear if the second situation is simply a suturing device or if it implies something more sinister. That Lona is a high-class "call girl" suggests a lesbian affair since it is Sheila Heindricks, on the other end of the receiver, who has Sapphic interests. The credits now roll and the camera tracks Lona through crowded afternoon streets while Bruno Nicolai's mellow, upbeat, jazzy score accompanies her to her rendezvous. Lona's murder in an elevator is a companion piece to the death of Marilyn, Jennifer Lansbury's roommate, which takes place on a busy street in Genoa, although in the English-dubbed version, no mention is made of the city, giving the large metropolis a universality similar to the folk tale's "in a certain kingdom." The murder sequence is sutured through seven shots of the illuminated floor panel as the lift makes its way from "T" (terra/ground floor) to the 20th floor. The first two shots move from outside the elevator to the inside to establish spatial perimeters, but the contiguity among the people in the elevator through successive shots is not established nor is their proximity to Lona, the intended victim. The crush of residents and the close shots of Lona trap her in the confines of a small space, which becomes an index of the character's security or lack thereof. A great deal of space leaves the character vulnerable to attack from outside the frame, while a tight space projects a claustrophobic situation where the character has no place to turn if threatened. However, if the victim is immobilized by the crowd, so is the killer. Carnimeo has atypically set us up for the murder by situating it in a familiar, congested locale so as to preclude violence. These first ten shots, consequently, explore, not the space, but the individual faces of mostly male passengers, and, with one exception, all other shots are close-ups bordering on the extreme so that a delimited environment is quickly established.

Because of one extreme low-angled shot, the ceiling of the lift appears to constrict the passengers' heads, giving the illusion of constrainment. Shots of Lona in an exceptionally compact area ironically afford little spatial connection with the others, exemplifying the loneliness and isolation found in a megalopolis before the age of social networking.

The constant allusion to the lift's upward ascent through the illuminated panel over the door is a forewarning that a critical incident will occur on or before the 20th landing, the turning point occurring with the introduction of the killer whose countenance, unlike the others, we never see. Concentration on Lorna's face slowly builds up. Sometimes the close-ups are in pairs with a shot of a self-absorbed Lona looking up at the killer as he turns to face her followed by another close shot of her head in profile adjacent to the killer (out of frame). Other times, her close-ups are separated by several shots but all forming a progressive pattern toward the sequence's climax. When the elevator reaches the 13th floor the mayhem begins. The audacious killer, before the doors have closed and all the passengers are out of sight, covers Lona's nose and mouth with chloroformed cloth. This signals the major struggle embellished through the next several shots with alternations between the killer's hand and the woman's face occurring in rapid succession. The killer presses his body into Lona's, his black-clad figure towering over the woman menacingly. She looks up with terror-filled eyes at the appearance of his scalpel. The knife, suggesting a perverted symbol of the male organ, a pernicious variant for orgiastic penetration, is thrust into her pelvic area countered by close-ups of her anguished face. Shots of Lona's countenance juxtaposed to the killer's scalpel culminate when he slashes her throat as though this figurative rape by scalpel has satiated the killer who now climaxes in this manner. While not as sanguinary as some *gialli*, the sadism directed against the woman is deeply felt through shots of her expressive face and eyes. If the pairing of sex and violence is rare in slasher films,[5] the partnering of sexual metaphors with graphic violence isn't. In a coda, the director passes over the 180-degree axis, and by doing so disorientates us with a reverse positioning of characters so that Lona, usually blocked to right of frame, is positioned on left and the killer on the right. As she sinks downward, her hands caress his body in a parody of sensual fulfillment. The assassin leaves with the self-assuredness of one who doesn't expect to be caught.

The shots of the floor landings outside the lift suture the other shots inside clustering around the elevator's ascent to the 20th floor where three of the film's prominent characters are now introduced while chancing upon Lona's body: Mizar Harrington, a black woman who is an exotic dancer/stripper; Mrs. Moss (Maria Tedeschi), who buys horror comics for her disfigured son, David; and Professor Isaacs, a violin player who lives with his lesbian daughter, Sheila Heindricks/Isaacs. None of the three recognize the woman's body, reacting to it at slightly different times. It is first viewed by Mizar, then by the professor and finally by Mrs. Moss. A hierarchal trajectory is established through their gaze at the victim: the first is a long shot of Lorna's entire body; the next begins with a long shot but then, through a zoom in, concentrates on her face and slit throat; the third shot of Lona starts at her face but the camera then tilts down her torso to the incision in her stomach, each of these three shots directing us to a specific wound.

There is a segue to a close-up of Arthur's hands as the fashion photographer, looking for a model in a group of shots, holds a picture of Mizar, the next victim. Arthur tries convincing Andrea, the architect, that he needs sex to sell his apartments. At this photographic studio we also meet the dizzy redhead, Marilyn Ricci, and her roommate Jennifer Landsbury, posing for a motorcycle ad which draws Andrea's attention to her. The cut to Mizar Harrington's act in a night club is not as jarring as it might sound since both the photographic session and the nightclub act deal with women as a commodity to sell a product. In the studio the nudity is used to market a motorcycle; in the club it is used to bring in customers and to sell drinks. Mizar urges the men in the club to come and get her as their slave. It is here that spectacle is turned into sexploitation as men are encouraged, in so many words, to try to rape her for the pleasure of the clientele. She taunts the males to prove themselves, begging to be dominated by a he-man. The notion of female empowerment is thus abrogated by the display of Mizar's anatomy in a skimpy bikini and her enticement to the males to subjugate her by sexual domination in a three-minute wrestling round. That she is too strong an opponent for most of the men doesn't mitigate the fact that she is selling her body like some unobtainable prize at an amusement park. She, in fact, does take down an all-too-eager male (Enzo Mondino) who rips off her bra and attempts to make violent love to her, but she, through sheer athleticism, clobbers him. As he tries to regain his pride by demanding a return match, Andrea pulls him back, and Mizar thanks him with a smile and a nod.

Both the nightclub and photo studio operate on the Lacanian principle that "woman does not exist," only as a fantasy of femininity. Woman, in Jacqueline Rose's theory, "becomes the place onto which lack is projected and through which it is simultaneously disavowed, reduced to being nothing other than this fantasmatic place."[6] This is what Mizar's act reduces her to: a scopophilic fantasy of the Amazon whom one can ravage through phallic subjugation. Mizar, as part of the illusion she fabricates, projects the need to be tamed of her primitive African sensuality by the white man. And to the men, Mizar symbolizes the castration threat by her absence of a penis and, therefore, someone to be "enslaved" (her terminology for the power play between the sexes). She is at once Laura Mulvey's nightmare about woman as the place onto which *lack* (of a penis) is projected and its opposite, the

Giuliano Carnimeo's Perche quelle strane gocce... (1972)

Jennifer's (Edwige Fenech, right) and Marilyn's (Paola Quattrini) painted-on blouses for a motorcycle photograph shoot set the theme for the commodification of women as scopophilic objects of desire to sell products (Guiliano Carnimeo's *Perche quelle strane gocce di sangue sul corpo di Jennifer?*).

embodiment of the strong female who doesn't need men to complete herself. On both accounts she symbolizes, for a patriarchy, the non-male through which men can live out their fantasies. For daring to do this, Mizar is tortured and killed. At the nightclub, as Andrea gazes off-screen to frame left, there is a cut to Jennifer at the studio posing and looking to frame right so that Mizar, the center of attention up until now, is replaced by the model as we hear Arthur's instructions to Jennifer to look teasing so as to torture her male readership. Jennifer is turned, by the photographer, into a Galatea, becoming all men's desires like Mizar. The irony is that the modeler of flesh and bone is gay, beyond the lure and love of his creation, turning our modern Pygmalion-photographer into a pimp who caters to men's desires with Jennifer as the consumer bait. Both Mizar in the club and Jennifer in the studio are eye candy for the male gaze much like the intended customers for the *giallo*. It is in the studio also that Jennifer has a disturbing glimpse of Adam watching her pose which sends the model into a paroxysm of fear. The director emphasizes "the gaze" of Adam and Arthur as well as drawings of women in sunglasses, photographs of a woman's eyes and a prop of a naked clay male figure all looking at Jennifer. With this pervasive "looked-at-ness" of Jennifer's body, we have come full circle from audience scrutiny of the semi-nude Mizar at the club to that of the model at the photographic studio.

Jennifer, walking home after her photo shoot, encounters her ex, Adam, and a cat-and-mouse game ensues. Outside a shopping complex she spies an iris lying on the floor, a symbol of the past she is trying to forget, and of a husband she has left. "Iris" likewise refers to a Greek messenger of the gods, similar to Adam's flowers which also become emblematic messengers from Jennifer's previous life. As soon as Adam speaks, the camera focuses on an extreme close-up of his mouth and then zooms back to a tight shot of his face as he tells her he thought she appreciated flowers. There is a cut as the camera zooms in to an extreme close-up of Jennifer's terrified eyes. Two zooms correlate to the two organs of communication: Adam's mouth which hints at Jennifer's relationship with him through his reference to the iris (a play on the organ of sight), and her eyes which lead into a flashback insinuating the impetus for her leaving the cult. A flashback reveals her life with Adam through a hallucinogenic haze of flowers, painted mirrors and nude male and female bodies. Multiple superimpositions of a naked Adam, recalling the Genesis story, are seen in sharp focus, throwing an armful of white irises in soft focus at the camera. Equally naked and ecstatic, Jennifer, filmed in swirling kaleidoscopic images, becomes the new Eve of this reinvented Bible tale for the '70s flower people. Lying down, she is the recipient of a cascade of irises over her body, suggesting her wedding-night defloration. Once more Adam throws irises at the camera with a cut to Jennifer, now in sharp focus, her naked body covered with the flowers. She seems enraptured under drugs that create an altered sense of time visualized through slow motion and supported by the sound of drums and a synthesized score. As Adam hands Jennifer an iris, his voice-over intones that the blossoms are symbolic of a single body with many members like the flower's petals. Naked men and women kneel down in a circle as if in prayer. Adam, as the cult's high priest, tells Jennifer this commune is her body and is one with the group in a parody of the Christian Eucharist. Trancelike she responds that she belongs to the group and the group to her. At this point she lies down and there is a cut to the present with a close-up of Adam saying that she belongs to the group and above all to him.

Adam's words suspiciously recall the Catholic Church's teaching of the "mystical body of Christ" reduced to the level of a countercultural commune communion ceremony. In Catholic doctrine, the "mystical body" constitutes a mystic union of all Christians into a spiritual body with Christ as their head. This scene is to be interpreted in a quasi-spiritual sense: one body, the commune, physically and spiritually united by group sex, with many members, being directed by Adam, its head, who exercises complete control. After the last member has made love to Jennifer, Adam tells her that only in this way can she be free like a beautiful wildflower; she is not one man's special woman because anyone can take her, yet she belongs to him as "an object," as a flower he can hold or discard at will. At this point Adam's explicit comparison between his wife and the iris will be recalled later when he mutilates the blossom: she becomes the white iris who, in order to remain free, must belong to him and his cult. This conceit comparing physical domination to freedom recalls Donne's "Holy Sonnet 14": "Take me to you, for I,/Except you enthrall me, never shall be free."

There is an overall paradox within the flashbacks. Traditionally the counterculture rejected violence and advocated harmony between human beings which translated into a communal lifestyle where traditional marriage was replaced by "free love." Thus, the film paints the traditional conception of hippie culture: they were pacifists, lovers, and espoused nakedness. While the commune settings suggest all of this, Adam's chauvinistic attitude toward Jennifer is antithetical to the traditional countercultural image that greatly advanced the women's rights movement.[7] His psychotic posture is due to the *giallo*'s attempt to stymie audience expectations by coercing it into speculating who the antagonist might be. In addition, the *giallo* takes place in a patriarchal society where Italian women's status is abnormally low in comparison with the rest of Europe. In February 2011, there were demonstrations in more than 250 cities around the world in defense of the dignity of Italy's women.[8] It is little wonder then that in 1972 Adam can make these demeaning statements to Jennifer who, as a model, is considered no better than a prostitute by those attracted to her, by those who hire her for work and by those in her apartment complex. She may be able to escape her ex-husband, but she can't escape society's judgment. Jennifer lives in a male-dominated Italian culture where even predatory women like Sheila see her as an object of desire. Later on Adam appears in Jennifer's apartment and begins to rend her clothes comparing her to the torn petals of the iris, an object that belongs to him. Each of Adam's five appearances metaphorically indicates a past of diminishing patriarchal dominance over her that Jennifer is running from to establish her own selfhood.

No sooner does Jennifer escape Adam than Mizar Harrington is attacked and killed returning to her apartment. The apartment's lack of lighting makes her immediately suspicious while the door to the flat, which she had left opened to shed some illumination, slams shut. In the darkness Mizar hears a tape of her enticing a male customer to overpower her on the club's stage. She is obviously being taunted for her aggressiveness in an inversion of societal gender roles. As a woman who is in control, she is regarded as an abnormality of nature which, when added to the belief that she is a whore, places her outside the pale of the patriarchate. This is indicated by Professor Isaacs as he informs Jennifer, before attempting to kill her, that women have corrupted his daughter, placing blame for Sheila's lesbianism on those females liberated from societal norms. Yet, as a counterbalance, the males in Carnimeno's film are a lamentable group that might make any female choose a same-sex companion: Commissioner Enci (Giampiero Albertini), more interested in investigating stamps than suspects; his assistant Redi (Franco Agostini), a blundering fool; Andrea Barto, an architect playboy with only sex in mind; Adam, a possessive psychotic; Arthur, a cynically misogynistic photographer; David, Mrs. Moss's son, a pervert; and Professor Isaacs, a serial killer. *The Bloody Iris* empowers women like Mizar only to punish them, featuring a villain easily found in the *Diagnostic and Statistical Manual of Mental Disorders* who uses cunning to establish dominance, takes pleasure in the tangible and psychic sufferings of others and demoralizes his victims through tactics of terror.

Mizar's torture and murder mainly rely on constrictive close-ups and point-of-view shots, the *giallo*'s vehicle whose murders constitute its tenor. Alone in her darkened apartment, Mizar must bank on her physical prowess to deal with the intruder, but is felled in an instant by a karate chop to the throat leaving her senseless. The opening shots build on the traditional synecdoche of the murderer's hands to portray the antagonist. Overhead close-ups of Mizar's fettered legs as she whimpers off-screen and of her face with rope around her neck emphasize the woman's torture juxtaposed to the impassive stance of the black-masked victimizer standing before her. He remains in perfect anonymity while the woman is completely exposed, not only because of her nakedness but because she is the object of her captor's gaze. Because of the killer's anonymity, the male spectator can project onto him any transgressive impulse he desires since the villain exercises his control over the visual register both overtly and covertly. The murderer, since he is in fewer shots, largely projects the viewpoint from which we are forced to watch, and if not through his eyes then through the extradiegetic narrator as when the camera, in a close-up of the killer's gloved hands tying Mizar's feet, suddenly zooms back to a long overhead shot of her in the tub with the killer bending over her. When the shot doesn't contain the perpetrator or the victim, depending on its angle, it can be assumed to be taken from the female's viewpoint as in a flat close shot of the running faucet which will lead to Mizar's drowning. The killer's mastery of the situation, even though not primarily in the picture, is manifested through his limited appearance which sutures both the beginning and end of a segment of shots all in close-up that circumscribe Mizar's suffering as she whimpers that she does not want to drown. The last series of shots all in close or in extreme close-up rapidly alternate between Mizar and the killer: Mizar's mouth as water reaches it, the killer's face with the sound of Mizar swallowing water, her face swallowing water, her face as she drowns, the killer's gloved hands and the sound of her cries as she takes in water concluding with a ghastly close-up of the dead woman's face, bubbles rising from her mouth. If the viewer can't endure watching a woman drown, the director is at pains to make certain we hear her die. A shot of the killer's folded hands patiently waiting for her death is more chilling than if he were to utter any sound. With the exception of two shots in the sequence, both Mizar's and the killer's bodies are fragmented but for different reasons. Mizar's splinted image is a visual correlative to the assassin's gaze who sees her not as a person but as an object, the sum of her parts. The killer's image is also ruptured through editing, not only evoking his lack of mind/body integration (an aberrant personality), but also due to the genre's conventions where delayed gratification of the murderer's identity is a function of its structure.

Coming home from a date with Andrea, Jennifer, like Mizar, attempts to switch on the apartment lights without success, signaling her imminent danger. In the darkness she is framed by a series of vertical poles evoking a sense of entrapment which proves to be a room divider once the lights are on. As Jennifer starts to lift her sweater over her head, a gloved hand reaches for her hands in an ensuing struggle. With her hands above her head, she is firmly grasped by an unidentified masked man (David) arriving from nowhere. As she pulls her blouse down, the man now places his hands around Jennifer's neck, but soon begins to caress her shoulders and tries to force her to kiss him. She pushes him away but David grabs her blouse and rips it off. Jennifer, in a bra and miniskirt, dashes out the door seeking help from Professor Isaacs's daughter. Sheila embodies the rapacious image of a vampire, seductive and suave, threatening the social and sexual order. She serves both as narrative stumbling block to the heterosexual partnering of Jennifer and Andrea, and as contrast in accentuating Jennifer's embodiment of heterosexual love.[9] Lona's tryst with Sheila at the film's beginning brings about her death while the lesbian's passionate letter writing to Mizar brings about the entertainer's death. Her attempted seduction of Jennifer also threatens the heroine's life since Sheila's deranged father can only see that other women have debauched his daughter and are, therefore, subject to punishment. Sheila, encoded as outside the hegemonic norm through her lesbianism, accidently dies by her father's hand, and her demise is propitiatory in restoring order and stability to the threatened heterosexual world of the two lovers. But to fully reestablish order, Isaacs likewise has to die. The professor, like his daughter, is an ethnic outsider and a subtle part of the film's underlying anti–Semitism. Mikel Koven reports that "he and his motive are encoded as being *different*, not *really* Italian, despite his citizenship."[10]

Once in Isaacs's apartment, Jennifer is fondled by Sheila. The heroine, in a desperate search for human comfort after nearly being raped, doesn't realize this. Sheila's initial response to Jennifer's plight seeing her in only a bra and miniskirt is playful, assuaging the other's fright by asking the heroine if her boyfriend got a little too over-zealous in his lovemaking. Ogling her prey, Sheila tells Jennifer that she is tantalizing. She then caresses Jennifer's shoulders much like the intruder had done minutes before. Her obvious gloating over the frightened woman's body emphasizes her insatiable sexual appetite, reminiscent of the vampire stalking its victim. For a second time she puts her hands around Jennifer's neck as the masked man had done, and

6. No Irises for Miss Landsbury

Sheila Heindricks (Annabella Incontrera, right) inspects the heroine, Jennifer Lansbury (Edwige Fenech). Sheila, coded through her attire, embodies the rapacious stereotypical lesbian, seductive and suave, threatening the social and heterosexual order (Giuliano Carnimeo's *Perche quelle strane gocce di sangue sul corpo di Jennifer?*).

raises her hair a bit off her shoulders as if to expose her throat like a vampire about to attack its victim. She brings Jennifer back to the latter's apartment with apparent designs on her, but Marilyn bursts in. There they discover a bloodstained iris on the floor and bloody fingerprints on a closet door which Jennifer opens causing Adam to fall out, a knife protruding from his stomach.

The misogynistic theme is reintroduced when Inspector Enci confronts Sheila with her love letter to Mizar, and she tells him it was a joke. In response he deprecatingly takes up her jest asking her to "joke with a man" because such a lovely woman would be squandering her gifts in a same-sex relationship. He urges Sheila not to be ashamed in writing him love letters. Since both films were scripted by Ernesto Gastaldi, Sheila's love note about being corrupted by Mizar's primal African beauty bears a striking resemblance to the notes in *The Strange Vice of Mrs. Wardh*. Sheila's sexual desire is articulated through her written notes and spoken words, but her lesbianism in this instance is discretely redefined by Enci in terms of deviance. Under his nonchalant delivery he is uncomfortable. In advising Sheila, he appears considerate but simultaneously ridicules her lesbianism because he knows of Sheila's embarrassment and recognizes his own unease in her presence. One might construe Enci's remarks as a means of lessening the tension between them, but despite this, the negativity emerges: he speaks to her about her misplaced sexual interest in women as "wasting" her time. He then moves his argument to another level of generality suggesting that she "jok[e] with a man," where "joking" is used euphemistically for sex. This is brought to the fore in the English translation's double entendre about "making out better" with a man, signifying both a more satisfying relationship and, more subtly, an erotic intimacy evoked by the verb "to make out." Her preference for women underlies his fear that she doesn't need men to be complete. His next step is to artfully move the discourse from relationships with men in general to a relationship with him. He tells Sheila to write him, where writing is an implied form of "making love," just as D.H. Lawrence called dancing "making love to music."[11] But Sheila's rejection of men becomes an underlying rejection of him when she abruptly ends the conversation. Enci's short speech creates, despite its banter and charm, a homophobic argument that reinforces the patriarchy's hegemonic values. Once rejected, he turns nasty, commenting that her father has enough problems without hearing about his daughter's deviancy. When he asks if Professor Isaacs knows Andrea Barto, there is a cut to the architect and Jennifer making love at his house. This juxtaposition of homosexual and heterosexual desire enforces Enci's argument through editorialization by spending considerable time on Andrea's and Jennifer's intimacy whose purpose is to expose the ideological apparatus. The love scene is framed through a reflected Mondrian artwork, mirrored in a television screen, seen through a vertiginous camera angle, in close-up and in long shot, all to celebrate heterosexuality while the commissioner's assistant, Redi, voyeuristically looks on from his car.

Marilyn Ricci, Jennifer's roommate, is the next casualty. Her slaying, audacious as the murder of Lona in the elevator, occurs on a crowded Genoa street one afternoon while she is shopping. In close-up a gloved hand takes a scalpel from a newspaper while the camera tilts up to a long shot of an arcade busy with people and flanked by shops. A handheld subjective camera moves into the crowd until it reaches Marilyn in close-up as she smiles with a "hello." A knife penetrates her stomach and in a facial close-up she tries to scream. Carnimeo cleverly appropriates material from the previous murder of Lona with the above sequence of Marilyn's death.

Marilyn on the Street

CU: gloved hand takes scalpel from a newspaper; camera tilts up to LS of a crowded arcade.

CU: knife penetrating Marilyn's stomach and then withdrawn.

CU: Marilyn's mouth open wide in agony. Camera tilts down to her stomach; her bloodied hands hold her midsection.

Lona in the Elevator

CU: camera diagonally tilts down from Lorna's face to the killer's pocket; he pulls a scalpel.

CU: killer's hand thrusts scalpel into Lona's stomach.

CU: Lona's mouth and eyes are wide open; she begins to look down.

CU: knife being pulled out of Lona's stomach by gloved hand and plunged again into it.

6. No Irises for Miss Landsbury

Marilyn on the Street	Lona in the Elevator
CU: over Andrea's left shoulder Marilyn's face looks up to Andrea's. She falls from his grasp.	CU: Lorna falls down as her hands seem to caress the killer's chest and body.
CU: Marilyn's face unable to speak. Places bloody hand on Andrea while leaning on him.	CU: Lorna's mouth and eyes wide open; she begins to look down.
CU: Marilyn looking up at him unable to speak.	CU: Lorna's face softly screaming in pain.
CU: Marilyn's opened but inarticulate mouth.	

The first shot of Marilyn walking down the arcade parallels a later shot of Jennifer walking down the same avenue. Presumably both are from the murderer's viewpoint, which unites the two women marking Marilyn and Jennifer for death. The sequence is divided into three parts, the first being the killer's meeting with Marilyn and her subsequent stabbing. The second section is transitional moving the action from the arcade to the streets. Once on the busy thoroughfare the third segment comes into play, Marilyn's meeting with Andrea. The sequence's finale involves two shots to accentuate Marilyn's death. Her encounter with Andrea is significant for it is the second time his morbid fear of blood is adverted to. The first happens when Jennifer accidently cuts herself on a tin can in her apartment where she and Marilyn are to lunch with Andrea.

Five shots specify the agony and isolation the dying Marilyn experiences. She is in the midst of people, but no one seems to notice her as she drops the packages, crouches, clutches her bleeding stomach and tries to walk to the curb as disinterested people file past. A facial close-up of her opened mouth reveals her suffering as do most of her close shots. Her bloodied hands hold her midsection until she grasps Andrea's arm. Once Andrea's face is glimpsed, the crosscutting in the remaining shots is deftly handled with either close-ups of each, over-the-shoulder shots, or shots that fragment Marilyn's body, emphasizing her bloody hand and inarticulateness. This shot–reverse-shot setup enables us to become an invisible mediator between a reciprocity of gazes, a fictive player in the illusion of the film. "From a shot of one character looking to another being looked at, the viewer's subjectivity is bound into the text."[12] Marilyn's final falling to the sidewalk begins with a long shot of Jennifer walking down the same mall as the camera zooms in to a close-up of her face. This is followed by a subjective shot from Jennifer's viewpoint as she approaches Marilyn who continues to fall while Andrea, temporarily rooted to the spot, is stunned by the profusion of blood. At the sequence's close, Marilyn is ironically surrounded by concerned people who can no longer be of help, meeting death alone with everyone watching.

Andrea, now on the run from the police, persuades Jennifer by phone to meet him in a derelict car lot. The director employs sound, light, minimal color and fragmentation of the human form to generate psychological terror, the lot's *mise-en-scène* substituting for the conventional Gothic ambiance of a cemetery. Once she is there, the place is a surrealistic nightmare with cars piled on one another as if they had been in a monumental crash. To add an uncanny effect, many light-colored autos give an eerie impression of a bone yard filled with the cadavers of old cars. Amidst this stillness, Carnimeo uses three sound bites and several fragmented shots of the human body to startle the heroine. At one point a car door, as if by devilry, opens on its creaking hinges terrifying her, at another, from out of the right corner of the frame, a hand appears resting on one of the wrecks, and then a close-up of a man's shoe is accompanied by its sound on the gravel. Jennifer is beset by abandoned metal heaps, sounds and disembodied images. At times her figure is either so insignificant amid their motionless bodies or barely seen as she moves from the safety of an unspecified light source into the night's darkness, the *noirish* lighting taking precedence over the human figure by reducing it to an immaterial shadow. The camera, at one point, tracks Jennifer as she looks about since startling sounds connected with the autos precede, by a fraction of a second, the image that causes them. As with the resonance produced by the car door's opening, another car's open hood mysteriously slams shut causing the woman to panic. Jennifer calls out Andrea's name but receives no answer. A zoom in to Andrea's face half hidden in the shadows looking straight at the camera is matched with a zoom in to Jennifer's face in the foreground with a soft-focused background. The camera then rack focuses on a now sharp-focused background where Redi, the commissioner's assistant, is seen emerging from behind a small house while Jennifer is in soft focuses. Andrea ducks below frame making clear that he is not hiding for some sinister purpose but knows the police have followed Jennifer. His action also informs us that Jennifer is ignorant of the surveillance. At this point a third startling sound is heard as a car perched above topples down as if by design to frighten the woman, while the background music imitates the car's crashing with the loud twang of an acoustical guitar, turning a clandestine meeting of two lovers into a nightmare concert.

Jennifer then runs out of frame and emerges at a massive stone-columned building complex. The oneiric quality of the car lot is matched by the monumental architectonics of this scene where a simple edit allows for a fluid melding of vastly different locations not governed by the laws of physics. So large are the stone columns and so massive the building that she is overshadowed by their presence and frightened by the cavernous space's lack of human activity. Jennifer runs onto a desolate street scene lighted by various neon signs believing she is being followed. These scenes' ambiance recalls film noir which aesthetically creates an underlying mood of pessimism and an existential outlook of loneliness and dread devoid of moral absolutes. In this world Jennifer's closest friend is murdered in broad daylight, the man she loves is suspect, her ex-husband has been murdered in her apartment, someone has tried to kill her, a masked man has sexually assaulted her, her neighbors seem to despise her and the police are using her as bait to capture her lover. On this deserted street she meets Sheila, dressed mannishly in a shirt and tie who confides that she would love to share an apartment with Jennifer to get away from her father. In so doing, Sheila becomes the controlling partner insinuating herself in Jennifer's life after the model feels betrayed by Andrea.

Once in their apartment's elevator, the women find it heading to the basement. The door opens on a dimly lit boiler room. While Jennifer is all nerves, Sheila assumes command taking Jennifer by the hand and leading her out of the lift. A noise is heard and then footsteps. The close-ups mainly deal with the women turning their heads in various directions indicating an off-screen presence awaiting them. The "heroine-in-distress motif" is nothing new, but what makes this different is that Carnimeo has paired off two women. Nowhere in the film is Jennifer's "distressed damsel" more evident than with Sheila as her protector. Their entwined hands are seen in close-up; significantly Sheila disentangles her hand from Jennifer's grasp, taking the initiative and walking ahead to investigate. This one shot tells us of Jennifer's dependence and her reluctance to be separated from Sheila, and although Sheila is coded as predator, she is not stereotyped as "butch" either through iconic or indexical signs in spite of her apparel. In fact, her masculine garb is also mimicked in Jennifer's androgynous outfit. In this sense Sheila is attracted to a reverse mirror image of herself. Whereas the model is passive, Sheila takes command, where Jennifer is artless in her simplicity, Sheila is devious, where Jennifer has a faithful friend in Marilyn, Sheila has no lasting friendship with any woman; where Jennifer wants to belong to one man, Sheila is promiscuous; where Jennifer's parents are never mentioned, Sheila constantly complains about her father, intimating unresolved repressed conflicts.

While investigating the boiler room, Sheila is enveloped by scalding steam and screams out in pain. The shots have, up until now, been taken from a flat angle, but this one of her engulfed in steam is from a high angle, ambiguously evoking an unseen presence that has observed the women since they entered the lift. Later, the culprit, Isaacs, claims that he meant the steam for Jennifer, but in the basement, Jennifer is not near Sheila. Perhaps in the darkness the two women look physically alike, but the act also implies subconsciously Isaacs's way of chastising his daughter's transgressive behavior. So burnt is Sheila that her face resembles Mrs. Moss's scarred son. Her death is sparingly handled in ten shots. The situation defies logic, but the *giallo* isn't one to stand on logic. Why doesn't Sheila move away from the steam instead of remaining there? Nothing bars her way. Why doesn't Jennifer push her friend away? Interestingly, given the sexual role reversal, Jennifer acts like celluloid heroines of old when their men were in danger: she looks petrified and screams. Bracketing Sheila's death are close shots of Jennifer shrieking. The subsequent shots are not taken from Jennifer's viewpoint: a gloved hand turning the steam on and off, a high-angled long shot of Sheila on the floor screaming as the camera zooms down to her figure below, a low-angled close-up of the steam pouring out of a funnel as Sheila's cries are heard off camera, and a shot of the steam coming out of a pipe. The one shot from Jennifer's viewpoint is a flat-angled long shot of steam enveloping Sheila's body, but once this is established, Jennifer is detached from the proceedings, incapable of aiding her friend, and the lack of POV shots delineates this. In the dark, Sheila, unable to cry out, grabs Jennifer's leg and when her horribly disfigured face appears amidst the boiler room's gloom, the heroine screams. These female fatalities are related: Sheila's inarticulateness evokes that of Marilyn Ricci and the prostitute, Lona, while the scalding water vapor is a variation on Mizar's death by drowning.

The second half of this basement sequence deals with Jennifer running from the sound of footsteps through a maze of half-lit corridors. The passageways are lighted in various color combinations from soft green to a softer amber, from high contrasts of light and dark to shots quite devoid of color, from a magenta-lit avenue that she runs through to a perfectly amazing cave-like entryway with streaks of light gliding over the passageway's pipes comparable to the slit-scan photography of *A Space Odyssey*'s (1968) "stargate" sequence. The issue of artifice in the *giallo*, much like '40s film noir, arises here through lighting whose source is unseen and whose hues are more theatrical than realistic. The genre's color palette has usually been quite varied to suggest expressionistic states or to portray the familiar as fantastic with or without a supernatural factor. Here, the design and elegance of the lighting never degenerate into subterfuge. The chromatics usually serve a purpose appropriate to the environment by appearing to heighten the melodrama. If these stylized plots do not always assist the cause of realism, even when laying claim to being realistic, it is the lighting, hovering between reality and fantasy, that bolsters this illusion.

Back in Jennifer's apartment, Isaacs's violin playing can be heard through the walls. As Jennifer listens to the music, there is a cut to a close-up of the professor on the verge of tears as he plays. The camera pans to his shadow on the wall, a Jungian archetype seen as the inverse of the ego image containing qualities that the ego does not identify with but yet possesses. This shadow self embodies a ferocity of character which may plunge things into chaos. Outwardly the father's ego image projects a stern, powerful, controlling figure which castigates his daughter's lifestyle, but as Sheila pays no heed, the father's shadow side meets punishment not only on those whom he believes have corrupted her but on Sheila herself. As Jennifer combs her hair, a rubber-gloved hand in close-up parts the curtains across her balcony door while on the sound track Isaacs's violin continues to play, throwing doubt on his culpability. Jennifer escapes the killer's chloroformed handkerchief and runs out of her apartment. The violin playing has subtly been employed as asynchronous commentative sound to indicate Isaacs's presence and, by extension, to indicate his home as a place of refuge. She runs into the professor's apartment, locks the door and screams when she notices David seated on a chair with his throat cut wearing the same rubber gloves as the killer who entered her room. The camera zooms in to the dead man and then Dutch angles the shot to show the confusion Jennifer is in. When she sinks to her knees she observes that the violin playing has been taped and realizes that Isaacs is the killer. He enters, takes off his mask, explains everything and then chloroforms Jennifer. Isaacs throws David's body over the stairwell and drags Jennifer out intending to do the same. She awakes, shrieks, and from out of the elevator Andrea arrives, struggling with the professor. Isaacs pulls a knife but Andrea turns it against him and cuts the professor's hand. At this point a 21-shot montage explains in flashback Andrea's aversion to blood.

The Shots	*Analysis*
1. Andrea in the present 2. The boy, Andrea, trapped in car	Pattern initiated by equating the adult Andrea (#1) with the child in the car (#2).
3. Andrea in the present 4. The boy and his father trapped in car 5. Andrea's father in the car	Next three shots (#3–#5) establish a pattern: Andrea followed by the boy and his father followed by a shot of the father alone.
6. Andrea in the present 7. The boy and his father trapped in car 8. Andrea's father in the car	The above is repeated in shots #6 to #8.
9. The wreckage. First establishing shot outside the wrecked car.	
10. Andrea in the present 11. The boy and his father trapped in car 12. Andrea's father in the car	The shot pattern #3–#5 and #6–#8 returns in #10–#12: Andrea as adult, boy and father, and father alone.
13. Single shot of the boy in the car 14. Wreckage 15. Andrea's father in the car 16. The boy in the car	Finale (#13–#16) emphasizes boy (#13), the crash (#14), cause of trauma [his dead father] (#15). Ends on boy calling father's name. Boy bookends last segment (#13 and #16).

Four repetitive shots, #1, #3, #6 and #10, occur during Andrea's fight with Isaacs recalling his past traumatic experience as a boy in a car witnessing his father's death. As Andrea begins to recollect the incident, the flashbacks take over with only one more shot of Andrea in the present sandwiched in the 21. The first two shots of the sequence parallel each other: from a close-up of drops of Isaac's blood on Andrea's face as he looks up to the top of frame right, there is a cut to a close-up of Andrea as a child with drops of blood on his face as he looks up to the top of frame left. Three shots isolate the boy in the auto as blood continues to drop on his face (#2, #13, and #16), while three more shots (#4, #7 and #11) widen the scope to show a close-up of the little boy and above him in the car, a portion of a man's face, his blood dripping onto the boy. While #5, #8, #12 and #15 deal exclusively with the dead man in the car, two are taken with his face circumscribed by the steering wheel (#8 and #12). Two others have him looking directly at the camera (#5 and #15). All shots form perfect symmetrical patterns of information in their pairing off. The conclusion comes in #16 with its zoom in to the boy calling "papa," revealing their relationship. Uncharacteristically, the establishing shot of the wreckage is not at the beginning but comes in #9 and is repeated in #14 of a white car totaled with a parked car in background as a police vehicle's lights play on the wreck.

The last five shots (#17–#21 not listed above) deal with the fight between Andrea and Isaacs over the stairwell's railing, giving a sense of the danger each faces in falling over, necessitating either extreme long or long shots taken from a multiplicity of angles. Shots #17 and #20 partner off and are the most spectacular ones: #17, an extreme low-angled long shot of the apartment stairwell looking up as the camera zooms in to a long shot of Isaacs attempting to push Andrea over the balcony. The zoom upward indicates the depth of the stairwell and what awaits one of the two paralleling #20, another extreme low-angled long shot, showing Isaacs's body plunging downward toward the camera as he hits various landings. The result of the fall (#21), a tight close-up on the bottom floor, accentuates the killer's signature gloved hand in the foreground and in midground the back of his bloodied skull.

The closing segment of the scene, outside her apartment, Jennifer asks forgiveness from Andrea for not believing in him as they caress. He tells her, signaling the finale, that the nightmare is over. That statement sums up previous *gialli* that introduce us into a personal nightmare of one character whose adventure implicates many people in his/her misfortune before order is restored. We can only presume that ultimately Andrea and Jennifer will wed.

There are two codas to the story, one ending humorously, the other more problematically. The first concerns the standing joke about Redi's intelligence as Enci suggests that he join the firefighters, prompting the assistant to ask if he needs brains to join. Enci only gives a sigh. Following this we are treated to another woman in the crowded street making a telephone call at a public booth just as Lona did at the film's inception. The same jaunty opening theme music is playing. A woman answers and, without inquiring who the caller is, invites her up to her apartment saying that she is alone. This sutures the film's cyclical structure that, while returning the audience to the opening, proposes a cautionary tale about female companionship and empowerment. What women require, it subtly suggests, are the right type of men who will not have to tell them the nightmare is over, so that the *giallo*, despite its sexual openness, is inherently pro-institutional and delimited by patriarchal conventions that make it political, for its goal is to repair, with the support of the male, the disorder created initially by the narrative.

Carnimeo's film conforms to Propp's taxonomy of the folk tale in the following ways.

1. **A member of the family leaves home (I).**

    This form of absentation is again centered on the more commonplace occurrence of leaving home and "going to work." Many of the *gialli* deal with working people in white-collar jobs that, before the age of the computer, take them away from their own dwellings which, in a big city such as Genoa, are not that removed from their professions. We observe them going about their work: Andrea is an architect first seen with the photographer, Arthur, looking at pictures of models who might advertise Andrea's new apartments; Jennifer and Marilyn are modeling for a motorbike advertisement—as roommates engaged in a specific career for a specific company, they constitute "family."

2. **An interdiction is addressed to the heroine (II).**

    Interdictions can be in the form of an "order/command" given to the protagonist. The interdiction comes in the form of a request and turns into an order by Jennifer's ex-husband, Adam, to return to a lifestyle she has come to detest and from which she has run away. It is the first of several interdictions by Adam.

3. **The interdictions are violated (III).**

    The principal antagonist, Isaacs, enters the story early on right after the murder of Lona, although the audience cannot be expected to know this. Therefore, the first bona fide substitute antagonist for the real one is Adam, Jennifer's ex-husband, who seems volatile enough to have murder in mind, although there is no logical connection between him and the murdered women. Adam's persistence in demanding Jennifer back into the cult and her violation of his dictates eventually places her in the hands of the killer because in fleeing from Adam she is driven into the arms of Andrea with his suggestion that she and her roommate, Marilyn Ricci, live in the apartment where Mizar Harrington was murdered. Through this move she and Marilyn become acquainted with Sheila and her murderous father, Professor Isaacs, and encounter Mrs. Moss's son, David, who is a voyeur and rapist.

4. **The villain receives information about his victim (V).**

Isaacs's information gathering is seen through his daughter Sheila's involvement with women whom he then kills. He believes they have corrupted her and perhaps have turned her into a lesbian. Since the women in Sheila's life are invited to the apartment she shares with her father, he knows the victims: Lona who has been coming to see Sheila, Mizar to whom Sheila is writing passionate letters, Marilyn who lives on the same floor as Sheila and whom she has met with the professor at a shop, and Jennifer who seeks aid from Sheila after David attempts to rape her. At this point Isaacs sees his daughter with Jennifer, suspecting that she is another one of Sheila's conquests.

5. **The villain attempts to deceive the victim in order to take possession of her (VI).**

Isaacs's "cover" is his status as a professor of music, as his interest in the violin might suggest. It is presumed that the women he kills know who he is and would not seem to be threatened by his presence, and thereby he takes his victims unaware. He appears to be a righteous, moral man who does not countenance immorality. Yet he disguises himself to resemble David wearing the selfsame black hat and black stocking mask along with flesh-colored rubber gloves that conceal his identity in order to commit murder. His disguise is useful in pinning blame on David should the need arise. He especially deceives Jennifer by taping his music so that she believes he is in his apartment when the murders take place.

6. **The victim submits to deception and thereby unwittingly helps her enemy (VII).**

Jennifer is deceived by the false facade Isaacs projects. When she is attemptedly raped by David, she manages to escape to the professor's apartment where she meets Sheila who immediately takes a romantic interest in her just as the professor arrives. His disparaging tone of voice signals his displeasure with his daughter, but also marks Jennifer as one of Sheila's love interests and one of her corruptors. The second time Jennifer submits to the antagonist's deception is when she is attacked by the masked Isaacs. She eludes him only to run to the professor's apartment for aid, not realizing that he is the perpetrator since she hears him playing his violin. This playing, however, is a recording to get the neighbors to believe he is in his flat. Only when Jennifer is in his apartment seeing David's body and the taped violin solo does she realize Isaacs is the killer.

7. **The villain causes harm or injury to a member of a family (VIII).**

Once more, the words "member of a family" must be taken connotatively. "Family," first of all, designates those women who live/frequent the apartment complex who are either prostitutes (Lona) or, by society's standards, promiscuous (Mizar, Marilyn, Jennifer). Jennifer's roommate, Marilyn, is the closest thing to "family" that the story presents. Mizar and Marilyn, part of the family of models/performers, are eliminated because of their association with Sheila and because Isaacs believes their promiscuity is morally contagious. Jennifer is attacked because of similar reasoning by the professor.

Function VIII is important since by it the actual movement of the tale is created. The story's complication is begun with Isaacs's villainy in murdering Lona, for Sheila then transfers her affection to Mizar, whom her father kills resulting in Jennifer's moving into her flat in an attempt to get away from her ex-husband's demand that she come back to him. The absentation of most of these murdered women from their families, Jennifer's casual relationship with Sheila, and the success of Isaacs's deceit all prepare the way for facilitating attempts on Jennifer's life (subcategory #6, "The villain causes bodily injury"). Other subcategories of this function are also pertinent in defining the patterns that villainy takes: subcategory #14, "The villain commits murder," in four instances and "the villain torments at night" (subcategory #18) in three instances: when Mizar is tortured and drowned in her bathtub, when Isaacs stalks Jennifer and accidently kills his daughter and when Jennifer and Andrea are attemptedly murdered in the apartment complex. Adam, as a subsidiary villain, terrorizes his ex-wife at night while he spies on her during the day.

8. **The heroine/hero is tested and attacked which prepares the way of her receiving a helper/donor (XII).**

Andrea is threatened by Adam with a knife telling him not to get involved with Jennifer. Jennifer is threatened physically by Isaacs and sexually by David, both of whom she does not immediately suspect since they are masked. This incident prepares the way for Jennifer to receive a helper in Andrea, for he has rented her the apartment where the attacks take place, although afterward Andrea himself is suspected of murder both by the law and Jennifer. Andrea interrogates her (#2, "The donor greets and interrogates the hero") in a car about her former husband and advises her to let the police take care of Adam. But his devotion to her, despite Jennifer's suspicion, pays off at the conclusion as he, and not the police, is able to rescue her from Isaacs. Jennifer's second donor are the police who interrogate her regarding Adam after he is found dead in her flat. Enci wants her to stay against her inclinations in the apartment with her roommate as a decoy for the killer. The police are there in the building's boiler room and mistakenly protect her from Andrea instead of Isaacs who has been stalking her and has accidentally killed his daughter. Therefore the heroine is attacked in the first half by her ex-husband, Adam, and in the latter half by Isaacs.

Propp lists ten subcategories under XII. Jennifer is tested in several ways beginning with her ex-husband. She does not acquiesce to Adam's demands, but actually fights him off (#9, "A hostile creature attempts to engage the heroine in combat"). The means used by Adam are physical, beginning with his asking Jennifer back to the commune (#7, "Other requests"), but this degenerates into force by attempting to inject her with drugs to facilitate her kidnaping.

9. **The heroine/hero and the villain join in direct combat (XVI).**

Isaacs endeavors to kill Jennifer in her apartment only to be thwarted by her tenacity in defending herself. She runs unknowingly into the murderer's home seeking refuge and is followed there by him. Overpowered and chloroformed, she is dragged to the stairwell and attemptedly thrown over when the donor, Andrea, comes to her rescue and engages the villain in combat.

10. **The villain is defeated (XVIII).**

It is the donor, Andrea, who struggles with Isaacs to the death in open combat (#1) for his own life and that of Jennifer on the apartment landing.

7

Jealousy as Cruel as the Grave

Andrea Bianchi's *Nude per l'assassino* [*Strip Nude for Your Killer*, 1975]

Yet hopeless love must mate with jealousy...—Pierre Corneille, *Polyeucte* (Act 3)

Andrea Bianchi's film opens literally between a Milanese woman's spread legs having a backstreet abortion while over the soundtrack is the thumping noise of a beating heart. This is a bizarre type of "sex scene" for a *giallo* in that the director inscribes within it, through monochromic blue tinting which appears nowhere else, the suggestion that we are about to watch a porno, a "blue movie." Whether or not the term "blue movie" was employed in the trade at the time is questionable, but the expression was not confined to the U.S. industry. The common idiom among today's Italians for a pornographic film is *luce rossa* (red light).

Considering the opening abortion, a thorny topic at the time since abortions on demand during the first 90 days only became legal in Italy in 1978, *Strip Nude* embarks immediately on a taboo subject especially since the operation goes awry. When the model, Evelyn, has a coronary and dies despite the gynecologist's efforts, a further idea is subtly evoked: abortions must become legal if endangering a woman's life is a possibility. With this reading, a sensitive political subject matter seems camouflaged under *giallo* sensationalism and Evelyn, whose death is central to the action, becomes a national representative of "every woman." Ironically, the woman's name contradicts the very act performed: "Evelyn" means "life" in French or "life giving" in Hebrew. While menacing electronic organ music plays which modulates into an upbeat melodic phrase, Dr. Julio Castelli (Filippo La Neve) telephones Carlo Bianchi (Nino Castelnuovo), a photographer, to help him stage the woman's death in her own bathtub as if through natural causes. At the woman's home, there is a quick zoom out from the nude model in the tub as the water is flowing. The film changes to full color as the camera zooms in on the bathtub spigot which, with the dead body, becomes a leitmotif interjected throughout the film. The director interestingly enough, who also wrote the story, has given the protagonist, Carlo, his own family name. And why not? Both are in the profession of creating glamorous images of women and both are in command of their environment by manipulating the photographic material to their own advantage.

Film credits now roll over images of a garishly lit Milan at night seen through a car's front window. A jazzy trumpet, snare drum and small band underscore the flashy visuals. Bianchi knows how to capture the nocturnal rhythm of the city making it by turns tawdry and exciting eye candy. The driver, the doctor previously seen, parks his car in a secluded residential spot and begins to walk up the stairs to his house to a dimly lit interior seen through large glass doors. There is a jarring cut to a displaced diegetic insert of a bathtub spigot's running water with another shot of Evelyn's body. Its function is to invoke a time prior to that of the image with which it is correlated. Over the soundtrack now comes the amplified breathing of another individual; a helmeted figure accoutered in a black motorcycle outfit rushes up the stairs and jumps the doctor as he opens his door while on the soundtrack is an unusual amalgam of weirdly mechanical orchestrated notes. The restraint in the depiction of the murder is cleverer than it first appears. In long shot the killer knocks the doctor down as he opens the front door stabbing him multiple times. This camera setup alone distances the viewer from the action. The killer also knifes the man in the throat in close-up, but the victim is so blocked that his throat is not seen, only the upper part of his back. Only when the bloody blade is pulled out and thrown to the carpet do the previous discretionary shots give way to a close-up of the man's head and chest with blood streaming out of his severed carotid artery. This is followed by a reticent medium shot of the black-clad figure bending over the off-frame body, but the viewer can hear the sound of flesh being rent and the killer's labored breathing. The assassin rises and bends to frame right succeeded by a cut and a right pan to streaks of blood on the floor, while the camera, continuing its swift motion, reveals bloody severed genitals as they splatter on the foyer's rug. Clearly the director toys with his audience, the camera coyly avoiding the mutilation taking place but baiting the viewer's imagination through the soundtrack. Bianchi first denies the voyeuristic impulse to view the stabbing and the severing of the genitals only to reveal them shortly afterward. In this way we are encouraged to become complicit in a despicable act by postponing our expectations only to feel disgust when they are gratified by the riveting sight.

7. Jealousy as Cruel as the Grave

At an indoor pool, the photographer Carlo Bianchi, accomplice of the abortion doctor, is formally introduced. He is attracted to the bikini-clad Lucia Cerrazini (Femi Benussi), who pays no attention to him as he follows her up the stairs of the bathing complex photographing her derriere. He seduces her with a hint that he can get her into haute couture magazines; has her strip in the sauna, pretending to take pictures; and takes off his bathing suit to get between her legs for an extensive interview. This soft-core sex has been set against the previous scene of hard-core violence, where the dismemberment of a male's "member" is now juxtaposed to a jocose scene of a male getting his member up for an "interview." The two scenes are paired off for a dialectical reflection on male virility and the price men have to pay for their physical potency over females in a patriarchy. Carlo affirms pornography's major thesis of "male power ... expressed ... in and through ... the degradation of the female [as] the means of achieving this power."[1] *Strip Nude* has been compared to the crossbreeding of Michael Powell's *Peeping Tom* (1960), equating scopophilia with rape and murder, and Antonioni's *Blow-Up* (1966). All have main characters who are photographers, all three experiment with the limits of provocativeness, and all three focus on photography as a key in solving its protagonists' central issues.[2]

In *Strip Nude for Your Killer*, the assassin, Patrizia (Solvi Stubing), is a model at the Albatross agency where her sister, Evelyn, worked and whose cardiac arrest during an abortion prompted Patrizia to seek vengeance on the entire group, not knowing who the killer might be, similar to the antagonist's technique in *Seven Bloodstained Orchids*. Carlo, at the film's conclusion, tells his girlfriend and assistant at Albatross, Magda Cortis (Edwige Fenech), that Patrizia had more than sisterly feelings for her sibling and became demented after her death because she felt betrayed by her sister's involvement with a man instead of her. This disclosure changes the playing field considerably by turning Patrizia into an incestuous, man-hating lesbian in another *giallo* that pits a heterosexual male against a lesbian villain. Apropos of this, lesbians can be viewed by the male spectator as rivals to the heroine, appropriating male prerogatives in their desire for female partners, thus becoming suitable villains sanctioned by a patriarchal code. Patrizia is Sheila Heindricks (*The Case of the Bloody Iris*) on steroids, serving as a deviant polar opposite to the heterosexual couple, Magda and Carlo.

It is not accidental that these individuals appear familiar for they bear some similarity to those in *The Case of the Bloody Iris* as well as other *gialli*. As each genre has its own stock characters, so too does the whodunit especially when so many center on the fashion, modeling or photographic industry. These individuals assume common social stereotypes relying on cultural rubrics for their personality, manner of speech, and other idiosyncrasies. There is the gay photographer, Mario Ferrari (Claudio Pellegrini), only less flamboyant than Arthur in *The Bloody Iris*, coupled with the head of the Albatross agency, Gisella Montani (Amanda, aka Giuliana Cecchini), the rapacious lesbian reminiscent of both Sheila Heindricks in her aggressiveness, and Françoise Ballais, the conniving power behind the fashion house in *Seven Shawls of Yellow Silk*. Carlo is evocative of *The Bloody Iris*'s Andrea Barto, but much more an anti-hero. He is manipulative, sexually aggressive, decidedly self-centered and, although a lady's man like Andrea, Carlo has less scruples and is more inclined to be faithless than Andrea. There is no comparison, however, to Gisella's corpulent, sweaty and impotent husband, Maurizo (Franco Diogene), who can reach potency only with an inflatable rubber doll.

In fact, the aberrantly sexual aspects of *Strip Nude* stand out more than the usual violent set pieces which are not as florid in their detailed blending of realistic and surrealistic expressions of murder. This fact can be ascertained in the two deaths that have occurred during and since the opening credits. Bianchi would rather concentrate his set pieces on sexual titillation than on morbidity. For example, he positions his camera to contemplate two semi-naked women at a club bathed in a red spotlight making love to each other as Maurizo and Patrizia, his pickup for the night, watch on. Bianchi treats this in loving detail with the deliberate attention that a *giallo* would normally handle in a murder emphasized by a mosaic of numerous cuts. As the women on stage perform, an unseen orchestra executes a slow, dreamy piece which accompanies the swaying of their bodies to its rhythm. Although the scene does not contain the accustomed violence, other elements have been substituted for the familiar mayhem. Fascination within the canonic set pieces is usually predicated upon close-ups during the murder. However, in *Strip Nude* the traditional close shots of weapons and mutilated bodies give way to more sensually provocative images. The pattern of reiterative shots in most *gialli* is directed to the murder weapon which is customarily seen in the assassin's hand before, during and after the crime. The audience thus knows at the onset the victim's danger through foregrounding the weapon which triggers an immediate emotional response. In this scene at the club, the bloody weapon has been transmuted into a red spotlight shown seven times accentuating the bare flesh of its "victims" in its reddish glow while recalling the numerous bloodstained bodies penetrated by a knife. The spotlight also signifies the highlighting of a public act in a communal space set apart from the spectator for performance.

In other *gialli* scopophilia is tied into the act of murder usually in an isolated area but, nevertheless, becoming a performance piece for the audience. Another trope of crosscutting between the murderer and the victim has been modified in *Strip Nude* by having the two female performers coming slowly together through a series of crosscuts that climax in their sensual kisses and embraces displaying the entirety of their bodies for the first time.

In the conventional *giallo*, the female is undressed or quasi-clothed by the end of her clash with the killer; in *Strip Nude* both women are naked except for their G-strings. The director, through editing, has carefully disrobed the women for audience delectation. First we see only their faces for five shots, then part of their torsos with an extreme low-angle shot of their sensuous and prolonged kissing, followed by the camera's tilt down to their crotches with glittering G-strings and naked derrières bathed in the spotlight's reddish glow as they dance and grind their pelvises into each other. Finally, through a rear shot of their backs and naked buttocks bathed in the red spot, they are now so blocked as to become a framing device for the club's customers directing the audience's gaze back to the drama as the camera zooms in to Maurizo and his date. During this 14-shot interlude, with its jazzy horn, piano and violin accompaniment, all narration has ceased while the women have become a scopophilic extravaganza. Bianchi, consequently, has transferred the customary horrific set piece into an erotic and non-violent display of female flesh, not simply for sexual stimulation but as a means of foregrounding the particular sexual appetites of the characters.

With the recurrent theme of females as a saleable commodity, the story moves from the red spotlighted women in the nightclub to Carlo Bianchi developing prints in the studio suffused with the red glow from a safelight. Magda enters, takes off her dress, revealing a black string bikini and matching black mesh garter belt. She, like the women at the nightclub, invites Carlo to look at her as a different commodity: a model. He in turn, as in the nightclub, directs a desk light on her to emphasize her physical charms. They begin their lovemaking as she, kneeling down in front of the photographer, fellates him. With a jump cut, the crimson color is now picked up with Magda's red auto, accentuated by the surrounding darkness, as the two stroll out of the studio. There is a cut back to the studio; an unidentified black-clad figure carries a flashlight whose red plastic perimeter casts a scarlet glow that recalls the nightclub's crimson spotlight. The individual comes upon a photographic negative of the Albatross's employees which he reprints, bathed in the red light of the equipment so that this color continues as a nexus between interior and exterior scenes. But not only are the sequences joined through color; they are joined psychologically. Red is a strong color that evokes an array of ostensibly incompatible sentiments from wanton passion to ferocity and armed conflict. These conflicting sentiments are at the heart of the *giallo* since people, incidents and dialogue are made to appear what they are not, where morality is in contention with immorality, where lovers can't be trusted and where love is subject to paranoidal anxieties as in '40s film noir, their ideological precursor. In a world of pessimism with few moral absolutes, these ambiguous situations even undercut the *giallo*'s attempted happy ending. Central to this, the hero loses awareness of ties that bind him/her to

Andrea Bianchi's Nude per l'assassino *(1975)* 135

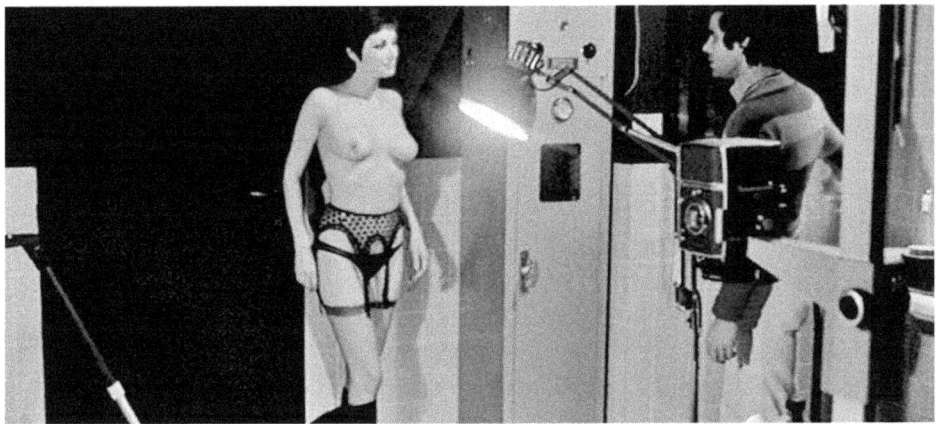

Magda (Edwige Fenech), looking to become a model, undresses before her boyfriend, Carlo (Nino Castelnuovo) at the Albatross studio. Her position in the frame, the lighting and even the spotlight recalls the ambiance of a previous strip club scene (Andrea Bianchi's *Nude per l'assassino*).

communities like the modeling agency, fashion house, photographic studio or apartment complex, and he or she must stand alone or accept a "donor" who serves as a folk tale plot device. But the *giallo* takes the folk tale one step further so that even the donor comes under suspicion as the hero/heroine doubts his integrity, becoming subject to pressures that sometimes drive him/her to the brink of insanity. Into the *giallo*'s world lurks the surreal as seen in the antagonist's ubiquitous presence akin to seemingly omniscient arch-criminals like Fantomas, created by Marcel Allain and Pierre Souvestre.

The killer, from a small park, now spies on Mario Ferrari, the intruder from the photographic studio, as he enters his apartment building. Visible only is the antagonist's black helmet and the sound of heavy breathing misleadingly coding the figure as male. This extended murderous set piece (23 shots) is singularly bloodless although menacing enough. With the exception of an establishing long shot of the living room, most are close-up or medium, imparting a hemmed-in sensation by blocking Mario through the murderer's foregrounded image or by photographing him in shallow focus leaving no depth for him to function. The second shot, a close-up, tracking black boots walking up the apartment steps with the sound of heavy breathing, typically introduces the killer through synecdoche. The assailant's gender, coded as masculine, becomes less certain as the scene plays out. In keeping with the diminishing space, shot #3 begins as a long shot of Mario in a chair holding a rolled-up paper; then there is a zoom in to him in a medium shot as he picks up a glass of liquor. A knock is heard. Mario gets up, the camera tracks with him in medium shot as he approaches the door, putting down his drink before answering. He, in close-up, opens the door, and the camera zooms away from him a bit; he looks bewildered and the camera zooms again in to a tighter shot of his face, constantly reducing the victim's spatial field. The sound of the visitor's heavy masculine knock suturing the interior of the apartment with the exterior stairwell is intentionally misleading. Mario's face appears bewildered but he knows the party; his puzzlement is not due to the visit but to the visitor's outfit. Since the *giallo* is no stranger to stereotyping, Mario's exclamation, "Darling," might suggest a female caller, but coming from a man coded as "gay," the comment is ambiguous. Mario remarks that he has the requested photos of the Albatross staff, giving the reason for the antagonist's call. Two inserts are presented: one of the studio personnel lined up for the photo, and a second, a few shots on, of a close-up of Evelyn in the same snapshot. More significantly, however, it connects the cyclist in some manner with Studio Albatross's employees and in particular with Evelyn because of the prominence given her. So intense is the connection between the cyclist and Evelyn that, at the mention of her, the visitor loses all track in pouring a scotch. Four shots illustrate this impact with the liquor flowing from the glass onto the table while Mario vocally upbraids his guest. The pouring of whisky triggers an insert to the scene of water pouring from the bathtub spigot with Evelyn's body slumped inside.

The psychological tension in Mario's apartment is not generated by the act of murder, but by its anticipation with the camera zooming in to the back of the motorcyclist with her raised arm opening a switchblade. As soon as the flashback of Evelyn occurs, ten shots of the killer approaching the victim within the small room constitute the mounting melodramatic spectacle. These ten leading to Mario's death are framed by the killer's raised forearm and end on that forearm while in between are regularly repeated close-ups of Mario's face and the knife which extend time and thereby increase viewer edginess. Only in the first half of the sequence (the first nine shots) is Mario in control of the situation. Once the flashback to Evelyn's body occurs, the emphasis is on Mario's subordination to the killer. Mario shares three shots with her, and although the killer's image is only partially foregrounded by showing either her helmet, arms, back or gloved hand, her figure predominates, making him, through blocking, less significant by occupying a background/midground space, or because he is periodically soft focused. While the killer is also fragmented, she appears dominant in four shots as well as being foregrounded in those of which Mario is a part. In short, the director, through the visual register, informs us that the conflict is not between equals, that the outcome is preordained, and that the traditional fragmentation of the villain is in direct proportion to the victim's plight.

Mario's murder, through repeated stabbings, is less graphic than the slaying of the doctor. In the final two shots, both the victim's and intruder's images are fractured but in different ways. Mario is at first presented in a medium shot that quickly changes through a zoom to a facial close-up severing his image just as the killer does with a knife. Of the killer, only her left arm and back are seen. The knife stabs are not further probed by the camera; only the motion of the cyclist's arm is evident while concentration is on the murdered man's face recording the effects of the wounds. The final shot is employed expressionistically, soft focusing Mario's visage to optically signify his losing consciousness as the music swells up.

When Mario's body is found face down by Patrizia, his pants have been pulled to his knees, and there is blood between his legs indicating that he too, like the doctor, has been castrated. There is a cut to the Albatross agency with an inverted image of two models, Doris (Erna Schurer) and Stephano (Wainer Verri), in fur coats posing before a motorcycle taken from Carlo's camera and assisted by Magda. The inverted frame becomes a perfect correlative to the *giallo*'s chaotic world where no *prima facie* evidence has an epistemological certainty. Maurizio looks at the beautiful blond keenly as if he were considering purchasing the "merchandise." His voyeuristic stance conflates the mechanical means of production with the merchandising of young, nubile bodies in the advertising industry. Although female nudity in the *giallo* is ubiquitous, the process of turning people into commodities has never been so conspicuously pronounced.

The vitriolic-erotic encounter between Gisella and Carlo's new find, Lucia, has them both naked in bed, the latter writhing in ecstasy as a mournful sax plays a slow solo. Gisella, jealous of Lucia sharing her affections with Carlo, sadistically smacks her partner calling her a "bitch" while Lucia passionately acquiesces, enacting the role of submissive partner to Gisella's dominatrix. Gisella's enviousness mirrors that of Patrizia's jealousy over her sister's involvement with other men while the characters playact a near-perfect roundelay of sexual relationships where Gisella is involved with Lucia who is involved with Carlo who is involved with Magda. The only missing link is Magda's sexual involvement with Gisella, but it would be narratively and ideationally inappropriate for a heroine coded as the prototypical example of heterosexual love and polar opposite of Gisella to do anything else. Having said this, those listed above, let alone the males, are necessarily flawed individuals: Gisella, as administrator, sexually dominates Lucia; Lucia, aspiring to be a model, sleeps with her boss for advancement; and Magda, hoping to become a principal photographer, seduces Carlo, her supervisor.

Once Gisella leaves her home, the scene is set for the murder of Lucia. Because of Lucia's prominent nudity, the blatant exploitation of her body leaves her more vulnerable, fetishistically accoutered only in high heels as she preens herself before a bedroom mirror recalling the classic images of Venus before her looking glass painted by Rubens and Velázquez. As a Venus

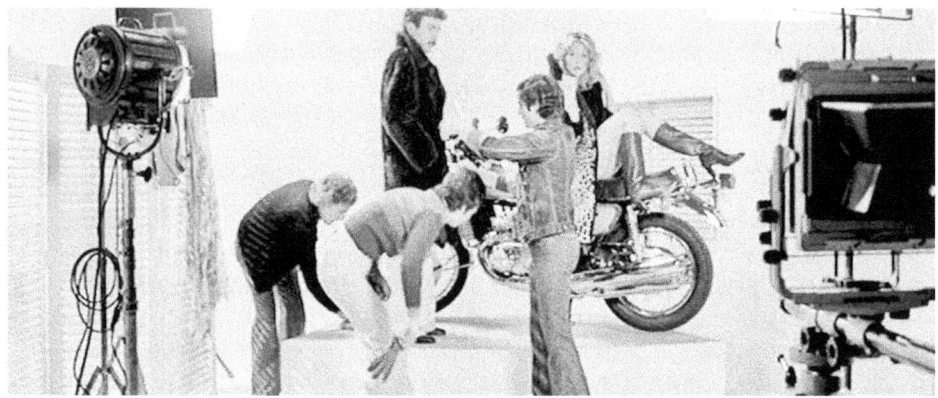

The photographic studio as a trope. The neatly blocked but dense scene with camera equipment juxtaposes the activity of Magda (Edwige Fenech, center) and Carlo (Nino Castelnuove, center right) in the foreground with the relaxed pose of the models, Doris (Erna Schurer) and Stefano (Gianni Airo), in the background that belie their tumultuous lives and violent deaths (Andrea Bianchi's *Nude per l'assassino***).**

reference, Lucia is the love object of Gisella and Carlo, and, for different reasons, the envy of Magda and Patrizia. Novels as early as Nicolas-Edme Restif's *Le Pied de Fanchette ou le soulier couleur de rose* (*Fanchette's Foot or the Rose Colored Shoe*, 1769) speak of *retifism*, a sexual attraction to footwear. The high-heel fetish is common in S&M literature as a dangerous implement to inflict pain. By solely wearing those heels, divested of any other bondage paraphernalia, Lucia is coded as an object of Sadean pleasure, but she is also subject to a sadistic lesbian killer's phallic weapon. The conventional S&M image is then turned on its head and Lucia, while signifying the dominatrix in heels and a motivator of desire, also becomes the persecuted woman, uniting both conceits into one.

Visually counterpointing the image of Lucia's commodified body is the sound of the murderer's presence, first emerging as an indistinguishable noise but shortly after segueing into the now familiar sonority of running water. It is this placement of sound within the diegesis (*point d'écoute*) that signals Lucia's preordained fate and that leads Lucia on her investigative journey. Acousmatic sounds are slowly revealed through the character's perambulations, but at each point in the discovery of the sound's source, Lucia puts herself into more danger. As in previous films, the old, dark, dusty and lofty spaces often recounted in Gothic novels by the heroine wandering through innumerable deserted rooms of an estate give way in *Strip Nude for Your Killer* to the small, cramped and contiguous room structure of a modern home. In place of a candle held by the protagonist in her investigation, we have electric lights; in place of the white flowing garment worn by the virginal heroine of the novel, we have a nude figure who has just had sex with another female; in place of the seemingly supernatural element of ghostly sounds, we have a unequivocal number of noises being made by a killer whom we only glimpse.

The first eight shots are crosscut so that the noise in the first shot is juxtaposed to an undefined source outside Gisella's house, eventually establishing a human referent with a definitive viewpoint exemplified by heavy breathing heard over the image of a black-gloved hand. Where the first four shots contrast interior with exterior, the next four, while continuing the alternating syntagma between Lucia and the killer, are all interior shots of the woman and house's entranceway. A figure is glimpsed through the front door suggesting the killer's means of entrance and that the proceeding events will be orchestrated within. While the crosscutting hints that the killer's entrée will be through that door, another series of shots are crosscut to imply that the stalker is about to enter from behind the living-room drapes.

In a series of shots that begin with a continuous take, Lucia, prompted by a noise, searches through the house. At this point the traditional crosscutting between victim and assassin is eliminated. The driving force of the shot is in the tracking and panning camera which follows Lucia, once she has left the bedroom, through the living room, onto the entranceway, into the dining room, through the kitchen and finally into the bathroom. The camera zooms from a medium shot of Lucia to a long shot of her walking toward the camera as she puts on the living-room lights. In the foreground is a room divider with metal horizontal and vertical bars. The camera pans with her as she moves frame left around the divider and then to the entrance to make sure the door is closed. The sound of water is now heard. She turns from the door as the camera pans with her entering the dining area and in a medium shot she, back to the camera, stares at running water in the kitchen sink; the camera stops before the kitchen entrance. Lucia, panting in fright, walks through the dining room and into the kitchen finding the tap open. Her progress is momentarily disrupted by two subliminally displaced diegetic inserts of the water faucet and Evelyn's body in the tub seen before each of the previous murders, visually reiterating that the killings are closely connected to Evelyn's death and the members of the Albatross studio. As Lucia closes the kitchen tap another sound of water is heard and she moves toward the camera and out of the kitchen, fearfully looking left and right. The camera, from the rear, pans with her as she enters the dining room; we look at her back as she turns the corner into the living room and to the open bedroom door she is approaching. She walks up two stairs to the bedroom and disappears, turning left inside. The camera zooms in to a bedroom mirror reflecting her image as she, back to the camera, stares into the bathroom. In a close subjective shot we see the bathroom sink; the camera zooms back to Lucia in long shot in the bedroom approaching the sink. The camera zooms in to her rear as she enters the bathroom, followed by her hand turning off the water. There is a zoom out to a long shot of Lucia hearing an off-screen noise while framed by the bathroom doorway which virtually imprisons her within a narrow space. Eleven shots are crosscut between close-ups of the frightened woman in the bathroom's confines, instancing her lack of motility, and long shots employing a zoom to the bedroom's rustling drapes that Lucia is observing. Each time a shot of the drapes concludes by zooming out from them; the next time they are shown the shot continues from the previous one as though from an uninterrupted point of view revealing a bit more of the bedroom area. Lucia's face is in a tight close-up as she continues to retreat to the apparent safety of the bathtub. Unanticipated, the killer, from behind the shower curtain, pulls it noisily aside as Lucia turns around. There is a close-up of the killer raising her arm repeatedly with a knife and the sound of the weapon entering Lucia's midsection, but denying the audience a detailed view of the slashing. There follows a medium shot of Lucia's bloody body on the floor with a knife entering her midsection, the killer gasping from exertion. This constitutes the "money" shot where the inflicted carnage is presented in savage detail, the knife penetrating Lucia's body acting as a substitute for the sexual climax in pornography. The audience now understands the byzantine reasoning in back of the lengthy crosscutting between the woman and the bedroom drapery which has groomed viewer expectation to look for the killer behind them. The cyclist's sudden appearance behind the shower curtain is more frightening because of the sound of its metallic hooks being pulled back swiftly as well as its unexpectedness. As witnessed here, Bianchi's females are first paraded around in nothing more than their alluring vulnerability for a male audience's delectation before being murdered under the most sadistic circumstances.

Since one of the *giallo*'s aims is to furnish as many suspects as possible, every piece of dialogue or non-verbal communication is textually imbedded to equivocally communicate misleading information about the characters' involvement in the mayhem. But this is not the only means. Another avenue is through camera positioning and framing. Immediately following a scene in Magda's studio apartment where she questions Carlo's involvement with the murdered Lucia causing him to throttle her for this and throwing suspicion on his intense irascibility, there is a cut to him looking frame left while smoking a cigarette at the Albatross studio. The police commissioner (Lucio Como), with his assistant, is interrogating him. Both officers momentarily remain off-screen. The camera pans slightly right and slowly pulls back in an arc from a close shot of Carlo to a medium shot of the back of the assistant's head so that he is in the center-foreground, Carlo is in the midground to the left of the frame, and the commissioner is to frame right in the background.

The blocking is sufficiently dense to connote the constrained and uncomfortable feeling experienced by Carlo as he is being questioned, isolated to the far left of the frame yet wedged between the two law officers. The camera then moves in to a close-up once more of Carlo's face as he nervously makes an excuse to distance himself from the slain Lucia. Parallel to this in the same room at a different time, Gisella is questioned and reacts identically to Carlo as the camera performs a similar movement with the selfsame blocking to make both suspects appear vaguely culpable causing one to distrust the other.

There is also a similarity in the murders of Maurizio and Lucia. Maurizio picks up Doris, a blond model, and drives to his retreat where he attempts to persuade her into sex; it is clear that she has been there before with his wife, Gisella, the same house where Gisella made love to Lucia. Maurizio cries when he can't perform with Doris, his impotency seemingly attributed to his mother fixation. Bianchi ridicules another sacred cow, the *mammoni* or "mother's boys," adding a perverse ingredient to this mix: Maurizio achieves orgasm only with his inflatable doll, making him at once pathetic and ludicrous as he invokes his mother in distress. After Doris leaves, Maurizio, blowing up his doll, hears the sound of running water recalling not only Evelyn's death but those subsequent images of other victims whose deaths were heralded in the same manner. As Maurizio proceeds from the living room to the dining room and then into the kitchen where the tap is running, one is reminded of Lucia's walk through the same house, likewise attracted by the sound of running water. As Lucia wore only high heels, Maurizio wears only his briefs; as Lucia carried Gisella's earring in her hand, Maurizio carries a partially inflated sex doll; as Lucia was a beautiful woman whose state of undress could only elicit desire, Maurizio is a middle-aged corpulent man whose state of undress can only elicit amusement or pity. The camera on the previous occasion stopped at the kitchen doorway while Lucia went up to the sink. As Maurizio enters the kitchen, the camera zooms in to the faucet as he closes the tap. On this action there is a flash cut to a close-up of the tap in Evelyn's tub followed by the recurrent shot of the dead woman. As Maurizio continues to blow up the inflatable doll, the same electronic rattle-like noise is heard as at Lucia's death. The camera zooms back to see him isolated in the small kitchen looking insignificant despite his immense size, blocked by the kitchen door frame as Lucia was blocked by the bathroom door. He then hears still another running faucet. Getting hold of a knife, he proceeds to walk from the kitchen to the bedroom, the camera taking his point of view. As with Lucia, Maurizio in an objective shot enters the bedroom, turns to the left to go to the bathroom while his image is reflected in the bedroom mirror. A slow sax wails on the sound track while he cautiously walks toward the bathroom door, knife in hand. The audience, thinking back to Lucia's murder, expects the killer to come from behind the shower curtain, but before Maurizio gets into the bathroom, the cyclist jumps him from behind at frame right, stabbing him continuously in the chest; the infliction of wounds, however, cannot be observed from this angle. The camera zooms to a close shot of the killer's back as the stabbing continues; the obese man falls to the floor while the killer persists in knifing him. There is a close shot of Maurizio's face turned to the floor with a medium-close shot of the killer's back, arm and buttock to the extreme left of the frame still wielding the knife and then a quick fade to black. Besides the sounds of the knife, the man's groans and the electronically hyped music, there are no explicit visuals to evoke the man's plight.

Bianchi has led the viewer in past murders to expect a visualized culmination of the violence, but has softened the assault on Maurizio so that his stabbing as well as his castration is only inferred. Conceptually, the violence depicted in these films functions like sex in pornography. It should be varied enough so that the set pieces are not redundant, operating "to multiply the possibilities of exchange [violence in this case]."[3] Maurizio's stabbing, therefore, is even more discrete than the others, psychologically taunting us into desiring to witness the mayhem, but denying that expectation in the climatic shot. Subtly, this stratagem coerces the moviegoer to acknowledge his position as voyeur in an inherently voyeuristic medium. We have been misled into thinking that the series of events, based on past experiences, would suggest a predictable culmination of the action, but Bianchi thwarts viewer expectations. The murder has not culminated in a strategic aesthetic of explicit voyeuristic violence. It has not even been deferred as in Mario Ferrari's case; it has been eliminated.

Two important incidents now occur: Magda overhears a telephone conversation between Gisella and an unknown man who is blackmailing her for £10,000,000 and discovers, in a photo, the same earring on a model that remained in Lucia's hand the night she was murdered. When Carlo comes to the apartment she mentions this to him as he initiates foreplay. Electronic guitar and keyboard music with wordless female vocals and woodwinds further romanticize their lovemaking while camouflaging a pivotal point: the model with the identical earing found on Lucia. There are several reasons for this: Bianchi is making soft-core *giallo* porn, breaking older taboos by setting a new boundary where titillation is more important than information, and where the clues are given but not understood when they are introduced. The erotic situation in which the information is disclosed is not conducive to argumentation. If the murderer is an agency model, the cyclist might well be a female, and if a model she, is either friends with the deceased Evelyn or even more intimately connected since the retributive punishment met out is severe.

Gisella's death occurs in a lonely place. The build-up to this murder-mutilation is likewise engaging, for Bianchi once more has varied its staging. The action is photographed in silhouette, sound predominates as sensory substitution for the visuals and Gisella is symbolically and bizarrely castrated by having her ears severed. Equally important, Bianchi has photographed most of Gisella's murder in extreme long shot with an insert of the killer's arm repeatedly stabbing the victim who is off-screen, distancing the viewers from the crime while allowing them to hear Gisella's cries and the sound of the knife cutting through her flesh. Carlo is in the frame's foreground taking pictures while the murder occurs in the background producing an invocatory drive in the visually deprived audience depending exclusively on sound. Only in the "payoff" do we see the mutilation which evokes the earlier castrations of male victims. After the murderer departs, Carlo runs to Gisella; dying she curses him for not intervening. The police routinely arrive too late and witness instead the photographer's retreat, but lose him in the darkness. Once more, the police's ineffectuality makes way for the layman, Carlo, to uncover the murderer with Magda's help. Photography, quite naturally, proves a pivotal clue for both the amateur detectives and the killer: Magda recognizes the earring in the photo of the dead woman's hand, Carlo has photographed Gisella's murder, and the killer uses a group photo to track down her victims. Photographs within the film thus assume a privileged position as a source of visual information, whereas the film itself purposely misleads us with its visual information.

Carlo, escaping the police, is now pursued by the killer who runs him over, landing the photographer in the hospital. Disabled, he sends Magda for the infrared film of Gisella's murderer hidden in the Albatross's trash, adding another crucial photo to the list to be analyzed. From the hospital Carlo calls Magda at the studio where Patrizia has followed her and where she has turned off the fuse box placing the studio in darkness. In the darkened studio, Magda moves toward the fuse box as Patrizia, bursting through a huge poster that recalls the parting of the shower curtain in Lucia's knifing, knocks Magda down. Over the phone Carlo hears Magda's scream inaugurating quick cuts to the studio phone, to Carlo leaving his hospital bed, and to the killer burning Carlo's photos. From the burning film there is a rhymed cut to Doris, a model, wreathed in a haze of cigarette smoke linking the two disparate scenes. Doris is listening to the news on television at home about the latest victim, Gisella Montani, when an "intruder," seen as a shadow on a wall, enters from behind. Since it is shot in deep focus, the living room's space engenders uneasiness because the dramatic time is identical with the empirical time it takes the intruder, partially concealed by the low-key light, to make his way to Doris. When he finally faces her and shuts off the TV, she calls out, "Stefano." Once more, the director strategizes an aesthetic of deferred gratification; the moviegoer is drawn into a state of anticipation only to be deceived by an accumulation of suspenseful signifiers.

Briefly suspending this plot development, Bianchi cuts to Carlo searching for Magda at Albatross. Once Carlo enters the studio the camera (1) zooms from his face to an extreme long shot revealing it empty. As a rhetorical function this first zoom permits us to participate in the impact the empty studio has on him and his trepidation at the disappearance of Magda. Moreover, the zoom from a close-up of Carlo's face to an extreme long shot places the photographer in a threatening space where silence prevails and where his image becomes insignificant and open to assault as Magda was. Bianchi punctuates each new shot of Carlo entering various rooms of the Albatross with a zoom as a unifying aesthetic to join disparate locations. Carlo is again seen in close-up followed by a subjective shot of a broken vase with its flowers strewn on the floor accompanied by a (2) zoom back from the vase to examine the area around it. This second zoom draws us into the protagonist's psyche as he rapidly assimilates information about Magda's situation. Once more there is a medium shot of Carlo's face followed by a (3) zoom back which places him bewildered in an empty office. The scene in the photographic development room begins with a long shot of Carlo entering followed by (4) a zoom in to the burned remains of his film, then a (5) zoom out to a long shot of the hero grabbing the remains of the film and cursing. He walks over to the photographic negative of the staff when there is a (6) zoom in to it as Carlo, using a magnifying glass, sees Stefano in the picture as another potential victim. The six zooms in less than a minute in no way, even as an emphatic "gestural marker of narratorial performance," break the illusion of the "invisible narrator required for the suspension of disbelief."[4] The viewer experiences the scene through a central character's limited point of view, a Jamesian third-person reflector. It is through this restricted narratorial device that the audience understands what has taken place at the Albatross and its effect on Carlo. The thought that excessive zooming might destroy one's suspension of disbelief seems a trifle over-reactive, although its use can be a slippery slope. The zoom may call attention to the extradiegetic narrator or to the camera itself, but more creatively it contextually privileges the technique as an expression of psychological or emotional intensity.

As Carlo utters Stefano's name, there is a cut to Doris being slapped by Stefano when she asks if he saw Gisella that evening, arguing the possibility that he was the one who ran away when Gisella was attacked. Doris hints that his sexual preferences are somewhat abnormal, his sadism vividly presented in subjecting Doris to pain and humiliation like Gisella's smacking of Lucia. Although Bianchi delights in presenting sexuality and violence in various forms, he is also a moralist. He condemns Dr. Julio Castelli not because he has performed an abortion but because he covers up evidence; he condemns the lesbian and homosexual not because of their sexual preferences but because they are arrogant, deceitful and oppressive individuals; he condemns

Maurizio's kinky sexual proclivities, not because of his fetishistic practices, but because he preys on his subordinates. There is no one in the cast, except the romantic leads, whom he does not castigate including the police who use their authority to intimidate civilians. The story is one of class warfare packaged around morally bereft, misanthropic personalities. While the killer invites no sympathy because her motivation is based on revenge and incestuous jealousy, we likewise are not made to care for her victims. This is evident in the Albatross "family" who, although part of the same corporate enterprise, appear increasingly disembedded (especially the killer), without social or moral concern for their actions. In brief, whether the relationships are heterosexual, homosexual or sadomasochistic there is a sense of vacuousness.

Immediately after Doris's declaration of love to Stefano, crosscutting between the couple and the black-clad cyclist outside their home begins. Doris is weeping while a shirtless and unmoved Stefano stands over her. Outside, a handheld subjective camera launches the killer's approach to the house. Inside, Stefano, indifferent to Doris's pleading, pours a scotch. His ultra-masculine posing solidifies his hegemonic position; stripped to the waist with the ubiquitous bottle of J&B, he ignores Doris as much as he mistreats and sexually degrades her. Although it is uncertain how Italian women of the period would have received the portrayal of Doris, a woman probably without much education, and Stefano, a product of the Italian patriarchal structure of machismo's gendered relations, it is feasible Doris might have garnered some empathy from the less-educated female audience especially prior to the equal rights law of 1978 which gave women social and economic self-determination. However, among more progressive and educated women in large northern cities, it is more likely that there would be little tolerance toward Doris's reaction, though there might be some understanding and sensitivity to her in light of the ideology that produced it.

The double murder sequence is divided into six sections with a total of 21 shots illustrating the set piece's aesthetics. *Shots 1–2*: The trigger that launches Patrizia into action is an event the trigger is listening for, the traumatic memory of seeing Evelyn's body in a bathtub. This event conditions her rage over her sister's loss thereby causing her to act, even to the point of running tap water in the victims' homes before murdering them to simulate the primordial event under which she found Evelyn. *Shots 3–5* crosscut between the killer outside the house and the couple inside: the killer's hand with a glass cutter breaking through a window, the arguing couple, and the killer's hand pulling a circular portion of the cut window away. The "outside" corresponds to the dark unknown, the perilous, nebulous space inhabited by the murderer; the inside represents the illuminated "known," the safe and the defined space inhabited by the victims. When these two collide mayhem occurs signaling that the illuminated space is no longer secure. *Shots 6–13*:

Bianchi builds this threat quickly as the third and largest segment develops. The couple turns their attention to the sudden opening of the bedroom door leading to the living room after hearing the sound made by the killer. The living-room lights abruptly go out and Stefano proceeds to investigate (off-screen); his cries, the crash of breaking glass, and his body hitting the floor are heard. At this point crosscutting is confined within the house between the couple in their lighted room and the open bedroom door. Once the lights go out in the living room, the couple is invaded by the darkness, a reversal of the poetic theme in John's Gospel about Christ's advent in the world and the forces of evil: "What came into existence was Life ... the ... Light to live by. The Life-Light blazed out of the darkness; the darkness couldn't put it out." *Shots 14–16*: Crosscutting between Doris calling out her lover's name and the door leading to the living room now begins with the sound of running water. *Shots 17–20*: Four more shots are reserved for crosscutting between the screaming Doris and the mutilated Stefano reintroducing explicit carnage with his neck slashed, his rib cage sliced and his genitals severed. The sound of running water ceases. *Shot 21*: Doris's death concludes the sequence but is relegated to one explicit and lengthy shot. The killer grabs her arm and continuously stabs her in the stomach until she falls down dead.

The film concludes as Carlo contends with the assassin in three different locations seeming to meld into one another like some hypnagogic event. He is nearly killed by Patrizia with a sword in her home, from there she attempts to murder the intoxicated Magda in the park until frightened off by Carlo, and finally Carlo pushes her down a flight of stairs to her death in a shopping mall. As she calls out her sister's name, a form of visual hyperbaton occurs. There is a cut to a long shot of the dead Evelyn in her bathtub followed by the doctor and Carlo placing her in that tub as though Patrizia has finally connected the pieces of the puzzle and discovered who was associated with her sister's death. This is accompanied by Carlo's explanation of the mystery behind Patrizia's killing spree as he and Magda are in bed. The viewer is treated to another of Magda's disrobing scenes and the couple's lovemaking. In fact it is Magda who tells her boyfriend to stop the foreplay and begin intercourse because she is on the pill. He in turn pretends that he is going to have anal intercourse with her while she protests vehemently. The film began with a taboo subject of abortion and now ends on another controversy still fresh in the minds of the Italians, birth control. Pope Paul VI in *Humanae Vitae* (1968) reaffirmed the Catholic Church's continued condemnation of artificial birth control. In Italy the encyclical was welcomed, but feminists won the battle on the birth control ban in 1970, five years before *Strip Nude for Your Killer* premiered. Magda's remark to Carlo indicates that she is a modern, emancipated woman, and for Bianchi their banter is all in good fun.

Bianchi's film fits well into the taxonomy of the folk stories despite or because of its lurid qualities which were the fixture of many of these older narratives delineated by Propp.

1. **A member of the family leaves home (I).**

Since many of these films deal with middle-class people in white-collar jobs, the absentation is centered on their workplace. The distance between home and job is routinely not made specific, but the story is situated usually in a large northern city. *Strip Nude for Your Killer* takes place in Milan, the densest in all Italy, ranking with New York as one of the world's "alpha" cities. The main character, Carlo Bianchi, a photographer, absents himself from home by coming to the aid of a doctor friend of his, Julio Castelli, to help him get rid of the corpse of a model from the Albatross studio named Evelyn who has come for an abortion. Carlo is a member of the studio which, as in many of these films, becomes a surrogate "family" for the protagonist, a home away from home for many of the characters.

2. **An interdiction is addressed to the hero (II).**

The basic premise which sets off the multiple murders is the overall legislated interdiction in 1975 that abortions in Italy were illegal. Once Evelyn's abortion is performed and she dies as a result, it triggers the film's primary interdiction that is addressed to Carlo, the hero, in an inverted form of an "order" (subcategory #2) by Dr. Julio Castelli. The abortion doctor, knowing that Evelyn was one of Carlo's protégées, orders him to come to his office and help him dispose of the body by placing it in Evelyn's own bathtub to appear like an accidental death, saying nothing to the police. This solution to the problem serves as a "contrasting background for the misfortune to follow."

3. **The interdictions are violated (III).**

Functions II and III form a "paired element." Naturally, the fulfillment of this order to dispose of the model's body is to make it look like a natural occurrence which results in a cover-up of an illegal activity. Had the death been reported, Dr. Castelli and perhaps Carlo, his accomplice, would have to go to prison for five years and there would be no need for Patrizia to avenge her sister by killing the doctor and Studio Albatross members. Arousing her interest and ire, Patrizia's role now becomes the disturbance of the peace of the "happy family" comprising the studio staff and its models. So, therefore, the primary interdiction under which the doctor is working is the illegality of an abortion in Italy. When Castelli violates this, the interdiction to Carlo for help is its consequence. This also affects the second protagonist, Magda, as an Albatross member and Carlo's lover. The violation of the primary interdiction and the secondary interdiction not to inform the law propels the couple to find the murderer before they become the killer's next victims.

4. The villain receives information about his victim (V).

When we finally realize the villain is a member of Studio Albatross, it is inconceivable that Patrizia would not know something about the people on her hit list, especially since her sister, Evelyn, must have informed her about the studio "family." First, Patrizia is never in the spotlight at the studio because her prominence would lead to her being a suspect vis-à-vis the audience. She is almost forgotten as a character and can operate under the radar. Second, as part of the modeling staff, Patrizia would not be suspected by the others since it is mostly within the ranks of the models that the crimes are being committed. Patrizia has obtained the photo of Albatross members by Mario and kills him because he might possibly be the one responsible for Evelyn's death. The revenge motif guides the narrative to its conclusion. No one knows Patrizia is Evelyn's sister and no one is able, until the finale, to ascertain that Patrizia's motive is based on an incestuous desire for revenge.

5. The villain attempts to deceive the victim in order to take possession of him/her (VI).

The villain has deceived many of the characters in order to get them in her confidence by becoming a model at the Albatross. Her looks get her noticed by the head of the company, Gisella Montani, and her husband, Maurizio, takes Patrizia out expecting sexual favors in return. Patrizia also returns to the scene of the crime where she castrated Mario and feigns being overcome by the sight so that the police commissioner is convinced of her innocence.

6. The villain causes harm or injury to a member of a family (VIII).

Taken figuratively, the "family" is seven members of Albatross, and because none of them know that Patrizia is the sister of Evelyn, they are not able to tie the accidental death of this model to her vengeful sister. She is able to kill five of the Albatross's "family."

Dr. Julio Castelli's criminal abortion activity and his interdiction to Carlo about keeping quiet prepare the way for this function and facilitate its happening since their transgressive behavior results in the Albatross members' deaths that are tied into a community photo. Propp also states that the patterns villainy takes are considerably disparate. Those patterns of interest are several: subcategory #1—"The villain abducts a person." Patrizia doesn't wish to kill Magda but to pin the murders of Stefano and Doris on her and perhaps, by implication, the murders of the other Albatross members, so she overpowers her at the studio, abducts her and forces liquor down her to the point of inebriation causing Magda's sudden disappearance from the Albatross (subcategory #7) by "deceitful means." Also within this function is subcategory #14: "The villain commits murder" and, in the case of the hero and heroine, subcategory #6, "The villain causes bodily injury," when Patrizia attempts to run Carlo over and to frame Magda for the murder of Stefano and Doris. Included in this is still another form of villainy: subcategory #18, "The villain torments at night." This occurs in the stalking of Dr. Castelli, Maurizio, Doris, Stefano, and Gisella as well as the chief protagonists.

7. One member of a family either lacks something or desires to have something (VIIIa).

The two sisters, Evelyn and Patrizia, are the only bona fide family. That this family relationship appears dysfunctional is not the case in point, but the manner in which one sister's loss becomes the suffering and destruction of many. The lack, therefore, is the death of a sister. Patrizia's murderous rampage is the result of Evelyn's accidental death and constitutes the film's revenge motif. Whether or not Patrizia's love was reciprocated by her sister is not clear; the former has an incestuous desire for her sister and is angered by Evelyn's "betrayal" of her with another man. Not only has Patrizia suffered a loss; she desires, therefore, "to have something," namely, retribution against the company where Evelyn worked, as though all its members were responsible for her sister's pregnancy and subsequent heart attack during an abortion.

8. The hero/heroine are tested and attacked which prepares the way of her receiving a helper/donor (XII).

Propp lists ten variants to this function. Once Carlo doesn't inform the police about the model's death, he is tested by the deaths of members of his community and with his lover is eventually attacked. As donors, the police have interrogated Carlo, Gisella and Albatross workers without satisfactory results so that Carlo and Magda decide to find the murderer themselves due to the law's ineffectual handling of the case. Carlo assumes the role of helper by now questioning Magda (subcategory #2, "The donor greets and interrogates the heroine") when she notices the earring in Lucia's hand after her death, and a similar earring on a model in a photo. Carlo tries to put an obstacle in her way by arguing that there must be many women who have the identical style of jewelry. Magda, however, is persistent so Carlo informs her to start the investigation at the Albatross studio. Magda's taking charge, despite her boyfriend's questioning the advisability, gives her the edge as heroine over Carlo's role as hero. Since they work as a team, Carlo, when hospitalized, requests (subcategory #7, "Other requests") that Magda develop the film he took of Gisella's murder, placing Magda in danger as she is pursued by the killer. This feature is subsumed under subcategory # 9: "A hostile creature attempts to engage the heroine in combat." Carlo, from the photograph, recognizes Stefano who is blackmailing Gisella for her sexual relations with Lucia, but there is also an unknown helmeted individual he photographed at Magda's death. The cat-and-mouse game played by Patrizia with Carlo ends in his hospitalization when she tries to run him over. She subdues Magda and, with the heroine in a semi-conscious state, plies her with liquor and takes her to the murder site to incriminate her.

9. **The hero/heroine and the villain join in direct combat (XVI).**

Carlo goes to Patrizia's home where he is attacked by the cyclist and thrown down. The killer escapes the apartment and then attempts to strangle the inebriated Magda, but Carlo chases her off. He pursues her to a shopping mall where they stalk one another.

10. **The villain is defeated (XVIII).**

Carlo struggles with Patrizia, they fight and he throws her down a flight of stairs to her death. Taking off Patrizia's helmet he confirms his suspicions as to the perpetrator of the crimes. Magda, still under the effects of alcohol, cannot assist Carlo and so remains off-screen during the fight.

8

The Shadow of Guilt

Antonio Bido's *Solamente nero*
[*The Bloodstained Shadow*, 1978]

A priest is he who lives solely in the realm of the invisible, for whom all that is visible has only the truth of an allegory.—Karl Wilhelm Friedrich Schlegel

   Solamente nero's villain-priest is not unique in concept in Italian cinema which has both abused and extolled Catholic priests on numerous occasions. Well before new millennium sexual scandals covered up by the Vatican and its bishops, Italian film generally portrayed the clergy sympathetically, like the heroic Don Pietro Pellegrini in Rossellini's *Roma, città aperta* (*Rome Open City*, 1945), and his humble Franciscan monk in *Francesco, giullare di Dio* (*Francis, God's Jester*, 1950), as well as Julien Duvivier's humanist cleric in the 1952 *Don Camillo*. The *giallo*, while not turning the priest into a comic dupe like Don Mario in Dino Risi's *La moglie del prete* (*The Priest's Wife*, 1971), did more serious damage by portraying him as a misguided, malicious or deranged individual. In 1972 alone there were at least three *gialli* about malevolent priests, not including those in the "nunsploitation" subgenre that can function within the *giallo* canon. There was Don Alberto Avallone, who kills children in order to save their souls in Lucio Fulci's *Non si sevizia un paperino* (*Don't Torture a Duckling*), the nameless killer priest out for revenge against women in *Sette orchidee macchiate di rosso* (*Seven Orchids Stained in Red*), and Aldo Lado's Father James, a cross-dressing child killer who targets redheads, in *Chi l'ha vista morire?* (*Who Saw Her Die?*). The Italians exploited the more lenient censorship laws to vent antipathy through anti-clerical filmic portraits sometimes bordering on the surreal, and *Solamente nero* is no exception.
   Antonio Bido's film deals with ecclesiastical guilt and fashions a story about a Catholic priest, Don Paolo (Craig Hill), who has tried to sexually

151

molest a girl and in an attempt to cover up his crime has killed her. In later years when his life is threatened, Don Paolo murders those whom he thinks might have been a witness to the deed. The guilt comes to the man who, as a priest, "lives solely in the realm of the invisible," that is to say, a life of faith. But Don Paolo's visible world truly becomes an allegory, for all he sees are people who make his dedicated life to God a sham, reminding him of his crime and God's judgment upon him. If the film deals with a hypothetical guilt-ridden priest it is also set in "a hypothetical Venice ... that doesn't really exist," for Bido "never wanted to set [his] films in a precise city, but rather in an atmosphere."[1] In one sense his statement is odd. As a director of award-winning documentaries one would expect that the integrity of a geographic location is meaningful to him as an artist, to the story line and to the characterization. In another sense the *giallo* is pure fantasy where the *mise-en-scène* takes on a hallucinatory quality and documentary realism is not an indisputable necessity to attend characterization and action. To find any one ideal location is a sizable task, and to create an "atmosphere," a "Venice that doesn't really exist," is part of the illusory ambience of *Solamente nero* contributing to its own artificiality. His characters populate more evocative locales than precise indigenous neighborhoods through the film's manipulation of spatial continuity for dramatic purposes.

To some degree *Solamente nero* promotes its "Italianness" through foregrounding verifiable tourist locations in Venice that briefly arrest the narrative trajectory and operate as out-and-out spectacle, but also, by using Murano as its major setting, it promotes a "rural-historical" locale as a place of the fantastic.[2] Stefano D'Archangelo (Lino Capolicchio), a mathematics professor, returns to Murano, his childhood home, having been estranged from the small community by anxiety attacks rooted in an adolescent trauma that have worsened, persuading him to take a leave of absence from his teaching post to visit his brother, Don Paolo.

The film opens with a low-angled over-cranked pan shot from a country church to a girl being strangled by an unknown assailant in black shirtsleeves. Hurled to the ground, she grabs onto a book in her fall, tearing some pages out of it. The concluding long shot, with title and credits superimposed, has the deceased girl in the foreground and in the background a hilltop church. Obsessional shots from this scene become fixed narrative points of the film's focalizer, Stefano. Throughout the credits, acoustical guitar, keyboard and percussion instrumentation in an upbeat contrapuntive melody belie the seriousness of the implied image. The viewer, after the credits, is introduced to Stefano en route to Venice by train where he makes the acquaintance of Sandra Sellani (Stefania Casini), a painter, who is also traveling to Murano. There he is met by his older brother, the priest, and soon becomes swept up in Paolo's personal problems. Later it is discovered that Stefano had witnessed his brother's crime and now suffers from its persistent recollection, causing post-traumatic stress disorder.[3] In the restaurant where they go, several characters figuring prominently in the story are introduced: a bogus medium (played by Alina Simoni) involved in blackmail receives money from a young man named Thomas, the boy-toy of Count Pedrazzi (Massimo Serato); also seated is a doctor, Aloisi (Sergio Mioni), who has "accidently" killed his wife while cleaning his rifle. After dinner, while walking to the rectory, the priest continues to describe other townspeople: Signora Nardi (Juliette Mayniel), a midwife and abortionist living with her disturbed son (Gianfranco Bullo) whom she keeps hidden, and Count Pedrazzi, a pedophile, whom the priest detests. Strolling by Murano's Rio dei Vetrai, Paolo's recitation of other parishioner's sins skillfully boosts his own respectability, for how can he be so scornful of other's failings unless above reproach himself?

On a rainy night during Stefano's first day with his brother, the medium is murdered in a square behind the church just below the priest's window. She had been conducting a séance with the town's most notorious characters. The assailant attacks the medium, but only the culprit's arms are seen strangling her. Her screams amid the thunderstorm awaken Don Paolo from sleep, and the director crosscuts between the priest and the attack. As the *giallo* operates on its characters' voyeuristic tendencies, the priest looking from his window watches silently as the medium is killed. She calls for help, but only after he has witnessed her murder does he go down to investigate. Stefano, Paolo and his sacristan, Gasparre (Attilo Duse), explore the area but find no corpse.

The medium's throttling evokes the opening scene of the strangling of the girl by another unseen character, Don Paolo, years ago. The subjective shots from the priest's viewpoint, looking from his bedroom window at the murder, implicitly implicate the viewer who becomes an empty, absent subject with a pure capacity for seeing.[4] We feel helpless, as Don Paolo must feel, at the sight of the woman being attacked, but we participate in the spectacle as voyeurs, the reason for watching *gialli*'s set pieces. More importantly the scene buttresses his characterization. The association between his murder of the young girl and the one he presently witnesses is like an out-of-body experience. The attack diverts suspicion away from Don Paolo in the same way that his moral indignation about the townsfolk suggests his exemplary life. At one point he tells the pederastic count that he, as a priest, stands in God's place and feels sick just listening to him. The count, knowing more than he says, calls Paolo hypocritical. Paolo, as a celibate, brings up another interesting correlation between celibacy and violence. Psychological findings support the thesis that deprivation of bodily pleasure throughout life is closely related to interpersonal violence.[5] Paolo's killing of the girl suggests that violence becomes a substitute for genital love; the priest resorts to force as a means of assuaging sexually aggressive impulses. Paolo is momentarily paralyzed by the medium's murder in the square not only because of witnessing the act itself, but because he is reliving the initial act he committed. This paralleling of crimes is voiced by the police commissioner's (Alfredo Zammi) remark that the medium's strangulation is similar to the young Andreani woman in the meadow a few years back. Paolo's initial act of murder demonstrates priestly dominance through sexual exploitation. At the time, in Italy's nominally Catholic population, clerical privilege became a weapon to wield as a status symbol in empowering a priest into coercive sexual behavior.[6]

In the morning, after the theft of an incriminating tape from the medium's house used to blackmail her séance group, leading us to think it was one of them who killed her, a note is slipped under Don Paolo's bedroom door announcing that if he speaks out about the murder his own will be talked about. The second note, discovered by Stefano, unhinges Don Paolo a bit more, hinting at his part in the Andreani girl's death, the killer believing that Paolo has seen him strangle the medium. This message also is pertinent to the younger brother in a different way, for his past is linked to witnessing the death of the Andreani girl, but whereas the killer believes that Paolo has seen him commit murder, the priest does not suspect that his brother has likewise watched him commit a murder.

When the police find the medium's body, Stefano, Don Paolo and the sacristan are present. Stelvio Cipriani's synthesizer, at this moment, with its discordant notes, is orchestrated flawlessly by Goblin. It suggests the onset of Stefano's psychosis at the sight of the deceased medium. A close shot of the woman's head is cut to that of the young professor's; the camera then zooms in for an even tighter shot followed by an over-cranked zoom in to a distraught little boy (Stefano as a child) in the bushes with closed eyes and mouth opened in a scream. This, with minor variations, is repeated twice more. This recurring childhood trauma will eventually hold the key to the actual killer. The crosscutting between Stefano as a child and as an adult is so measured regarding focal distance, camera angle and speed that the correlation between the two events is categorically established. Because Stefano has witnessed his brother's crime that he has blocked from his mind, he has become depressed, going into a seizure[7] triggered by the sight of the medium's body.

Antonio Bido's documentary roots surface when Sandra takes a boat trip through Venice's canals on her way to see her stepmother (played by Laura Nucci). Through her viewpoint the moviegoer gets to see a touristy panorama of the city's broad canals bathed in an impressionistic greenish haze emanating from the water. Once on land, however, the topography conveys undertones of entrapment. Many of the shots of Sandra are taken with a wide-angle lens creating a deep focus so that walkways hedged in by walls on either side seem unnaturally long and narrow. There is no music, and only the distinct sound of her footsteps adds a disconsolate ring. The camera tracks behind Sandra through the twisting, narrow city corridors suggesting that someone is following her, pausing as she pauses and resuming tracking when she continues her walk as an electronic score intrudes. Even in long shoots Sandra is hemmed in by arches and waterways, and in close-up she furtively looks about as though pursued by phantoms.

In Val Lewton's *The Cat People* (1942), Alice Moore takes a solitary nighttime walk through Central Park, and, like Sandra, it becomes an increasingly nervous stroll accented by sounds of footfalls and climaxed by a commonplace noise. The film's editor, Mark Robson, described it: "A bus came by and I put a big, solid sound of air brakes ... cutting it in at the decisive moment so that it knocked viewers out of their seats. This became the 'bus.'"[8] In *Solamente nero* a man playing an accordion suddenly comes out of a doorway, and, like Lewton, Bido creates a "bus," producing an unexpected jolt of surprise and fear both in Sandra and the viewer. The impact on the audience is even more dramatic than Lewton's because the scene is set in broad daylight. As soon as Sandra walks up the central staircase and is out of frame, a man's shadow appears on the landing in the background. She picks up the apartment keys under the mat, accidently drops them and immediately gasps as a hand picks them up. It is the second startling incident on her trip, but, as with the accordion

The "bus" scene. Sandra (Stefania Casini) frightened by an accordion player suddenly appearing from a doorway pays homage to *The Cat People* (1942) where the sound of a bus's air brakes is employed to frighten the character and viewer by its unexpectancy (Antonio Bido's *Solamente nero*).

player, the intruder proves only to be a shamefaced Stefano. The periodic use of a camera tracking Sandra from the rear calls into question whether or not Stefano might have been in pursuit of her or someone bent on doing her in, but if Stefano, he doesn't make his presence readily known. Inside the luxurious apartment, Stefano notices the stepmother's painting of a landscape with a girl beset by the devil while diagonally above her is an insert of Mary with the child Jesus. The rest of the canvas's scene, a church atop a stone cliff, is similar to that which opened the film and part of Stefano's recurrent nightmare. His startlement is emphasized by crosscutting facial close-ups with a zoom in to the painting.

The death of the pederast, Count Pedrazzi, begins after a candlelit living-room dinner served by Thomas who leaves when they argue. The count hears a noise, and from a subjective viewpoint red drapes part and someone looks directly at Pedrazzi sitting alone on a sofa with a glass of J&B. Quirky distorted synth music rises and we see a close-up of the killer's black shoes and pant legs walking on a tiled floor as the count's voice calls for Thomas. The core of the first half of his murder centers on facial close-ups of Pedrazzi continuing to call out amid a clock's chimes. From the opening, seven close-ups of Pedrazzi's face, extending almost halfway through the 36 that detail his death, demarcate his spatial perimeters as he looks about the sumptuous living room prior to his being stalked. This spatial restraint is enhanced even in long shots by narrowly framing the count through parted drapes which reveal but compress his field or where he, in midground, is juxtaposed to a looming foregrounded world globe reducing him to inconsequentiality. Ironically when an unobstructed shot of the count does occur it is from a high angle that minimizes his figure so that Pedrazzi appears exposed and alone in a large space. Even in flat-angled shots he is framed by doorways or medieval pikes that restrict him by their configurations. In short, the *mise-en-scène* deprecates the count's control over the situation. Intercut with his close-ups is statuary which acts as signifiers to his mounting anxiety. Two times cherubs' smiling faces, followed by their solemn ones, are intercut with the count's so that blocking, editing and set design create a correlative that externalizes Pedrazzi's internal escalating fear. A close shot of Pedrazzi's face where, in a more commanding tone, he admonishes Thomas to end his joking is a turning point in the action, for now the count is on the move as well as the killer. The count's progression through corridors of his mansion increases a spatial dimension to the proceedings as the camera tracks with him revealing chivalric heirlooms of war and destruction, inserted early in the sequence to foreshadow his death. The weapons are somewhat at odds with the effete count whose only passion, outside of music, is handsome young men and lovely children. The suits of armor consisting of visors, rerebraces, vambraces and gauntlets imply a courtly time when men in combat or in jousting met on the field face to face, not stalking one another in rooms filled with memories of medieval valor.

The director builds upon a number of incremental images besides close-ups of the count and framing devices to demarcate Pedrazzi's limited space. Close-ups of the murderer's shoes appear early on giving substantiality to the antagonist rather than playing with the audience's emotions through images that only imply his presence as with parting drapery or the rustling of halberds. Four close-up tracking shots of the criminal's shoes complement an equal number of tracking shots devoted to the victim. The synecdoche of the killer's black shoes creates its own parallel visual structure through movement, fashioning an "enclosed" rhyme scheme where the first and fourth lines, and the second and third rhyme. This rhyme in turn mirrors the confined atmosphere of the mansion.

> Shot #6 The killer's shoes **moving away** from the camera. A
> Shot #24 The killer's shoes **moving toward** the camera. B

When the killer's shoes reappear the arrangement is reversed:

> Shot #27 The killer's shoes **moving toward** the camera. B
> Shot #29 The killer's shoes **moving away** from the camera. A

The instrument of death is foreshadowed by a close-up of halberds rustling as though someone had brushed passed them. *Giallo* directors frequently use foreshadowing to give the audience clues to the killer's identity or the manner of death the victim is to undergo. For instance, the assassin's black shoes and pants are not a disguise to confuse the moviegoer, but ordinary street clothing worn by a cleric. Regarding the count's death, the rattling halberds stacked against a wall are returned to in a latter shot where the camera dollies in to them to stress their significance, preparing us for the climactic moment when a halberd is thrust into Pedrazzi's chest. Bido temporally extends the death of the count by editing it into six shots as a denouement: (1) a medium shot of the halberd entering the count's chest; (2) a close-up of the halberd in the count's chest (3) a medium shot of the count crying out and dropping to the floor; (4) a close-up of the count's face as he falls, his head hitting a wall; (5) an extreme close shot of the count's eyes looking up, then closing; and (6) a close-up of the count falling face down to the floor. The number of shots devoted to the count's death is the visual equivalent of a melodramatic embellishment in its appeal to the emotions. As Ayn Rand expressed it, "a drama involves primarily a conflict of values within a man ... a melodrama involves only a conflict of man with other men."[9] These six shots are the crowning consequence of the conflict among men. The first of these shots, the sudden embedded halberd in Pedrazzi's chest, establishes the action. The shot has the capacity to make the audience gasp since the viewer's pent emotions have been progressively hyperbolized from the beginning to expect a catharsis to the action. After the halberd penetrates the victim, the next shot embellishes it with a close-up followed by a shot illustrating the effect on the human body as the count begins to drop to the floor. To prolong the emotional impact, this fall is broken up into the final three shots until the body strikes the floor. His death again finds the law baffled in its search for the perpetrator.

When Don Paolo, during mass, finds a sheep's head in the tabernacle, the familiar typed note alongside the animal warns the priest to be silent. The letter "T" in the note idiosyncratically hooks down only on the left side and Stefano believes that if the typewriter is found they will find the killer. This leads into the next set piece, the attempted murder of Don Paolo which is reminiscent of the death of Count Pedrazzi. The locations differ, but Bido makes good use of the church's space to create the sort of uneasiness he maintained in the count's mansion. As with the killing of the count, sound plays a significant role. The sequence opens with a noise that Don Paolo hears as he is eating in the rectory, thinking it to be Gasparre, the same way the count believes the sound to be that made by his male lover. The assault on Paolo, comprising 50 shots, has been divided into four sections to illustrate the incremental repetition that creates suspense: #1–#5 (5 shots), #6–#12 (7 shots), #13–#24 (12 shots), and #25–#50 (26 shots). Occurrences taking place in one section are amplified in another constituting a canonical trajectory of escalating uneasiness within this set piece. Once inside the church most of the sequence is observed through Paolo's (beginning with #14) and the killer's (beginning with #17) perspectives, and even if shots are from a seemingly objective viewpoint, so pervasive does audience paranoia become by odd-angled framing that they appear to be from the assailant's position since it is only the sound, camera movement and the motion of objects in the frame that signify the whereabouts of an invisible intruder.

The first five shots set the scene for the attempted murder of Paolo, the interior of a quiet church devoid of parishioners. Bido begins with an establishing shot of the (1) main aisle looking to the altar; the remaining four shots are key images that will reappear at climatic moments: (2) the statue of St. Anthony of Padua holding the infant Jesus together with (3) the violent slamming of the cabinet door bearing the saint with no visible agent present, and (4) three rows of lit candles along with the St. Anthony statue composited into one shot when the priest is about to be killed. Other shots of St. Anthony are presented with and without the priest in the picture. The second statue of (5) St. Francis of Assisi will similarly appear again later. The statues substantiate the place's sacredness, but this ambiance is juxtaposed to the profanation of the space by the attack on Don Paolo.

Shots #6 through #12 act as a nexus between the rectory and the church to place Don Paolo in the sanctuary because of the noise he hears as he is eating dinner. As Pedrazzi is murdered by one of the treasured objects in his home, a medieval halberd, the priest is attemptedly murdered by the dropping of a large crucifix on him, one of the objects he venerates. Both the count and priest call out endeavoring to learn the identity of the intruder. Both men are hunted down because of their involvement with children. The count is killed, while the priest eventually commits suicide realizing the enormity of his guilt and the psychological damage he has inflicted on his brother.

The next 12 shots (#13–#24) give the clear impression, through point of view, that someone is stalking the priest. His calling out to the intruder hints at an unknown presence and brings us closer to the climactic moment of Don Paolo's near fatality. Once in the church, there are abundant shots from diverse angles of Paolo looking about for the cause of the disturbance. The flat-angled shots of the priest, numbering six, convey a normalcy suggesting Paolo is in command of the situation, although even here his furtive glances subvert a sense of his assurance; the low-angled shots numbering five likewise appear to give him a dominating presence equal to the challenge, but they are few in number and again are undermined by his constant gaze off-frame. The more numerous high-angled shots, numbering seven, steadily attenuate his figure so that he appears inadequate to the situation and convinces us that they are taken from the unknown assailant's viewpoint. Certain shots, prefaced by a high-angled zoom from the priest to the organ loft, indicate that they are taken from the killer's vantage point: a close-up overhead shot of an aged organ keyboard with bits of paper crumpled on it, an extreme long shot from a high angle looking down at the priest from the organ loft and panning with him as he walks below, and finally an extreme high-angled long shot looking down at the priest before votive candles through the organ loft's latticed railing. The slamming of the cabinet door and the swinging sanctuary lamp, similar to the swaying halberds at the count's mansion, also indicate an unobserved presence, leaving us with the supposition that the killer is sadistically toying with his victim before doing him in.

Shots #25 through #50 represent the sequence's climax. We have observed throughout the comparison between the sightless statuary filling the sanctuary and the incessantly searching eyes of the priest and that of the camera. While Paolo challenges the nameless presence he senses is there, the statues have mouths, but they cannot speak to warn him of the danger and eyes that cannot see for him. Scriptures are turned back on themselves in a mocking portrayal of Catholic pietism's devotion to the saints recalling the psalmist's injunction against idol worship (Psalm 135): "They have mouths, but they do not speak, eyes, but they do not see, ears, but they do not hear.... Those who make them will be like them." The final affront to Christian iconography is the crucifix which cannot save; in fact it is turned into a murder weapon in the last eleven shots. The rapid alternating shots between the priest and the crucifix and the priest and St. Anthony's statue terminate in the falling crucifix (taking six shots) juxtaposed to Paolo (four shots), both sharing the same space in shot #45 when the cross hits the priest, felling him to the ground without seriously injuring him.

The next murderous set piece of Sandra's stepmother is quite gruesome. As with Count Pedrazzi and Don Paolo, the victim is lured to her death by a noise which initiates the sequence's 31 shots of virtually wordless action. The first 11 shots typically alternate between the killer and the old woman. The stepmother, dozing off in her bedroom in a wheelchair, is observed in long high-angled shots, stressing her diminutive size and defenselessness, abutting flat-angle close-ups that spatially hem her in to designate her precariousness. Throughout these initial 11 shots, the killer is represented by the flashlight he carries or as a monochromatic figure in black. Within this grouping, three more shots signal the stepmother's awakening and realization that someone is in the apartment. Unlike Pedrazzi and Paolo, the woman is not ambulatory and therefore cannot investigate on foot; she is only able to move her wheelchair to the bedroom door's entrance.

Shot #12 initiates the characters sharing the same filmic space. The woman asking "who is there?" recalls the other two victims with their similar inquiries. This apportionment of space by the killer and his victim is mainly done through metalepsis. The killer's torch, for instance, becomes the person himself while concealing his identity from the audience. The metalepsis is exploited in conjunction with synecdoche: the archetypal black glove, mask and coat of the *giallo* killer. The substitution of the torch for the assassin, indicating phallic power, ends in a medium shot of it shining directly into the camera until a zoom in to it blankets the frame in a close-up. From here on, the killer's image is fragmented in various ways: arms, hands, a portion of his torso, and a partially silhouetted image. Shots #16 through #19 inaugurate the manner of death in store for the old lady as she retreats in her wheelchair into her room moaning/screaming, her back to the camera as it dollies in after her. As she turns sideways in her chair to look toward the camera, the flashlight shines in her face. The killer, an amorphous black object, approaches behind her chair. In close-up a cord is pulled around her neck as she screams, turning her head about. From a long shot the camera dollies in to a close-up of the brightly lit bedroom fireplace. The killer, strangling the woman, pushes the wheelchair toward the fire, just off-screen. Finally in long shot taken from behind the hearth looking out into the bedroom, the woman screams as she is pushed headlong into it by the killer, toppling both wheelchair and occupant into the flames. This constitutes the macabre payoff of the set piece. The camera privileges three principal subjects within these shots: the victim, the fire, and the killer. Emphasis on the woman in flames is ceremonialized by the camera. Even when the killer is positioned within the frame, the eye immediately is drawn to the brightness of the fire and the old woman's burning body. Four more shots deal exclusively with her torture: a close-up of the woman's burnt head in flames still screaming, a medium shot of her back with her head in the fireplace as her body struggles to free itself, a close shot of the woman's back with her head on fire as she thrashes about, and lastly a medium shot of the back of the woman, her head engulfed in flames. While the killer's black-gloved hands are represented only once in this section, the woman's hands, indicating the agony she is experiencing, are accented through three shots. Earlier on there are two shots taken of the flames alone to telegraph her death. The final two shots, employing synecdoche, signal the victim's painful death: the woman's back and head inexorably sink into the flames and her hand's convulsive clasping of the rug that covered her legs relaxes its grip and ceases to move. This final shot is the only subtlety the set piece possesses which is not to negate its impact. All through this, the synthesizer's soundtrack by Goblin richly augments the horrific action. Later, sound will be emphasized once more to "awaken" Sandra to the presence of the killer in her home.

It has been previously established that the key to the murders of several of the town's citizens lies in the painting stolen from Sandra's stepmother's house, and Bido now pursues this lead. Sandra has a photograph of all her stepmother's artworks, and Stefano, recognizing that the landscape painting recalls some childhood incident he witnessed, cannot make the association. Later that evening after Stefano has left, Sandra is alone, painting the head of a woman whose hair is composed of streaks of flame (recalling her stepmother's death). The killer enters the house's ground floor to steal the photo of the original painting as diegetic classical music plays on Sandra's radio. The killer knows exactly where to go as the stealthily moving subjective camera reaches a bookcase and a black-gloved hand takes the bound copy of the photographed paintings. In doing so, however, the intruder knocks over a silver bowl. The sequence combines elements from the count's wandering through his house with the sound of rustling halberds, the priest roaming through the church because of the slamming of the cabinet door, and the killer prowling through the stepmother's apartment knocking over a painting. To investigate, Sandra, like Don Paolo proceeding down the stairs into the church's sanctuary, walks down a flight of steep steps into the lower part of the house, and like Count Pedrazzi, she is surrounded by works of art. At one point, a statue of Marcus Brutus, ready to stab Julius Caesar, frightens her as she treads along a corridor of marble busts. Abruptly the lights go out and nondiegetic music begins. A policeman suddenly opens the outside door with a gun pointed at Sandra, frightening her while his partner declares that he lost the track of the intruder. This short sequence, a *trompe l'oeil* of sorts, is placed here to deceive the viewer into thinking that the killer is on the other side of the door. This intended deception is staged as a murderous set piece during a tense narrative moment, already seen in *Seven Shawls of Yellow Silk* and other *gialli*.

A paradox exists for the viewer in the films under analysis. Most everyone avoids physical pain in life, yet goes to these films to be captivated by the physical pain of others. The typical moviegoer, viewing the brutal death of Sandra's stepmother, for example, experiences not sadistic delight, per se, in seeing her suffer, although that can't be ruled out, but the pleasurable pursuit of fear. Such drama is meant to give audiences a feeling of release and vindication in relation to the degree and kind of violence that is perpetrated. Aristotle calls this catharsis, an "emotional cleansing," occurring as the result of the viewer undergoing strong feelings of fear which are at the root of the *giallo*'s set pieces. The circumstances leading up to the set piece are more important in advancing anxiety levels while their release occurs immediately after the actual mayhem terminates. The anticipation of such cruelty produces a pleasurable fear, and perhaps "pity," depending on how fully delineated the character is. Fear and pity are subtly enhanced by the situation, the music, the cinematography and the editing. Taking only one of these aspects, let us consider the editing process. During these set pieces, there are constant cross-cuts between the victim and the killer, splintering the space so that the victim's assault is temporally protracted while through the repetitive editing patterns more fear and pity are generated than through the actual bloodshed, which only repulses. These dual emotions are prompted by the expansion of time and, concomitantly, of space to reach an inevitable point where the antagonist and the victim spatially share the frame. Audiences identify, however ambiguously, with the imperiled character, a cause of their pity and fear, by being positioned helplessly in their seats with information that the victim is not privy to and which can't be communicated to the character.

The next victim is the gambling addicted "wife murderer" Dr. Aloisi. This may be illustrated in an atypical manner, but emblematic of those set pieces where the highly structured spectacle is constructed like the format of a five-act play, a mini-drama within the principal melodrama, as is demonstrated below with an (1) exposition, (2) rising action, (3) turning point, (4) falling action and reversal and (5) resolution. The structure is the familiar one used by Shakespeare and is grounded in the concepts of unity in Aristotle's *Poetics*. The German novelist and poet Gustav Freytag described it as a "pyramidal" structure, with act 3 at the apex.

1. **EXPOSITION** [shots #1–#6]. The murder begins with an exposition, where we meet the principal characters and establish the location. Coming out of his office at night, Aloisi is bludgeoned by a black-clad figure along

the canal's waterway, emerging from the darkness. The doctor, falling to the ground, is then kicked into the water. Attempting to climb out, the killer steps on Aloisi's fingers and he falls back into the canal. A barge comes down the canal headed in the doctor's direction with two sailors manning the barge. This constitutes the antecedents to the action directing us toward the dramatic conflict. A bit of the conflict is seen in Aloisi's ability to latch on to the barge, and a second conflict presents itself: will the killer attempt to follow the doctor and complete the assassination?

2. **COMPLICATION/RISING ACTION** [shots #7–#11]. The course of the action becomes more complicated and the events accelerate in a definite direction causing the tension to mount and the mini-story's momentum to build up. Aloisi grabs hold of the barge's port-side rope and is pulled along, although the two men on the barge remain unaware of the doctor. As the barge turns the canal's corner, the camera pans to a speedboat parked at the canal's side. In effect this boat is the murder weapon of the killer who will use it against the doctor.

3. **CLIMAX OF ACTION/TURNING POINT** [shots #12–#18]. The development of conflict reaches its high point. Aloisi is at a turning point leading to victory over the killer or defeat and death. The villain now pursues Aloisi via speedboat. The anticipation is amplified by the killer's intentions against Aloisi through a series of five close-ups: (a) black shoes enter and walk down stairs into the speedboat, (b) a black-gloved hand turns the speedboat's ignition key, (c) the speedboat's turbulence caused by the propellers emphasizes its swiftness, (d) a black gloved hand manipulates the throttle, (e) a bit of the speedboat's aft and turbulence caused by propellers accentuating its power, (f) an extreme long shot of the topside of the barge as the doctor continues to hold on to its side, (g) a shot of the two men manning the barge. At this point we know that the killer is out to run the doctor over with his powerful speedboat.

4. **FALLING ACTION/REVERSAL** [shots #19–#25]. The consequences of act 3 play out, and tension is heightened by false hopes/fears. If it's a tragedy, it looks like the hero can be saved. If not, then it looks like all may be lost, the consequences of act 3. The conflict between the killer and Aloisi reaches its highest point when Aloisi realizes that the villain is going to run him over. As the villain's boat approaches the victim, more emphasis is placed on the speedboat's swiftness, decreasing Aloisi's chances of escape. Aloisi is in the water in the foreground, in the background the speedboat approaches causing the doctor to turn his head in that direction clinging to the rope. There are a series of shots of the bow of the speedboat, the killer's black-gloved hand manipulating the throttle and wheel, the lower side of the barge with the speedboat gaining (doctor not in frame), the doctor off port bow holding the rope, the killer's hand on the throttle, the wake of water from the speedboat's aft.

5. CATASTROPHE/RESOLUTION [shots #26–#33]. The conflict is resolved in the downfall of Aloisi when the villain's speedboat runs Aloisi over beginning with the shots of the speedboat gaining on the barge by coming along port side, the speedboat's bow with the doctor in the water, the port bow of the speedboat, Alosi screaming as he shields his face with his arm from the oncoming boat. The villain's breaking away from the barge commences with shots of his black gloves at the wheel (seen five times in 33 shots), the starboard of the barge and the port of the speedboat and finally a long shot of the speedboat pulling away.

The next note Don Paolo receives informing him of his imminent death is in the votive box containing money deposited to light a candle as, sardonically, the sacristan is reciting the *Litany of the Blessed Virgin* imploring Mary's help on all Christians. After speaking to an architect (Antonio Bido) about plans for the crypts in the cemetery, Paolo walks through its fog-enshrouded grounds, a setting worthy of Hammer studios. He hears footsteps and in close-up are seen the same black shoes and pants worn by the killer, ensuring us anew that the priest is not the murderer.

Various shots (opening three) give superficial views of the cemetery at night to establish location. The next shot establishes the padre's walk through the graveyard; crosscutting ensues between Don Paolo and the killer which expands the action's temporality to increase anticipation. The ubiquitousness of the killer is presupposed as he assumes a preternatural hegemony over his victims. The pattern of shots depicting the villain seldom varies: four close-ups of his shoes and pants with one medium and one full shot of his back as he runs away, the fragmentation contributing to his nebulousness. Interspersed with the villain are a variety of shots of Don Paolo: four close-ups of his face juxtaposed to six long shots of him rambling down paths. The only consistent shots (outside of close-ups of the killer's shoes) are Paolo's incessant looking about. Despite a semblance of reality by placing the cleric in quasi-contiguous spaces, Paolo's reiterated movements through the cemetery emerge as surreal through the manipulation of space. He appears en route to an exit, yet he returns to pathways already trod, giving the impression that for all this meandering the padre seems to be going nowhere fast. Only the final shots bring some semblance of unity to the space and closure to the sequence. In a medium shot the priest's back is to the camera tracking behind him as he looks around. The killer jumps at him from a mausoleum doorway, but Paolo is able to fend him off. In the final shot the killer runs to the frame's background turning left to exit.

A curious layout of shots is instituted between the priest and the villain. We start out with two shots devoted to the priest followed by one shot of the murderer. This is repeated. The paradigm now shifts alternating between one shot of the priest and one shot of the murderer only to return to two shots of the priest followed by a shot of the murderer. The finale is reached with two shots of the priest followed by a two-shot of the priest and the murderer spatially uniting them. The sequence, therefore, is constructed through its preoccupation with the priest and his growing fear of being followed in a precise formulation of images that actualizes this unease in us. Sound is conveyed through the pounding musical soundtrack and not through sonic signifiers of the assassin's footsteps, the creak of shoe leather or the breaking of debris under his feet, begetting a sense of unearthliness. The concentration of shots on Don Paolo is expected, for he is an ersatz protagonist, and the audience is expected to identify with him. Close-ups of the priest's upper torso are complemented with the unvarying close-ups of the killer's lower torso insinuating one composite shot of the two men from head to foot by uniting them in a kinship of crime.

The long shots of the priest, numbering five, are more numerous, but they hardly give any sense of location, tending instead to obfuscate the cemetery's spatial parameters. From the tracking shots of both the priest and villain we assume that one is following the other since most of the lateral tracking of both men moves from right to left of frame. At other times the lateral tracking of the priest suggests that the killer is walking alongside him unobserved, watching his movements. Further obfuscating spatial directions, at the sequence's culmination when the murderer appears from a mausoleum's recesses immediately before the priest reaches that point, it is assumed up until then that the killer has been following behind the priest, for the camera tracks the cleric's movements from behind as though from the killer's subjective view.

Those alternating shots between the priest and murderer are meticulously balanced which gives the episode its own rhythm through the repetition of images, motion and sound occurring in a regular pattern. This pattern has as its sole purpose to engender pity and fear which is only released in the culminating shots of the cleric besting his attacker. The tempo of the sequence, determined by the content of the scene, the frequency of the cuts and the duration of the shots between the cuts, is quite uniform, but it is precisely this invariability that gives the piece an edgy quality as we wait for the inevitable clash between the two, rather than calling attention to itself by percussive edits, odd angles or distorting lenses. When that clash does come, it unexpectedly ends in the attacker's hasty retreat, marking the second time the cleric has had a near-death experience.

During the intervening time, Stefano finds letters addressed to Sandra, with the odd-typed *T* and surmises that Signora Nardi, the midwife, wrote the threatening notes. Opening up a cabinet in her son's (Gianfranco Bulo) room, he discovers the typewriter, hears a noise and turns. This movement is match cut, linking him to Paolo in church sitting in a pew and turning around as though he has heard the selfsame noise; he gets up and moves into the aisle as two hands spring out of the confessional and attempt to strangle him. There is a cut back to Stefano at the top of the staircase in the Nardi house, much like his brother earlier at the head of the rectory stairs hearing a disturbance in the church. Paralleling the present experience of his brother in the chapel, Stefano suddenly is confronted with the midwife springing from a closet, a pair of scissors in her hands ostensibly to strike at him, only for the audience to discover her throat is slit. There is a cut from the dead woman on the floor to Paolo on the floor struggling with Nardi's son, trying to avenge his mother's death. The priest, saved a third time from death, knocks him unconscious with a candlestick. It is revealed that the priest has been killing prominent townspeople who attended the medium's séances because he wasn't sure who had seen him murder Andreani's daughter. Stefano enters the church as the son is taken by police to a hospital. Seemingly the mystery is cleared up, but Bido has some surprises left.

At Sandra's apartment, Stefano takes out an old newspaper clipping stating that a girl was strangled by a maniac, showing the hillside church depicted in the stepmother's painting with the deceased girl lying in the grass and clutching pieces of paper. Thinking about the original painting, as Stefano runs back to his brother's church, his childhood memories of the murder vividly return in a series of slow-motion flashback shots counterpointed to the swift tracking camera of his running through the town's streets. Stefano reveals the real murderer of Nardi's mother to be Paolo and not the demented son; in fact the son had attempted to avenge her death by killing the cleric. Furthermore, Signora Nardi killed the medium because she was being blackmailed by her for performing abortions, but seeing Paolo at the window she thought that he had recognized her. It was Nardi who kept the cleric's prayer book with its torn pages as insurance which she took from the medium and which Stefano had taken from Nardi's closet. It was Nardi who had written the threatening letters to Don Paolo. The three breviary pages torn by the murdered girl matched the pages ripped from the priest's breviary that were described in the caption under Stefano's old newspaper account of the killing. Paolo, likewise, couldn't be sure which three who frequented the medium's home knew he had murdered the girl, so he killed them all, like the cleric in *Seven Blood-Stained Orchids*.

Bido, in the end, creates a portrait of Paolo as a man tortured by guilt, in despair of salvation, and in fear of discovery, a villain who is not only the principle of destruction for others but for himself. For Don Paolo there is "only darkness": a darkness of soul which isolates him more from the rest of humanity than any physical deformity. The tragedy about the priest is that he can't seek forgiveness from God or from his fellow human beings. In one formidable montage the audience is made aware of his conflicted spirit as a flashback begins; Paolo, in close-up, turns away from Stefano and Sandra staring down the empty church aisle. This is one of the few non-set pieces where Bido employs a percussive editing style as images flash through Don Paolo's mind. His despondent face is constantly returned to in 12 shots as he stares into the empty church and remembers the parish communicants he has murdered (seen in nine shots), and parishioners who accusingly stare back at him from their seats (six more shots). Paolo, in his mass vestments, seems to stare back from the past into the present at the profligate priest he has become. Seven other close shots of Paolo's face giving out communion are as accusatory as that of the parishioners, not only of their lifestyles but of his own, as he recalls his sins. The palpable estrangement he feels from God and his parish is clearly visualized where, in the present, his figure in the church is dwarfed by the prominent dead space surrounding him. This is contrasted by two extreme long shots of the priest with a church filled with people. The film doesn't have to verbally explain the shame, indignation and loathing the cleric feels for himself; visually this cognitive and emotional conflict raging in Paolo is conveyed in 40 shots. Even during mass he seems to accuse himself of what he has become. To palpably convey this in the present, Bido has a sharp close-up on the priest's face shift to soft focus emphasizing his isolation and reprehensible nature by literally blurring his image.

Paolo runs to the bell tower and, in a cinematic equivalent of Hitchcock's Madeleine Elster in *Vertigo* (1958), climbs to the top as the pleading Stefano, in the "Scottie" Ferguson role, runs after him. In three shots (one in close-up) the audience views the cleric's fall to his death.

Again we turn to Propp's paradigm to examine Antonio Bido's folk tale structure.

1. **A member of the family leaves home (I).**
Professor Stefano D'Archangelo leaves his home in Rome to visit his older brother, a priest in Murano, a small town near Venice where they were raised. This absentation is significant insofar as Stefano has been experiencing flashbacks of a murder he witnessed as a child. On the verge of a nervous breakdown, he has taken the trip to forestall the consequences.

2. **An interdiction is addressed to the hero (II).**
The town of Murano is postcard picture perfect and "serves as a contrasting background for the misfortune to follow," as Propp remarks. The hero is Stefano D'Archangelo while Don Paolo, his brother and the major villain, is seen as an ersatz hero, honest and righteous. The other scoundrels include Signora Nardi and, to a lesser degree, her unhinged son. Signora Nardi, believing that the priest witnessed, from his window, her killing the medium/blackmailer, places under Don Paolo's bedroom door a note telling

him not to say anything to the police or he will be killed. This interdiction, the first of three sent by her, personally involves the real hero, Stefano, because his brother is being threatened and because it leads to the uncovering of Stefano's repressed traumatic experience as a child.

3. **The interdiction is violated (III).**

Although Don Paolo is the chief villain and enters the picture once Stefano reaches Murano, Signora Nardi is the film's second villain. Her interdiction is left unheeded by Stefano since his life and his brother's depend on whether or not he complies with the prohibition to stop interfering. Consider what has transpired when the interdiction is addressed to the priest and, by implication, the young professor: Stefano is experiencing an ongoing trauma of the murder he witnessed as a child, and someone has murdered the medium/blackmailer right before his priest brother's eyes. He and Paolo, therefore, violate Nardi's advice for two significant familial reasons: first, Paolo's life is in danger and Stefano desperately wishes to aid him, and second, Stefano, implicated even more than he knows through the threatening letters Paolo receives, by connecting the deaths of the medium and the girl will discover that his brother is the town murderer and will rid himself of his suppressed childhood memory. Nardi's interdiction causes both brothers to bond together to solve the mystery of the murdered medium that develops into the amateur sleuthing trope.

4. **The villain receives information about his victims (V).**

First, Don Paolo, as parish priest of a small town is the major villain and knows much about the lives of his parishioners: through the sacrament of penance, through his own parishioners who inform him of the lives of others in the community, and through his ability to be present at most communal functions in the role of parish priest. Despite this, once the accusatory letters are sent to him, he is uncertain what parishioner has witnessed his murdering the Andreani girl. Don Paolo's own brother is likewise a victim of the cleric's machinations since Stefano has suffered throughout his life with a repressed memory about the murder he witnessed. Second, in a small town, Signora Nardi has enough information on Don Paolo to blackmail him into silence since she has the torn pages of his breviary that connect him to the murder of the girl.

5. **The villain attempts to deceive the victims in order to take possession of them (VI).**

Although there are several villains, the priest, Signora Nardi and her son, the main antagonist is Don Paolo. Paolo's "disguise" is both a physical and a moral one. Dressed in his clerical cassock he is literally able to get away with murder as the robe is a symbol of his dedication to God and humankind, his separation from the world and a sign of God's presence working through a human agency. But Paolo also uses a moral disguise with the hypocritical stance he takes against his sinful congregation. His air of piety and a semblance of indignity against the pedophile, abortionist, blackmailer and the wife-murdering, gambling-addicted doctor aids his deception as he systematically eliminates them to save his own reputation. The abortionist's unsigned, threatening notes also paint the cleric as a victim in his brother's eyes, giving the priest a perfect alibi. Paolo is able to deceive Stefano in this way because the threat to his life is real.

6. **The victim submits to deception and thereby unwittingly helps his enemy (VII).**

What is interesting about *Solamente nero* is that the victim, Don Paolo, is the hero's brother, and therefore, Stefano D'Archangelo, the film's amateur detective, is very willing to "agree to all of the villain's persuasions." In fact, the dire straits the cleric finds himself in prompts Stefano to uncover the murderer who is the man he wants to protect. Stefano, as well as the audience, is deceived by the priest because, in reality, his life *is* being threatened by poison pen notes. The irony in the film is the commissioning of Stefano by the killer-priest to find out who is threatening him.

7. **The villain causes harm or injury to a member of a family (VIII).**

Propp considers this function "exceptionally important since by means of it the actual movement of the tale is created." Stefano's trip to Murano is linked to his traumatic childhood memory. The event triggers his quest and involves him in the threats against his brother, the priest. Don Paolo, as older brother and killer, has already caused psychic harm to Stefano seen in a puzzling flashback at the film's opening. That the priest doesn't know what has triggered his younger brother's traumatic experience, which Stefano is unable to recall, is a sardonic commentary on the iconic image of the priesthood and the commandments he is bound to uphold. Paolo is responsible for the younger man's repressed memory, thereby affecting Stefano's physical and mental health. But as Propp reports, the initial murder of the Andreani girl is "only an accompanying form for other acts of villainy, serving to intensify them" (subcategory #14). Because the priest is uncertain who had seen him strangle the girl and does not know who is sending him intimidating notes, he kills the remainder of the medium's circle. Added to this, and characteristic of most of the *giallo*'s villains, Paolo "torments at night," (subcategory #18) if we take this to include stalking his victims first.

8. **The hero is led to the whereabouts of an object of search (XV).**

Propp states that "the object of search is located in 'another' or different kingdom." Since this kingdom lies "far way horizontally," Stefano, the hero, "travels on the ground and on water" (subcategory #2). His search is for peace of mind through the unraveling of a mystery that has haunted him since childhood and he attempts to find it in his hometown. He discovers that the source of his physiological difficulties is his priestly brother, and the object that convicts Paolo are the torn pages of his breviary in a dead girl's hand linked to a painting in Sandra's stepmother's apartment. In addition to subcategory #2, Stefano fulfills another of Propp's subcategories, "mak[ing] use of stationary means of communication," which includes acts of locomotion like: "climbing stairways" (subcategory #5) to uncover new information leading to the link among the murders, walking up a flight of stairs to Sandra's stepmother's apartment and coming upon a key painting, investigating Signora Nardi's stairwell after she has been murdered and, in both instances, unearthing clues that will point to his brother. His climb up the rectory stairs to discover that his brother is receiving threatening letters parallels his climb up the bell tower stairs to save his brother from committing suicide.

9. **The villain is defeated (XVIII).**

Don Paolo's defeat is psychological as well as moral. Stefano confronts Paolo in the church and in the presence of his girlfriend, Sandra, and Gasparre, the sacristan, describes the cleric's crimes to him and the revelation that it was Stefano who had seen his brother murder the Andreani girl. If anything, the villain is defeated through the logical presentation of facts by the professor. Paolo has a flashback/fantasy in which he is giving out communion at mass and the parishioners silently accuse him of his crimes. But Stefano cannot bring his killer-brother to justice; it is up to Paolo to turn himself in. The priest's despair is so great and at the same time his pride is so pronounced that he cannot let the townspeople know that he, respected among them, is the murderer.

10. **The villain is punished (XXX).**

Don Paolo punishes himself by committing suicide in a leap from the church's bell tower as Stefano attempts to run after him to dissuade him.

9

A Night at the Opera ... Without the Marx Brothers

Dario Argento's *Opera*
[*Terror at the Opera*, 1987]

Murder is born of love, and love attains the greatest intensity in murder.—
Octave Mirbeau, Le Jardin des supplices

Dario Argento's *Opera* is built around the mystery of Betty (Cristina Marsillach), an overnight opera sensation, catapulted into stardom by Alan Santini (Urbano Barberini), an admiring police officer, who hides his features under a mask and speaks to her as a disembodied voice over the phone, recalling the character in Gaston Leroux's novel, *Phantom of the Opera* (1910). From childhood memories Betty vaguely remembers her mother's relationship with a masked man born out of lust where torture and murder became the ultimate expressions of unattainable desire. *Opera*, consequently, is a hymn to memories of a sadomasochistic affair that in Argento's world is the stuff dreams are made of.

"Murder is born of love" becomes a mantra for two damaged individuals, Erik in the novel and Alan Santini in the film, whose worship of two young divas turns them into killers. Argento, in reworking Leroux's novel, presents us with an opera house phantom, not unlike Erik, whose possessive love for Betty has turned into sadomasochistic desire and murder. While Alan is young and handsome, he too, like Eric, becomes disfigured, wishing to hide his face from his beloved. In Rupert Julian's *Phantom of the Opera* (1925), the phantom's voice is heard by Christine Daae through a wall in her dressing room, while in *Opera* Betty first hears the killer's voice over the phone. The Phantom, like Santini, wants to dominate the all-too-willing Christine by commanding her love, while in *Opera* Betty is forced to obey. In the silent film it is not the opera *Macbeth* that has a curse on it, but the opera house itself where *Faust* is being performed.

Argento had to settle on the Teatro Regio opera house in Parma for his setting because La Scala's premises were unavailable during the theater's extremely successful season.[1] Leaving the real location aside, it is *Macbeth*'s stylization that correlates with the theatricality of Argento's set pieces of carnage, ramified beyond the scope of the opera's proscenium arch into the private lives of the performers. In effect, each new setting becomes a histrionic expanse upon which the events of the *giallo* are enacted. The characters' larger-than-life offstage activities involving murder and fetishistic transgressions make their real lives as sensational as Verdi's *Macbeth*.[2] Furthermore, the S&M motif, seen in the film's flashbacks, is subsequently carried out in Betty's Lady Macbeth costume with "an absurd medley of chains, studs, jewels and dark black cloth ... which suggests avant-garde dominatrix drag."[3] These accoutrements mimic the relationship between Betty and Santini who desires to replicate the perverse scenario he had with the star's mother, a correlation that finds a parallel in Lady Macbeth's coercive relationship with her husband in his rise to the throne.

The film opens with an unseen opera diva, Mara Czekova, complaining about Marco's (Ian Charleson) direction of an anachronistic production of Verdi. Julia, the costume designer (Coralina Cataldi-Tassoni), even says that he has overdosed on weirdness. As the unseen Mara leaves the opera house in disgust, she gets hit by a car. The oddity of not showing Czekova's face is that through synecdoche she is treated as the cinematic equivalent of a villain, a tactic primarily used for *giallo* assassins which heightens viewer belief about her untrustworthiness.

In the opera house there is a cut to a huge, black rectangular digital clock as it is being raised from the stage floor with the time "16:30" on it and a match cut to "6:30," in close-up of a stereo's clock, two hours later. The camera tilts down the stereo playing a tape with classical instrumental music, then moves down still further to a digital volume readout, pans across a table with various bric-a-brac on it including a marble reproduction of Canova's *Cupid and Psyche* to a telephone as it starts to ring. This camera movement is the first yoking together of the opera's enormous theatrical space with the private space of Betty's apartment where theatrics of a different nature are to unfold. The linkage is disorienting because no establishing shot of the apartment building is provided, but what is observed in Betty's bedroom notifies us that the occupant is conversant with operatic music and that the objet d'art lingered over by the camera foreshadows the deadly relationship between sexual love (Santini/Cupid) and the soul (Betty/Psyche) that is to be played out. Apuleius's tale of *Cupid and Psyche* might also be looked upon as the struggle for love and trust. Santini, loving Betty, mistakenly attempts to gain her trust by involving her in his sadistic rituals.

Argento appropriates a considerable time in continuing to build up the audience's expectations of the apartment's tenant. A hand picks the receiver up and the camera slowly tilts upward as a disguised male voice congratulates Betty on her debut as Lady Macbeth, and only then, on her questioning the caller, is the movie-goer permitted to see the young woman's face asking if this is a joke. The caller hangs up. In long shot Betty lies back on her canopied bed as the camera dollies to her in a medium shot but then tilts upward to a louvered grille near the ceiling where a shadowy figure in the air duct watches her. The leisurely buildup revealing the main character emphasizes a languorous camera movement that is counterpointed to the sinister urgency of the voice over the receiver, augmented by the melodramatic opera music. That the opera house and Betty's apartment have been spatially fused by the digital clocks signals that the two-hour time lapse is connected to Mara Czekova's mishap; that the speaker on the phone, because he has disguised his voice, is responsible for the diva's misadventure; and that the startled young stand-in has nothing to do with it.

As Betty lies on her bed, the sound of an opening door is heard off-screen while the camera from the hallway of the apartment swiftly tracks into Betty's bedroom. Only when the diva's understudy calls out her agent's name does the viewer realize he is watching this from Mira's (Daria Nicolodi) point of view. The usual objective shot of the character followed by a subjective shot of what she sees has been omitted to create an unsettling ambiguity hinting that the subjective camera might represent the voice over the phone or even the silhouetted image spying from the air duct. Only after Mira's name is spoken do we see her reassuring presence. But this allaying of fear is offset by the camera cutting from the bedroom to a low-angle shot of the grilled vent in the ceiling and then to a reverse shot looking down from the duct into Betty's bedroom indicating an observer. The conceit of observing others in private moments will be amplified when Betty is forced to watch the gruesome deaths of people in the opera company; if anything, *Opera* is much ado about "noting." As he does later when speaking to the police inspector about reality and film, Marco, the director of *Macbeth*, informs Betty that becoming the star overnight only happens in the movies. This reinforces that idea that chance is not the substance of fiction, but a plot device with a long history of screen dramatization. "Break a leg" was never so ironic a statement as it is when Mara Czekova, hit by a car, breaks her leg, thereby giving Betty a chance at stardom.

As everyone leaves the bedroom, the camera moves circularly around the perimeter of the room focusing on various objects and then tilts up to the air duct, dollying in to the same indistinct observing figure. This turns into a subjective point of view looking again at Betty's bedroom from a high angle through the louvered air duct. The camera quickly pans left into the darkness of the duct and tilts upward into the opera house looking through a prompter's box at the conductor. In an identical movement as that performed in the bedroom, the camera pans 180 degrees around the well-attended opera boxes and then to the stage as the curtain parts on the opening scene of *Macbeth*. This is the second time that a correlation between the opera house and Betty's apartment is established, suggesting a theatrical relation between the melodrama within *Macbeth* and the melodrama inherent in Betty's private life. There is also a voyeuristic parallel in the act of "noting": an unknown person spying on Betty in her apartment parallels an unknown observer spying on her at the opera. For Argento, all space is theatrical inasmuch as all space is cinematic. Argento, as a horror film director, is directing a film called *Opera*, and Marco, a horror film director, is the director Argento is directing in the direction of *Macbeth*. Marco equates Betty's becoming a star overnight to being in a movie, but likewise maintains that movies are not a guide for reality. The two statements diagnose film's singular gift in that it is able to take a trope like Betty's instant success to affirm its fictionality through its content and the means by which that content is presented while denying it by creating a reality where *Opera*'s staged horrors, in order to seem plausible, require a suspension of disbelief.

Thus the film establishes that Marco, a horror film auteur who has turned to the stage, is a surrogate for Argento himself, orchestrating the means by which the identity of the murderer is revealed while deriding the viewer's voluntary suspension of disbelief, the film reviewer's search for a rational plot and motivation, and the censor's protests about cinematic violence. Argento is having sport with the legal assumption that films frequently depict conduct that would be criminal if actually performed "in a public place," for films are a "depiction of conduct not the depicted conduct itself."[4] Argento had a rough time with the censors on this film so that Marco knew from whence he was speaking. This symbiotic relationship between Argento and Marco paves the way for Marco to become the surrogate hero-outsider invading a world that considers him out of his class, and who pays for this transgression with his life by solving the mystery.

Opera is redolent with references from other Argento films, including the deceptive nature of vision associated with scopophilia; past traumas as a key to the mystery's solution; psychological themes of madness, alienation and paranoia; evil houses of architectural richness (the opera as metaphor for the fantastical); colors of deep reds and greens; incongruous heavy-metal music; plots driven more by surface associations than by inductive logic; and a reliance on the causal logic momentum of what Deleuze calls the "action-image," where the amateur detective's mission is to uncover a succession of misleading clues and resolve the narrative disruption by revealing the killer's identity. Finally there is an escalating engagement with the dialectics of feminine subjugation and identity in patriarchal society.[5] This chapter will discuss some of these ideas in the delineation of the director's set pieces.

On the opening night of *Macbeth*, the camera backstage moves among performers and technicians in little, agitated maneuvers not only producing a synesthetic involvement in the spectator, but suggesting the uneasiness among those staging the opera. There is a swish pan to one of the many opera house staircases leading to the box seats; the Steadicam glides up the stairs, pauses for couples to depart, and advances through red-carpeted corridors in direct contrast to its previous frantic maneuvers backstage, ambiguously offering either an objective investigation of space or a subjective viewpoint through the eyes of an unknown individual. As with all Steadicam shooting, the camera's disembodied peculiarity does not approximate human movement, which erroneously lends itself to the idea that we are objectively exploring space rather than an individual's point of view. This idea proves false, but only at the conclusion of the camera's perambulation. There are cuts to the audience, the musicians and the stage, and then the camera returns to its ascent of auxiliary stairs not used by the patrons. A door opens, as if by itself, revealing in long shot a man in livery just closing the door to an opera box. The camera pauses until he has left and proceeds again tracking though red-carpeted floors with heavy red velvet draped hallways dissolving to a box seat containing a spotlight on a stanchion. On a red velvet balustrade a black leather gloved hand, a representation of the killer's own fractured self, places a pair of binoculars on the railing. Two observations can be deduced from this: (1) the camera corroborates Argento's deliberate dalliance with his audience, ambiguously creating a space which might be examined subjectively or objectively inculcating viewer paranoia, and (2) The camera's subjectivity places the viewers in the uncomfortable position of the killer allowing them to become an accomplice to his actions.

The unknown individual, only represented by his gloved hand, watches and listens. The camera concentrates first, in long shot, on Betty singing, then cuts to various shots of her (most of which are objective), the orchestra, the onstage ravens making a din and finally zooming in to the killer's binoculars from a low angle on the orchestra floor. In a reverse-point-of-view iris shot, the unknown looks through the binoculars at Betty and enigmatically states that she has returned. The subjective camera tilts down from the singer lingering briefly at her midsection then moves to her feet. The momentary halting of the camera's tilt at her pelvis will be repeated later as the assailant watches her on videotape, this time using a knife on this anatomical area to register his sexual frustration. As the camera begins to move up her body again, there is a quick cut to a circular stone staircase, startling in its abrupt incursion into the *Macbeth* opera sequence. The film's equation of pleasure and pain is inaugurated in a series of four dominant flashbacks with three fragmented flashbacks or subjective inserts which take on the aspect of a film-within-the-film. The fragmented flashbacks arise from Betty's recollections while the dominant ones originate from Inspector Santini. A camera tracks up a stone spiral staircase with a stone balustrade; there is no one in the shot but, along with the synth music, a sound of rushing water is heard, then a cut to a young frightened woman in a dark blue dress crawling to the top of the staircase. She looks toward the camera and screams as though being pursued then rises from the floor still looking at the camera. There is a cut to a woman bound by her hands and strung up with an expressionless face appearing as if she is observing the young woman. The low-key-lit setting seems to be a storage area. Crosscutting continues between the woman in bondage and the frightened woman; each time a cut occurs the camera zooms in a bit more to their faces: the young woman's panicked countenance is plainly seen; the bound woman's visage is mostly in shadow.

Logic demands that the scene should correlate to the opera in progress as a displaced diegetic insert temporally and spatially dislocated from the series of shots in which it is interjected. This "recollection," disrupting the main flow of the narrative, is a real image but is out of context to events at the opera. The displaced insert may be nuanced further. The young frightened woman and the bound woman constitute a subjective insert from the viewpoint of a particular character (Inspector Santini) at the opera as yet unknown to the viewer. Without this correlation there is no connection between the two spaces and the action that ensues. The insert of the terrified woman and the bound one, without a focalizer, erroneously suggests, then, simultaneity of action with the performance at the opera, an alternating syntagma spatially disengaged from the main action but aesthetically connected with it. The images within the two scenes do not progress from one to the other in a linear advancement of the story, but build up psychological associations that are not immediately perceived. The viewer at this point does not know if he is watching a flashback, a simultaneous action or a flash forward. Where the structural thrust of most films has been toward continuity through an invisible editing style, Argento fractures the space and time between the opera and storage area, affronting traditional editing by annihilating narrative description and its meaning.

At the conclusion of this murder-bondage scene another abrupt cut brings the moviegoer back to the opera house with a shot of Betty in profile singing, resuming the camera's focus at the exact spot where it had previously left off. The entire murder-bondage scene just described is bracketed by the image of Betty being observed by an unknown individual first through a subjective viewpoint with binoculars and secondly through the camera's objective point of view. The bracketing suggests that whoever is watching Betty is also fantasizing about a bondage incident that has taken place or is about to take place.

At the performance's conclusion, the murderer's gloved hand drops the binoculars on the red velvet balustrade, this act of observing emphasized by over-cranking the action and reminding us about the way individuals look at one another. Betty's performance is observed on TV as an object of beauty by a little girl, Alma (Francesca Cassola), sitting on her bed; Betty's triumph becomes an object of jealousy by Mara Czekova (only identified by a shot of her leg in a cast) who angrily throws a wineglass at the TV, while the murderer, after the performance, watches her on tape, running his knife over Betty's image. More instances are placed on the act of observing others throughout the film: Betty and Mira watch out of the apartment door's peephole at the building's residents and the suspicious police officer who flashes his ID card; Alma watches Betty through the apartment air ducts; Marco, the opera director, watches a man on the street watching Betty's window; Betty's mother watches Santini torture victims for her while little Betty spies on this scene; Julia, the opera's wardrobe mistress, watches Betty bound by Santini in a glass display cabinet; and finally, Santini, from off-screen, seems to watch everyone.

The killer's viewing a tape of Betty's performance ushers in the second subjective insert/flashback through a surreal close-up of a pulsating brain that slowly dissolves into the Steadicam exploration of deserted stairways finally descending (instead of ascending) down the same spiral staircase seen in the first flashback. The camera maneuvers through abandoned rooms and dollies in to a young woman asleep in a large bed. A gloved black latex hand removes the sheets revealing an almost completely naked female. A woman's hand (Betty's mother) gives the gloved hand a knife to cut the rope that will bind her hand. The woman on the bed awakens and sits up screaming while the knife in the frame's foreground threatens her menacingly. There is a cut to the present of the videotaped image of Betty singing at the opera, thereby conflating it with the insert, a different theatrical event involving a ritual killing. The need to kill is juxtaposed with the need to be seen killing, the need to supplant sexual penetration is juxtaposed with the need to inflict pain, all of which intimate the killer's abnormal drives and possible impotence. This act only underscores the psychosexual transferal between physical desire and its unattainability. These phallic objects, seen as instruments of penetration, are ubiquitously placed within oneiric settings. The staircase in the flashback is itself a symbol of sexual intercourse,[6] and Santini's recurrent memory of walking down the spiral staircase to the woman in bed enforces the symbol while paralleling his prowling around the opera house's stairs to voyeuristically observe Betty. But if Santini is watching Betty, Betty is forced to watch Santini's murders and we, the audience, are forced to watch what Betty watches. As she supplants her mother in the killer's mind and is constrained to observe the murder of the young stage manager, Stefan (William McNamara), by having pins placed under her eyes, the film's voyeurism is brought to the fore through the killer's sadistic pleasure in compelling the heroine to watch. Stefan's murder becomes the first extended etude on death orchestrated by Argento, a leitmotif of body parts divided into four phases befitting the film's musical theme and incorporating two other fetishistic ingredients already referenced: voyeurism and bondage.

The first and briefest accelerando begins with Betty's capture by Santini, with shots concentrating on her mouth and hands and his hands: (1) Betty's mouth grabbed from behind, (2) Betty's mouth taped, (3) Betty's hands tied behind her. This first phrase quickly ends in a ritardando with Betty left trussed up and alone on the bed. The tempo again accelerates upon Betty falling off the bed as the second phase leading to Stefan's murder begins with Santini tying Betty to a marble pillar. This comprises five rapid shots to various parts of her body as the killer's hands tie a rope around (1) her neck, (2) her waist, (3) the remainder of her midsection, (4) her head and (5) her knees.

The motif of subjugation is further developed in the third phase prior to Stefan's murder consisting of five more shots in close-up or extreme close-up to force open Betty's eyes to watch the slaughter. Emphasis is placed on her eyes and again on Santini's hands: (1) needles placed under her eye, (2) different angle: needles near one eye, (3) needles about her other eye, (4) needles adjusted about both her eyes, (5) finished results showing the proximity of the needles to her eyes.

The development of the subject reaches a crescendo with the leading motive in the fourth and longest phrase of 15 shots devoted to Stefan's death counterpointed to its effect on Betty registered only by her eyes. The accent is now placed on a majority of close shots of Stefan's slashed throat, the killer's hands knifing his body crosscut with close-ups of Betty's eyes. To initiate this conclusion, shots #1 and #2 comprise knife thrusts through Stefan's throat. The alternation of shots begins now between close-ups of Betty's terrified eyes and the continued stabbing of Stefan's prone body (#3 to #14) culminating in the killer's hand lifting up Stefan's head to show Betty (#13). A decrescendo begins with a subjective shot (#15) from Betty's view through needles, looming like prison bars, of the killer getting up from the floor to approach Betty, revealing Stefan's mutilated corpse. Forcing Betty to witness the murder becomes the real violence done to her,[7] recalling Buñuel's *Un Chien andalou* (1929) where the slicing open of a woman's eye becomes a metaphor for the familiar phrase "eye opener." Maitland McDonagh suggests that the needles under Betty's eyes metaphorically announce that *Opera* "is designed to knock your eyes out."[8]

Betty (Christina Marsillach) bound and forced to witness her boyfriend's murder. The florid setting and her iconic figure as a Christian martyr tied to the stake bring the opera's melodramatic ambiance into the characters' personal lives (Dario Argento's *Opera*).

The second subjective insert above of the woman's presumptive murder in bed is symbolically reenacted as the camera now cuts to Betty on a televised playback of *Macbeth*, framing the incident first with her live performance and now with her recorded performance. As Betty's voice is heard on the TV, the camera pans and tilts down to a toolbox lid which opens, and the same knife is seen as in the previous flashback together with a rope and a row of needles on a bit of tape. The weapon is taken and a finger presses the remote's zoom button so that the image of Betty is enlarged to the point where only her costume is visible. Santini "fondles" Betty's screen image with his knife. He lovingly maneuvers it along her midsection as though he were touching it with his phallus, not only equating sexual pleasure with pain but equating her unattainability with the hard surface of the screen, ritualistically repeating in symbolic form the relationship he once had with her mother and figuratively reenacting the torture of the young woman in bed. Santini's abnormal behavior presents a recurrent trope connected with desire and its lack of sexual fulfillment linked to his past history that is revealed only toward the film's end. He confesses to Betty that her mother taught him a cruel game of killing and torturing so he could be her slave, but wouldn't let him touch her. Argento's foregrounding of displaced female aggression is replicated through Lacanian psychoanalysis via a collapse of Santini's identity, mastery and sense of self.[9]

His enthrallment to his mistresses' sexual appetites conflates the relationship between lover and beloved with that of mother and child. But the lover/mother here becomes a *vagina dentata*, and depravity the prerequisite for entry into this orifice. Therefore, Santini requires a new bonding with Betty to recoup his selfhood after he has strangled her mother. The words he uses are expressive, for they signal the odd obsession he has come to avow. Betty, his nexus to the past, enables him to resume his perversions in the present for, as he says, she is exactly like her mother. *Opera*'s misogynistic trajectory is exhibited by Santini as he first attempts to dominate Betty, controlling her gaze by placing needles under her eyes, and then metamorphosing her into her mother's replica with their sadomasochistic love games. At the film's conclusion, the former police inspector, having transferred his dependency from Betty's mother to the young diva by allowing himself once more to become spellbound, has failed at both relationships and savagely tries to assault the young woman in the Alps. Where he enjoyed killing her mother, it is Betty who relishes smashing a rock over his head, effectively avenging her mother's death while repudiating her relationship to that woman. The whole experience, nevertheless, pushes Betty over the edge, as the film's coda attests.

Alan, when captured by the police, rationalizes that he didn't commit any crime but simply wanted to free his victims' souls. Santini believes his sadomasochistic relations with women, under the tutelage of Betty's mother, liberates their souls by going beyond the pleasure principle into the experience of the sacred. In Sacher-Masoch's *Venus in Furs*, Severin rhapsodizes about this type of relationship with Wanda:

> agony, gruesome torture seemed like a pleasure, especially when inflicted by a beautiful woman, since for me all that was poetic and demonic had always been concentrated in women. ... I saw sensuality as ... the only sacredness.[10]

Santini has conflated his behavior with Betty's mother and his subjection of Betty to his homicidal deeds with a form of sensuality that has thus sanctified his actions. He believes that murder is a holy act since "all sensuality [is] sacred." To say that he has freed their souls is, in effect, saying that he has fulfilled a sacred mission. There is something else that illuminates a link between Santini's remark and that of Severin in both Argento's film and Sacher-Masoch's novel. For the novelist pleasure and pain are "poetic" because they are "inflicted by a beautiful woman." For Argento violence is an aesthetic means for creating poetry, but it is violence *against* rather than *by* a beautiful woman that is poetic. "Poetic" has a diverse signification whose origins date back to Aristotle's *Poetics* (335 BCE). "Poetic" refers not to a work's content specifically but *how* the content is articulated through the creative impulses of the imagination in a highly charged way that results in a catharsis, producing a sense of wonder, pleasure and even enthrallment (*ecplexis*). The *how* by which a work is constructed refers to its style, and the Argento style is an exceptionally fanciful construct. Certainly he is one of the few horror film directors to use his camera the way an author uses his pen in what Alexandre Astruc in *Birth of a New Avant-Garde* (1948) termed *le camerastylo* which imagined film eventually breaking free of the concrete demands of narrative where images become a means of writing just as flexible and subtle as written language.[11] While Argento adheres to a narrative structure, what critics have complained about was his lack of logical exposition and his foregrounding of style. To counter this, the director claims his films are "dreams" that lack rationality so that his images advance from one to another not in the service of a progressive linear story line but by way of poetic associations. He has, in the past, broken "free of the concrete demands of narrative" and deliberately ignored, when it suited him, the rigors of narrative structure demanded by his detractors. In the process, he has become an auteur capable of expressing himself through cinematic images to generate, in the Aristotelian sense, awe and enthrallment.

If Argento considers his films dreamlike, McDonagh believes the psychology in his films is allied to magic.[12] Dreams and magic are closely linked to the early trance films from the New American Cinema of Kenneth Anger, Curtis Harrington and Maya Deren. In fact, Argento's heroine, Betty, lives a half trancelike existence preoccupied with recurrent childhood memories of a masked stranger during her sleeping and waking moments. Moreover, Argento employs a double ending in *Opera* that links it to the American trance films of the '40s, and although there is no indication that Argento had seen these works, they do, in fact, also contain dual endings: Deren's *Meshes of the Afternoon* (1943), Harrington's *A Fragment of Seeking* (1946) and Anger's *Fireworks* (1947). In Argento's doubling of narrative endings akin to those of the avant-garde, the first spurious conclusion in *Opera* occurs with the presumptive death of Santini at Betty's hands in the opera house. The second genuine ending occurs with his capture in the Alps as Betty, maternally, half coaxes and half conducts him by the hand after he has murdered Marco, her director. Moreover, Anger regards the projection of his films as ceremonies capable of intentionally invoking spiritual forces akin to "magick" rituals and as an evil force exercising dominion over people.[13] Similarly, Argento's "magick" lies in his desire to provoke people because it means he is making an impression on them which is another way of exercising dominion over an audience.[14] That the structure of the avant-garde should find its way into an Italian director's thrillers attests that Jungian archetypes transcend a variety of genres and decades.

Alan Santini's relationship with Betty is only one instance of a character's inability to make love in the normal way. Betty likewise is unable to have a satisfying relationship with Stefan Obrini, the youthful stage manager at the opera. The opera director, Marco, cannot relate to his girlfriend, Marion (Antonella Vitale), who calls him a sadist, arguing that killing turns him on. The other characters as well seem incapable of having sound associations with each other: Alma, the little girl who helps Betty escape from the killer, is at odds with her mother (Carola Stagnaro); Maurizio (Maurizio Garrone), the raven trainer, is eager to condemn Mara Czekova for the slaughter of the ravens at the opera; Julia, the wardrobe mistress, detests the director; the unseen diva enviously brands Betty as a "snake"; and Mira, Betty's agent, is distrustful of Santini's help (for good reason). *Opera* unfolds like a rondo of impaired personalities.

The third oneiric sequence that at first seems to disrupt the diegetic continuity occurs right before the death of Julia, Betty once again being compelled to watch. It transpires in the opera's wardrobe room and is orchestrated through a succession of subjective inserts. It begins with a zoom in to a close-up of a black-masked face, this ostensible camera movement continues into an extreme close-up to the bridge of the nose followed by a cut to a blank screen. The camera then zooms in to an extreme close-up of the temple on the side of the now uncovered masked man's face as it begins to throb, followed again by a shot of a blank white screen. The proceeding shot is a close-up of blood rushing through arteries followed by a third brief insert of a blank screen. This in turn is succeeded by an extreme close-up of a loudly throbbing human brain, after which the camera frames Betty in a medium shot, her back to the camera, looking at a life-sized female mannequin in a Japanese kimono within a glass-enclosed cabinet. The film frame starts to pulsate as the pulsating on the soundtrack increases. The camera then zooms in to a close-up of Betty still looking at the mannequin.

With these seven rapid shots Argento has composed a phenomenal montage. The cadenced sound of the killer's brain is translated visually so that through the camera's kinesthetic intervention, the frame literally throbs. This subjective sound emerges from within the killer to become a tangible source of tension expressionistically rendered through the palpitating film frame into the story space. The shot's purpose conveys the force of the intruder's raw emotions and sexuality as they materialize into a visible form. The sequence is a logical outcome of what Argento considers his most important cinematic influence: the German Expressionism of Lang and Murnau which made a profound impression on him even as a child.[15] While Julia is being attacked by Alan, Betty is incarcerated in the glass case that previously held the mannequin (a reference to *Madama Butterfly* that the soprano plays on tape) which in turn recalls her image contained within the TV screen that Alan Santini could not penetrate but only impotently run his knife over her recorded replica. Santini, of course, is able to get at Betty if he so wishes, but she is no good to him dead for she is his human recording device, unlike the mechanical film camera, of the atrocities he commits. The cat-and-mouse scene, whose rhythm in the first half is marked by the interplay between Julia and Allan in the opera's wardrobe department, is astonishing in generating suspense. The first half centers on gaining and losing, hitting and being hit: Julia has the ID bracelet from Betty's costume but drops it under a table when the killer attacks; he attempts to pick it up, but she snatches it from him before he is sufficiently able to grasp it; he forces it out of her hand the second time by hitting her with an iron and knocking her down. Sprawled on the floor, she throws away the bracelet and tells him to pick it up. Julia gets up and once he has gotten the bracelet hits him with the iron, sending him to the floor, and takes the ID.

There is now a phrasal pause in the action. Inquisitive Julia is beside herself whether to untie Betty or unmask the killer. She stares at the camera (in actuality, Betty's POV) as if to say, "What should I do?" The second half of this scene escalates the terror by the extended action of the bracelet's retrieval. Julia takes off the killer's hood, although his face is off-camera, but before she can convey to Betty who the assassin is, his hands rise up from below the frame to strangle her. There is a cut to his hooded face. As he stabs Julia in the chest with the scissors, the bracelet falls from her uplifted hand into her gaping mouth. The scissors now assume a more significant role with a mix of analogous and iterated sounds. Once Julia's mouth is closed, Santini attempts first to pry and then plunge the closed scissors into her shut orifice to get at the swallowed jewelry but to no avail, an ineffectual act of penetration. Failing that, he rips open her throat. There are crosscuts to Betty's eyes as she is constrained to watch. The deed is presented as a rape of Julia: her dress is cut with shears, the sound of cloth being ripped is magnified. To additionally underline the action, nondiegetic heavy metal music is intermingled with the muffled cries of the powerless Betty. This is followed by the sound of cutting Julia's throat and chest with the shears, mimicking yet another act of penetration until the bloodstained bracelet is retrieved. Santini then dangles the gory bracelet before Betty hissing that he can have her whenever he wants. So that we do not forget that violence is equated with sexual desire, Santini mimics the action he performed on Betty's TV image by running the bloody scissors down her throat, stopping at her midsection to slightly push the blades into her belly. He then cuts her bonds and, as she did after Stefan's death, Betty walks dazed through the city streets, but now the nondiegetic sound of a little girl crying clues the audience in on an aural association from Betty's childhood triggered by her present terrifying ordeal.

Another galvanizing set piece occurs at the death of Mira, Betty's agent, who visits her because of the singer's anxieties. The situation centers on the subjective shots of what Mira sees through the apartment door's peephole and objective shots of Mira looking through it. Wedded to this are shots of Betty pulling the telephone out of a room where Santini's assistant, Daniele Soavi (Michele Soavi), has disappeared. The wiring in the apartment has mysteriously short circuited plunging the two women into darkness. The scene takes up when the detective, claiming to be Soavi, shows Mira his police automatic through the peephole. The essence of Argento's suspense building involves five areas: (1) the close-up, (2) deep focus, (3) slow motion, (4) point of view and (5) editing.

The first idea that emerges is the rhythm established through the regular repetition of images, motion and sound. The shots contain no camera movement, real or apparent, nor are they tied to a customary musical score that generates suspense. There is, on the other hand, the report of the gun going off, the swish of the bullet as it moves through the peephole and the wail of a distorted scream in four consecutive shots through electronic amplification and sound distention: a close-up profile of Mira's face, the bullet passing through her right eye and out through the back of her head in slow motion; an extreme long shot in slow motion of Mira (in the background) falling backward. In the right foreground, Betty bends down to avoid the bullet; to the left, the telephone, hit by the bullet, shatters into pieces rising into the air; a close-up in slow motion as Mira continues to fall backward through the bullet's force, and finally an extreme long shot in slow motion of Mira in the background hitting the floor; in the foreground Betty, to frame right, ducks the bullet, to frame left the pieces of the telephone crash to the floor. Married to the sequence is a contrast in speech rhythms: Mira's dialogue is hurried, clipped, nervous and commanding while the voice of the police officer on the other side of the door is relaxed, reassured and measured, illustrating his control of the situation. Betty's agent is threatened and terrified lest the officer on the other side of the door be the killer while the killer must lull Mira into a false state of confidence. When the police revolver is introduced, the rhythm picks up. Mira becomes more agitated in her attempt to recognize the killer/officer, and sound effects are then added to the mix. The tempo of the scene contributes to the excitement generated. The cuts alternate at a steady pace between Mira's subjective viewpoint and objective shots of her. The majority of the shots are confining close-ups suggesting that Mira and Betty are trapped in the apartment. Four of the nine shots exclusively deal with Mira as the center of focus as she looks through the peephole while felled by the assassin's bullet, but she too becomes the audience focalizer since two shots stem from her view looking through the peephole at a hand holding up first an ID and then a revolver in the background. In an identical shot, seconds later, through the same peephole, the officer's gun, pointed directly at the audience/camera/Mira, is fired when she claims she knows who he is. A shot taken from a side-angle cutaway of the peephole, looking like the nozzle of a gun barrel, makes the bullet traveling in slow motion appear as if the distance between the outside and the inside of the door is sizable, temporally and spatially distending the movement of the projectile to hit Mira. The four shots devoted to her death, from her being hit to her fall to the floor, not only underscore the effect of the bullet, but the overlapping and over-cranking of the action accentuate and prolong this, forcing one's concentration on her downward trajectory. In two extreme long shots a wide-angle lens augments the distance between Mira, lit and framed by the door in the background, and Betty in the foreground's semi-darkness, thus focusing attention still further on the agent while isolating her and making her appear powerless.

A fourth flashback grouping is fragmented like all of the opera singer's remembrances. Heavy-metal music plays as Betty, emotionally distraught, walks rapidly through the congested cityscape. The music, delivered at shrieking intensity by a male vocalist, emphasizes her fear and isolation while surrounded by a throng of people. Filtering through Betty's mind are now fleeting close-ups of a hooded man. Moments later there is an unidentified multiple exposed image that seconds later clears to reveal Betty's mother, who has been repeatedly seen observing others she and Santini have victimized, now tied overhead by her hands, confining the opera singer's recollections to these two arresting images. As Betty continues to walk across a deserted street to enter the opera house, the camera dollies back and the viewer hears, through acousmatic sound, running footsteps and heavy panting. The camera tilts down and, in the foreground, portions of the Belgian street stones are painted red, acting as a nexus to the opera house's red-draped hallways through which Betty passes.

The fifth hiatus in the story appears in a flashback which reprises some of the images of the first while adding details of Betty as a little girl. Also reintroduced are Betty's mother, Santini wearing a black hood, and the unknown victim previously pictured in the first insert. It takes place after Betty has headed into her dressing room to lie down. The flashback presents not only a sadistic act as a theater piece with its own audience, but the gradual recognition of individuals detected in the scopophilic process. Little Betty initiates the gaze, but initially the viewer is not aware that the first shot is taken from her viewpoint as she explores ramshackled rooms and hallways via a tracking camera. She gazes at her mother who in turn is gazing at the torture of the young woman in blue who is gazing at the off-screen presence of her tormentor. Betty's mother seems to catch the little girl observing all of them, and the masked man in turn watches the little girl whose presence he perceives through her audible gasp causing him to silently withdraw. Nowhere do the characters ever occupy the same space but remain isolated from each other. None of them interacts with each other but all experience intense pain, pleasure or wonderment at what is transpiring. Little Betty doesn't seem to recoil from the torture of the young woman as much as she is startled by seeing the masked man. She doesn't try to hide or run away. This is troubling in itself and suggests that Santini might correctly assume that the opera singer would enjoy participating in the games he played with her mother. Betty can tell Santini later on that she is nothing like her mother, but this scene gives lie to the fact that the brutality of the situation has not frightened the little girl away. Betty is in denial at the film's conclusion when she, on her hands and knees, moves through the grass and underbrush saying that she loves every living creature and finally collapses upon the earth hugging it.

At the conclusion, Betty denies her inherited guilt and desires as she decries humanity. This is not the behavior of a woman in control of her life, but one who desperately wants to prove to herself that she is in control. The alternate conclusion of the Italian-language version where Argento does the voice-over has been derided. Alan Jones writes that

> after all the graphic mutilations ... this naive ... treatise really does strike the daftest note.... [I]n Rome ... the audience booed, screamed with laughter ... as this demented denouement unfolded.[16]

The voice-over, however, in the English-language version is that of Betty, which doesn't "strike the daftest note" because the words do not come from the intradiegetic narrator, a narrator who is not a character in the story,[17] but from a homodiegetic narrator, a character-narrator who appears as an actor in her own story. The scene now is simultaneously chilling, pathetic and beautiful. A young woman with a promising future has been psychologically destroyed from within and can't face the fact that she is, however remotely, responsible for the terror at the opera.

The last area to finalize is *Opera*'s place in Propp's morphology of the folk tale by pursuing the stages outlined in the previous chapters.

1. **A member of the family leaves home (I).**

Betty, Mara Czekova's understudy, is precipitously obliged to perform in a preeminent role in *Macbeth* and must go to work. Like Nora Davis in *The Girl Who Knew Too Much*, the heroine is a rather naive young woman relying on those around her for support in lieu of a mother. Propp considers "the death of parents an intensified form of absentation" (subcategory #2), and although her opera "family" constitutes her elders, all those whom she is most intimate with die.

2. **An interdiction is addressed to the heroine (II).**

The interdiction is initiated by the "accident" to Mara and the mysterious call that Betty receives as an order (subcategory #2) from a voice over the telephone which tells that she will make her debut as Lady Macbeth. This command is also tied into a second implied interdiction about *Macbeth* bringing harm to those who participate in it, but this fear is countered by a strong pressure from Betty's agent, the director of the opera, and the theater manager to disregard the superstitious sentiment. They are so vehement she play the role that their "prompting" her almost amounts to an order rather than a proposal.

3. **The interdiction is violated (III).**

Betty violates the implied interdiction not to perform in *Macbeth* because it brings bad luck. The soprano neither voices her agreement nor dissents but acquiesces non-verbally because of group pressure. The villain has entered the tale via his sinister voice over the phone. Betty is in no condition to refuse his offer, which is more of a command than a request as she is taken by surprise that the role is hers, thinking that the person on the phone is a prankster, not yet having heard of Mara's misadventure. After the performance the villain makes his presence known in the person of a police inspector. His dual role is to cause all forms of misfortune but at the same time to seemingly preserve order.

4. **The villain makes an attempt at reconnaissance (IV).**

As a police officer, Santini aims at ingratiating himself into the heroine's confidence. This isn't difficult since he has been able to manipulate the events of those connected with the opera house. He first introduces himself through a camouflaged voice over the phone, but then presents himself in person as a police inspector at the opera investigating a murder that he himself has committed in order to be closer to Betty. In reality he has begun courting her in his own deranged fashion, and at the same time is keeping an eye on his investment. Propp also speaks about an inverted form of reconnaissance demonstrated when the intended victim questions the villain.[18] Betty asks Allan if he is a fan and wants an autograph, which she is pleased to give. She accepts a flower from him but throws it away in disgust when she realizes he is a policeman investigating a murder, and is not there for the love of music. Allan seems without duplicity, is shy, apologetic and awkward in the presence of the young star which belies the sadistic stance he takes toward Betty in testing her to see if she is really like her mother.

5. **The villain receives information about his victim (V).**

This information comes from two sources. Santini's relation to Betty's mother has helped him understand his victim, for he knows little Betty has seen what he and her mother have done together. He intends to mold her in the image of her mother by submitting her to masochistic rituals he previously shared with her mother. Equally important is his role as police inspector because, by right, he is the one who asks the questions and expects to receive information. To take one example: after Julia, the wardrobe mistress, is killed, Allan meets Betty in the lobby of her apartment house and grabs her hands noticing the rope marks on her wrists. He questions her about them and sarcastically inquires if they are another manifestation of the curse. When she relates the story about Julia's death, Santini quizzes her as to why she didn't tell him. She replies that she has tried to wipe the incident from her mind. The inspector who has committed the crimes knows what has transpired, but he ventures to discover Betty's feelings at being bound and forced to watch a murder take place so that he can ascertain whether she is like her mother.

6. **The villain attempts to deceive the victim in order to take possession of her (VI).**

The inspector tells Betty that he needs her collaboration to find the murderer, but she cannot identify the killer because of his black mask. In presenting Betty as a guileless individual, Argento informs the audience that Betty is still very unsophisticated with personal problems that remain unresolved. It's her youth that enables her to be manipulated by Santini and others; she becomes a frightened child, terrorized not only by the past experiences buried in her subconscious, but threatened by present experiences of being pursued by an unknown killer and forced to participate in his depravity. In this sense Betty and Alan are two sides of the same coin: she trying to remember the past and what she has perhaps blocked from her memory, and he remembering the past and anticipating its reenactment with the young opera star. Santini plays on her naïveté to secure her confidence as her protector in his capacity as police inspector and then to initiate her into a sadomasochistic relationship.

7. **The victim submits to deception and thereby unwittingly helps her enemy (VII).**

Propp appends to this category "a special form of deceitful proposal" with its "corresponding acceptance" which he calls "the deceitful agreement." One direct proposal of Alan to Betty is that she remain in her apartment after he sees the bruises left on her hands by the rope he himself has tied forcing her to watch him kill Julia. Santini tells her he has to investigate the wardrobe mistress's murder, a ploy by him to throw off suspicion, but Betty doesn't want him to leave her after she has been coerced into watching several people killed. Alan soothingly instructs her to keep the apartment door locked until he sends another officer, Daniele Soavi, to protect her. She agrees to the villain's persuasions, leading Alan to kill Soavi and Mira and terrorize the soprano. The formidable situations the detective places Betty in are calculatedly spawned by him. In fact all of the difficult circumstances are caused by the villain from the outset when he presumably hits Mara Czekova with his car which catapults the young singer to the lead role of Lady Macbeth and leads to her calamity, which Propp describes as a "preliminary misfortune." Although Alan Santini is a complete outsider, Betty submits to his deception because he is a law enforcement authority and as such commands respect. The villain needs to get close to his victim in the role of a confidant to deceive her and discover her reactions to the situations he places her in.

8. The villain causes harm or injury to a member of a family (VIII).

The young singer is not given a living family. We know nothing about Betty's father, but we do know that her mother has taken on a lover/partner in aberrant sexual rituals and that Santini has finally been driven to murder her because of her demands for further bloodshed. Betty's family, therefore, is her agent and the theatrical group of performers and managers at the opera. The film constantly returns to the "family" scenes of torture and murder, of victimizer and victim, either through Betty's dreams or Santini's recollections. The villain commits murder against the singer's extended family (subcategory #13) and in doing so perpetrates bodily injury (subcategory #8) on the singer herself. In the concluding scene at the *Macbeth* performance, the villain abducts Betty (subcategory #1) to an isolated room in the opera house where he stages his death and plans to burn Betty in the conflagration. There are several instances where the villain torments at night (subcategory #18), when Betty is forced to watch the death of Stefan, when she sees Mira killed in her apartment, when pursued by Santini through the air ducts, when holding in her hands the dead body of the officer meant to protect her, when watched from below on the street by the murderer, and finally when followed through the crowded streets by the assassin as she walks to the opera house. If the first killing is excluded, that of the usher at the opera, and that of the policeman Daniele Soavi, all the rest of the murders are of Betty's extended family: Stefan Obrini, her lover and stage manager; Mira, her agent; Julia the wardrobe mistress; and Marco the director who later seems to have become her lover. In the end every person who meant anything to Betty has been eliminated.

9. The heroine is tested and attacked which prepares the way of her receiving a helper/donor (XII).

Throughout *Opera*, the heroine is continually tested and attacked, and those tests, administered by Santini, are to see if Betty's sexual proclivities resemble those of her mother. The villain, however, is also the donor, testing Betty (subcategory #1: "The donor tests the heroin") in a form of sadomasochistic courtship to discover her compatibility. Another factor plays a part in this particular morphological classification: "The donor greets and interrogates the heroine" (subcategory #2). In his double capacity of law enforcer and murderer, it is Santini's job to question Betty. Exhibiting no schizophrenic propensities, as a policeman he is gentle, almost shy in his interrogation of Betty. At his first meeting with her after her debut, he acts like a tongue-twisted schoolboy asking for her autograph. He has a tenderhearted demeanor about him that makes Betty confide in him and feel confident in his presence. As a murderer, Santini only envisions her as a mirror image of her mother whom he can take at any time.

Since there are a number of ordeals Betty is subjected to, there are also a corresponding number of donors that she has, but each is unsuccessful in fending off the killer and each in turn exhibits a distinct response to Betty's plight. Stefan approaches her trussed-up figure in amazement, ready to untie her, before he is stabbed through the throat; Julia wavers between untying the singer and pulling the murderer's mask off; she succumbs to her curiosity and is strangled and stabbed; Mira, with knife in hand, ferociously guards Betty's apartment door trying to make sure the police officer is who he claims to be, only to be shot through the eye; Marco, the director and the most proactive character in Betty's defense, rescues her from the burning room at the opera and physically assaults the killer. His recompense is to be repeatedly stabbed by Santini. The ravens also come to the opera singer's aid in attacking Santini by pecking his eye out as he fires wildly at the stage, killing several performers instead of her. In the end Betty becomes her own helper/donor by convincing Santini

Ironically the law enforcer is also the killer. Inspector Alan Santini (Urbano Barberini) has an eye gouged out by vindictive ravens purposely let loose at a performance of *Macbeth* to catch the killer (Dario Argento's *Opera*).

into believing that she is like her mother and then beating his head with a stone.

10. **The villain is defeated (XVIII).**
Santini tracks Betty to the Alps, killing the kitchen maid and Marco. Only through Betty's encouraging words does he go along with her. Seeing the police dogs and helicopter gives Betty the courage to put on another act; she hits Alan on the head with a large stone, and the police immediately take him into custody.

10

The Return of the Repressed

Lamberto Bava's Le foto di Gioia
[*Delirium: Photos of Gioia*, 1987]

The most loving ... relatives commit murder with smiles on their faces.—Jim Morrison

In Lamberto Bava's *Le foto di Gioia*, the word *gioia* is not only a proper noun, "Joy," but a common noun expressing "delight," "enjoyment," and "pleasure." These photos are a "delight" for the heroine, Gloria (Gioia's name in the English version), reminding her of the glamorous existence she spent before the cameras and representing a period in life where she was able to provide a home for herself and her brother, until she married a wealthy man who loved her unconditionally and supported her modeling career. The opening still shots of Gloria (Serena Grandi) attest to that former time, but will play a decisive role when a killer uses them to threaten her life.

Interspersed among the credits are numerous photos of Gloria by the world-famous Angelo Frontoni revealing various states of nakedness. Accompanying this is the heavy beat of Simon Boswell's synthesized dance music with drums and percussion as a bridge between photos and credits. The pictures objectify the woman so that voyeuristic fantasy and fetishism are authenticated at the start. Gloria's image in these stills, joined through wipes, has been coded for strong erotic impact in conventional exhibitionist fashion where women are marked for a powerful erotic impression signifying to-be-looked-at-ness. The photos produce two results: they glorify the flesh, freeze-framing it in a historical moment by preserving its transience, and secondly feed the models' narcissism through their self-gratification as erotic commodities.

Once the director's credit is listed, the viewer hears the sound of a still camera's shutter clicking off multiple photos of Kim (Katrine Michelsen) in a pool. Transitional wipes that unite them continue with a voice-over of the photographer, Roberto (David Brandon), as he verbally arouses the model while two black females caress the centerfold's breasts. The variety of women Roberto photographs through the day, without any significant time lapse, suggests that all female beauty is interchangeable, thereby negating individuality through eroticization of the human form.

Parallel with this photo shoot, Mark (Karl Zinny), seated in a chair by a window in his home overlooking the pool, observes Gloria through his telescope, reclining at poolside. From his subjective viewpoint the camera tilts up Gloria's legs as she begins to cross them, continues up her thighs noting the magazine, *Pussycat*, she is reading and then moves to her face. There is a cut back to a tight close-up of Mark's face with a smile, and then an extreme high-angled long shot with the telephoto lens protruding from the window and Gloria and her magazine supervisor, Evelyn (Daria Nicolodi), by the pool in the background. The extended lens, obviously and facetiously phallic, protruding outside Mark's window after his feverish examination of Gloria's body, augments his impotent sexual fantasies about her that he describes to her but does not dare carry out except through the safe distance of his telephone. The atmosphere is charged with sexual electricity from the shoot at the pool, to Gloria as she reclines poolside, to the *Pussycat* magazine cover displaying Kim in nude and semi-nude poses similar to that of Gloria's photos. We now realize that the magazine's photo layouts of Gloria, taken three years ago, and Kim, in the present, comprise the opening credits. Gloria's brother, Tony (Vanni Corbellini), also stares at his sister with desire while the camera slowly zooms in on his face oblivious to Roberto's voice repeatedly calling him. There are, therefore, four instances of voyeuristic subjects at the offset: photos of Gloria and Kim in the men's magazine, *Pussycat*; Roberto's camera lens capturing provocative pictures of Kim in the pool; Mark's observation of Gloria's body from the adjoining house; and Tony's gazing at his sister: people observing people so that everyone, including the viewer, is implicated in a voyeuristic act.

The dinner at Gloria's elegant house discloses critical information about the magazine's members: Tony's hostility to Evelyn's dictatorial nature as acting head of the magazine and his subservient position there; Roberto's chagrin when Tony tells him that he is bringing Sabrina (Sabrina Salerno), a model, back to their house; Roberto's homosexuality when Kim remarks that her needs in men are similar to his at a time when AIDS in Italy was barely a blip on the medical horizon[1]; Kim's observations on men hinting at her own promiscuity; and Gloria's return to the magazine after a year's absence because of a speedboat accident that killed her affluent husband, Carlo. Outside it rains heavily; the *giallo*, imitating film noir, employs rainfall as an objective correlative to the violent drama that is to come.

194　　　　　　　　10. The Return of the Repressed

Gloria (Serena Grandi, left) entertains Kim (Katrine Michelsen, seated in background), the first to be murdered by her pool. The framing already restricts their images creating an oppressive atmosphere where jealousy, revenge and incest lie just below the surface (Lamberto Bava's *Delirium: Photo of Gioia*).

As Gloria and Kim converse after the others have left, the camera is positioned outside the house. Filters are used over the shots alternating between the primary colors of blue and red while the camera laterally tracks outside the French windows to the accompaniment of a disturbing sound track of labored breathing and an evenly paced but decidedly felicitous piano and harp score. The change of color is meant to illustrate the perception of the killer whose features are not seen. Regarding this alternation of primary colors, a conducted study ascertained the psychological process through which color affects cognitive task performances using red and blue in activating different motivations on disparate types of tasks:

> Red is often associated with dangers and mistakes ... blue ... with openness, peace, and tranquility.... These different associations ... induce alternative motivations. ... Red ... should activate an avoidance motivation ... mak[ing] people more vigilant and risk-averse ... enhanc[ing] performance on detail-oriented tasks (...that require focused, careful attention). ... Blue ... usually associated with openness ... is likely to activate an approach motivation ... that encourages people to use innovative as opposed to "tried-and-true" problem-solving strategies.[2]

In *Le foto di Gioia*, the color red indicates the villain is task oriented; that is, there is a reason behind the persons he targets instead of a random selection. As in most of these films the murderer's modus operandi looks arbitrary so that no causal interconnection in the deaths can be determined, thus preserving the structure of the whodunit until the denouement. Second, the color blue indicates that the killer utilizes innovative methods of problem solving; that is, the variety of ways in which he dispatches his victims does not conform to the "'tried-and-true' problem-solving strategies" of orthodox murder mysteries. The alternating red-blue pattern likewise implies conflict within the killer because of red's "association with dangers and mistakes." The assassin is afraid of being apprehended, which is understandable, but also seems conflicted about the killings. This is the point at which psychological conflict brings emotional pain. Blue's "associat[ion] with openness, peace, and tranquility" indicates that he kills because it brings him inner serenity, but it also suggests that this experience is only transitory and that he must kill again. This is another facet of the psychosis that becomes ritualistic. These killings also confirm that the murderer is single-minded and a connoisseur in his approach: bodies are pitchforked, stung by bees, mutilated on elevators, hit by cars or found afloat in swimming pools.

As Kim exits Gloria's house, the music picks up with an upbeat acoustic score for guitar and drums. The camera observes her as filtered colors change from blue to red establishing the presence of the unseen assailant. At one point, as she is about to leave poolside, Kim's face morphs into a one-eyed Cyclops with heavily veined facial features. Presumably this is how the killer pictures her. According to the Greek poet Hesiod, the Cyclops was powerful and obstinate, becoming synonymous for brute strength and power. If there is a logic to the special cosmetic effects, this odd depiction of women intimates that the killer fears powerful, dominating women or else that he views women as a capricious and grotesque species. In slow motion the murderer thrusts a phallic pitchfork into Kim's pelvis, with its obvious sexual reference, so that she immediately vomits blood and is pitched by the force of the tool into Gloria's pool. Mark quickly phones Gloria of the model's murder. His tone, although breathless, hints at an orgasmic delectation in conveying the news, making him suspect and foregrounding the patriarchal power in the male's objectifying gaze. The models' bodies in life and in death become a source of spectacle even for a presumed wheelchair-bound youth like Mark. This response on his part has to be coupled with the weapons depicted in such films. For example, after Roberto's murder, Mark calls up Gloria and asks her how she feels being surrounded by death. As he enters his recreation room, the question he has posed to Gloria is ironic at best. Mark is surrounded by mounted rifles and trophies of animals bearing silent witness to the instruments of death and the victims that they have claimed as symbols of phallic power. The young man then throws the phone down and gets up out of his wheelchair as though restored to potency by the virile talismans in the den.

Phallic weapons are the stock-in-trade for *giallo* antagonists, at times testifying to an internal rage owing to sexual inadequacy. Gloria's brother, Tony, is one example of this impotency. He takes to bed a beautiful model but can't perform, insulting her when she lightly passes the incident off. Furthermore, in Gloria's dream filmed through a blue filter to simulate evening, a blond wig is thrown into her bedroom; Mark, another illustration of impotency, enters and gets up from his wheelchair, sticking his florescent wand between her legs in imitation of sexual intercourse. Pinning her to the wall when she attempts to escape, he tells Gloria that she "wants it" and jabs the instrument (below camera level), repeatedly into her vagina as she both cries out and moans. During this, bass violas play rapidly a rich melody taking on the tonality of a theater organ to express Gloria's agitation and ecstasy over Mark. Psychoanalytically dreams are the embodiments of repressed desires, tensions and fears that our conscious mind rejects which become manifest when the censor that guards our subconscious relaxes in sleep. These desires only emerge in disguise, as fantasies that are meaningless.[3]

Seen in this light, is Gloria's dream a nightmare or a turn-on? Is the supermodel's aloof demeanor toward Mark concealing her longing, or is she thoroughly repulsed by his phone calls? In some distorted fashion, she perceives him not as a cripple but as an aggressive lover desirous of giving her pleasure, but not being able to do so through his phallus but through a surrogate instrument. Gloria might harbor a desire for Mark but doesn't envision him presently as a potential lover, although we later learn that his paralysis is psychosomatic. Freud, addressing the theory about repressed wishes in dreams, observes, "the future which the dream shows us is not the one which *will* occur but the one which we should *like* to occur."[4] The dream also serves a structural purpose having its analogue at the film's conclusion when it is Mark who comes to Gloria's aid with his rifle as she is about to be raped with her brother's knife. Gloria's dream of Mark's illuminated wand has been transformed into the phallic rifle he later wields to save Gloria from the priapic knife used by Tony, while the blond wig in the dream recalls the one Tony uses in his killings so that the implication arises that he too has sexual designs on his sister.

Gloria, in fright, after Mark's call warning her about Kim's body floating in the pool, goes out there but doesn't see it. The musical accompaniment for this walk in the rain is for solo female voice supported by sustained ominous chords generating an eerie ambiance even as it captivates in its simplicity. The music, while not as complex and opulently assertive in melodic vocalization, recalls Villa-Lobos's *Bachianas Brasileiras (No. 5)* and Rachmaninoff's *Vocalise* and illustrates classical music's impact on Simon Boswell's score.[5] In *Foto* the ethereal sound of the female voice is counterpointed to Gloria's voluptuous body clothed in a white rain-drenched negligee that reveals her ample breasts beneath.

While the opening poolside photo shoot dealt with the female body's objectification by limiting it to a set of anatomical features, the sequence at the *Pussycat* emphasizes, even more, "woman" as commodity, for upon this feminine biologism the publication grosses its enormous revenues. It is a place where "woman" exists "as an absolute category and guarantor of fantasy."[6] The camera begins panning over close-ups of slides of a nude Kim wearing only red high-heeled shoes or draped in a floral print covering only parts of her anatomy. Each slide is seen through a magnifying glass as Tony and Roberto discuss what they can use. On the office walls hang pictures of nude women in various postures. While ogling her nakedness, Tony and Roberto treat Kim's torso as an object, a piece of architectonics. This constructedness of the feminine on one level justifies the phallocentric world for which these magazines are intended; on another it displaces the beauty of womanhood into a geometric fabrication that abstracts her into eroticized elements. Gloria, on her return as manager, is warned that Flora (Capucine) is waiting for her. Roberto bids her to tear into Flora, hinting that females are predatory jungle animals who must defend their space. Roberto is not far afield, for Flora wants to buy out *Pussycat*. Once in Gloria's office, Bava analogizes the earlier dining-room scene where Kim's response about Roberto's homosexuality is now paralleled with Gloria's response about Flora's lesbianism. Gloria's vehement salvos at Flora recall the older woman's sexual designs on her who, in retaliation, sarcastically informs Gloria that she will buy her old modeling pictures as souvenirs. Their verbal exchange fulfills Roberto's injunction for Gloria to tear Flora apart. Later on, Flora will cry over a nude photo of Gloria, cursing her because she is still in love with her. This unrequited passion of Flora for Gloria, of Roberto for Tony, and of Tony for his sister is one understated unifying factor in the narrative.

After the contretemps between Gloria and Flora, there is a cut to a close-up of photographic equipment, the sound of footsteps and the body of Kim, covered in a plastic bag, being dragged across the room. The scene is at first bathed in a blue light, but when the corpse is towed further along the floor, Bava blankets it in a red light replicating the two alternating colors used at the poolside when Kim was attacked. The close-up of the photographic equipment points to someone in the profession and, in all likelihood, somebody associated with the magazine. Hands prop up the dead model in her blue dress in front of an enormous picture of Gloria in a red dress, the dual colors played out once more in the clothing fabrics. Thus, the blue of Kim's dress animates the killer to use inventive design in positioning and photographing the corpse in the foreground while in the background Gloria's red dress predominates suggesting the task requires a focused attention to detail. The colors, as well as the meticulous positioning of the dead woman on a couch, indicate that the murderer is an ingenious artist, at ease with the situation and centered on the compositional elements of his job. Bava's use of these primary colors thematically sutures the murderer, his victim and the deed through a succession of signifiers.

The second murder is of the model Samantha, Tony's girl. He leaves the bedroom where he has failed as a lover, while Samantha takes a shower. Immediately nondiegetic heavy-metal instrumental music is played accompanying shots from the killer's point of view. He is dressed in a white protective suit, his face covered by a helmet with a dark visor, and his hands are encased in black gloves as he cuts the cords to the room's shutters. The room suddenly becomes a dusky shade of blue, and from no recognizable source a red glow bathes the apartment's various furnishings. The events are seen from the killer's perspective, but even with objective shots of the assassin, household objects are tinted red with no legitimate lighting source while the background remains unaffected. This time the killer pictures Samantha's face as a bee emerging from the bathtub. Tony, failing to perform sexually, now references Samantha as a queen bee and he the subservient drone who, in his humiliation, seeks retribution. He may, furthermore, see her as exploiting him to advance her career in *Pussycat* while Tony has a dread of anyone replacing Gloria either at work or in his esteem. He unleashes a small carton of bees that attack the nude woman who is brought to the floor as he pours oil of tuberose on her body to keep the bees on her. As with the first murder, Samantha's bee-stung corpse is placed before a large picture of Gloria's unclad figure, and similar crosscutting is used between the deceased and the cameraman's hands operating the photographic equipment.

The film's third homicide at a department store where Gloria has gone with her brother to look for modeling props can be partitioned into four quarters: (1) Entering, Gloria investigates the merchandise while Tony romances Susan, a salesgirl; (2) Tony's "death" while Gloria is menaced by an unseen killer; (3) Gloria, escaping the murderer in a freight elevator, comes upon the dying Susan; (4) Gloria's flight from the department store. The most significant shots occur when Gloria, alone, because Tony is chatting up Susan on a lower level, calls out but, receiving no answer, becomes worried. The alternating syntagma between the scene's focalizer, Gloria, and the object of her gaze, Tony, engenders the initial excitement. This internal ocularization places the moviegoer in Gloria's shoes so that initially we strain our neck, imitating her, to be able to see if her brother is coming up the escalator. In this long shot from Gloria's POV, the camera dollies to the moving staircase as the sound of its mechanism increases. Tony's bloodied "body" lies on an escalator between floors while Gloria's voice-over tells him to come to the next landing. Then three reaction shots of Gloria's face, interspersed with Tony's "corpse," explain its repercussion on her and, in turn, the audience by concentrating first on his body from the neck down and then on his upper torso, culminating, after another cut back to Gloria, in a close-up of Tony's bloodied head. In this monstration of sequential shots there is a slight jump cut between a long shot of Tony's body now at the head of the escalator, his face out of frame, to another long shot of Tony's head resting on the escalator ramp being slowly driven by the mechanism onto the floor.

The *giallo* also problematizes the role of the killer's off-screen space through the use of sound, camera movement and placement. The ubiquitous positioning of the antagonist in this space gives him an insubstantiality as though defining an all-powerful but disembodied agent. Gloria does not see the killer; she hears him, while the audience not only hears him but observes what appear to be his movements about the department store, presumably through his point of view. Tony's distraught sister hears the sound of breaking crystal replicated at Kim's poolside murder, followed by high-pitched recorded laughter with a menacing voice whose timbre, concealing the speaker's gender, informs Gloria that she is next to die. A camera tracks down a department store aisle striving to make us sense the killer's presence as he spies on Gloria, but there is no evident trace of him. A high-angle shot of Gloria taken from the head of the escalator on the floor above calls into question the presence of a focalizer. Long shots from Gloria's viewpoint of racks filled with men's apparel are likewise devoid of a human presence. All the while the same incorporeal voice persists in issuing threats, the killer ostensibly observing Gloria but not being observed by her. A dialectical edginess erupts between an apparent objective camera movement and the possibility that its mobility may denote the murderer's viewpoint.

Susan's death occupies the third quarter of the sequence in the confined space of a freight elevator in which the heroine finds herself. Bava has fittingly counterpoised the movement within the space of characters entering and egressing, with unenclosed but delimited spaces. When Gloria approaches the department store elevator, the lighting wondrously turns to a reddish glow with no diegetical governance to disclose its source, nor any indication that it stems from the antagonist's viewpoint; the lighting is manifestly stylized to connote its association with endangerment. The film's red and blue hues become a forewarning, a piece of showmanship not unlike that of producer William Castle to dictate to the audience when they are to become anxious.

In a medium profile shot, Gloria backs into a freight elevator with a hatchet clutched in two hands close to her breast testifying to her emotional perturbation. From outside the elevator, Gloria is seen inside the cabin as the door closes, intensifying the edginess of the situation because its focal length makes her look not only inconsequential but more marginalized by being hemmed within the lift's confines. The space outside the elevator is more extensive, yet its soft-focused foreground also negates the feeling of spatial openness suggesting that the safety of both areas is equally questionable. This sets the stage for the heroine's ride to the first floor, fraught with an anxiety on the cusp of erupting into full-fledged panic and only materializing on Susan's entrance into the lift. Once Gloria is constrained in the elevator her paranoia sets in. This is registered through close-ups with limited camera movement and enforced by vertical streaks of alternating red- and cerulean-colored light that simulate bars on the cabin walls as though she were incarcerated. Natural sounds are heard over the 21 shots; no music is played so that the visuals, together with the editing, camera placement and lighting, generate all the obligatory agitation.

Throughout the elevator ride, suspense builds by repeatedly crosscutting Gloria's image with the landing indicator. The pattern traditionally followed is an objective shot of the individual followed by a cut to what the individual is looking at. Bava confounds the viewer by first commencing with this model of five alternating objective shots of Gloria interspersed with three subjective shots of the floor numbers, a procedure mined in *Perche quelle strane gocce di sangue sul corpo di Jennifer?*, but then he abandons the paradigm resulting in a discordant sensation by waiting three more shots before showing the floor number again. In between we have shots of Gloria in profile backing further into the elevator followed by a close-up of an overwrought Gloria facing the camera and then looking relieved as the elevator continues its downward movement when she again looks toward the landing indicator. The director reestablishes the alternating format only to interrupt it once more by skipping a shot where the subjective insert of the floor number would normally reoccur, and substitutes a dolly-in to a close-up of the door as Gloria approaches it. The scene's climax reintroduces Susan whose sudden, bloody appearance comes as a shock. Many of the remaining shots are succinctly rendered and are devoted to Susan's three disparate stages of collapse before she dies from her wounds: the first presents her in a standing position grasping on to Gloria's neck, the second dramatizes her in a sitting posture on the cabin floor holding on to Gloria's leg for support, and finally the third has her prone on the elevator, eyes open in death with one hand flung over her head as Gloria walks over the corpse to leave. In between the last two mentioned shots is a close-up of Gloria, her mouth open in a scream, which functions not only as a reaction to Susan's death but, as an audience surrogate, she articulates a cathartic release of our emotions. As Gloria races through the deserted store in the final section of the set piece, the camera laterally tracks her in several shots accompanied by a progressive jazz score to underline the action until she reaches the street's safety.

When Tony's and Susan's corpses are placed before Gloria's six-foot picture, a comparable series of shots occurs similar to the previous photos taken of Kim and Samantha. This repetition creates a textural volume advancing the story by individual increments that restate the system of ten homogeneously cohesive shots to generate continuity[7]:

Photo of Gloria W. Corpses	*Photo Equipment*	*Photo Equipment/Gloria's Photo*
(#1) two bodies; the film camera tilts up to Gloria's picture.	(#2) profile of still camera	(#9) photo of Gloria's face turns a monochrome red; film camera tilts diagonally down to right of frame to table with photo equipment; film camera zooms in to box cutter which a hand seizes.
(#3) Extreme long shot of still camera in left foreground mounted on a table.	(#4) extreme close-up of still camera lens.	(#10) Gloria's face in photo monochrome red; an arm holding a box cutter slashes her face.
(#5) bodies and Gloria's photo in background; flash from camera.	(#6) profile of the still camera as in #2.	
(#7) corpses on couch; above Gloria's photo. Flashes from still camera.	(#8) extreme close-up of the still camera lens.	

Besides the picture of Gloria and the two bodies, one of the major codical components is the still camera, seen in part or in whole in five shots (#2, #4, #6, and #8). The repeated shots of the camera alternating between the profile of the camera and the lens through which the recorded image passes foregrounds the act of documenting, like the motion picture camera does. Despite this insistency on the verifiable reproduction of objective reality, Bava tricks us by not disclosing the person operating the camera, only the individual wielding the box cutter (#9, #10). But it is the missing synecdochical hand operating the still camera that provides a clue to the murderer. If the viewer is alert, Bava gives a hint as to his identity: the camera used to take the photos is on automatic. The motion-picture camera here proves to be an unreliable witness to the events, having omitted the setting up of the still camera. The absence of a human presence behind the still camera should indicate that whoever is orchestrating this macabre ritual of positioning the bodies before it is himself in the photograph, and consequently that the assassin, Tony, is the "corpse." For the first eight shots the camera crosscuts between the victims beneath Gloria's photo and the still camera, providing a rhythm that foregrounds the witnessing of the act of murder through a mechanical apparatus that objectifies the deed by reproducing a verifiable document. As a coda to the scene we become privy to the killer's state of mind by the use of a monochromatic red carried through both shots (#9 and #10) on Gloria's photo implying that the murderer cannot manage his anger because his "approach motivation" to solving problems has been deactivated. Shots #9 and #10 begin with close-ups on Gloria's face: #9 ends with a slight zoom in to the box cutter as the killer takes hold of the weapon; then the shot cuts directly to the same facial close-up being slashed with that weapon in #10. The knife becomes an adjunct to the photographic equipment; both "arrest" life: the camera by "freezing" it, the knife by terminating it.

The director circumspectly discloses more information as to who the murderer might be. Roberto, returning to the studio, decides to project some of the slides he finds on the table. Some include Tony at a stable with a horse, but also included are the very ones of Gloria that appear behind the posed murderer's victims. Roberto's facial response indicates two different emotions: the longing for the unattainable Tony and bafflement at finding Gloria's photos. The discovery leads to Roberto's distraught visit to her with the information. When the police arrive at the studio immediately after Roberto's departure, Inspector Corsi recognizes the couch and the enlarged photo of Gloria on a movie screen, but naturally assumes it is Roberto's because he sees no reason why Tony would embroil his own sister in these crimes. As the inspector phones her to warn her, Roberto appears at Gloria's window frenziedly demanding to talk to her. Gloria runs out pursued by Roberto to the front gate where he is hit by a car that speeds off. The police arrive before the dying Roberto is able to disclose what he has chanced upon. Evelyn's answer to Gloria's confusion about Roberto's apparent attack is that he must hate women, yet this adroit summation actually applies to Tony, although at this point his motivation is problematical.

At the denouement, while stalking Gloria at her poolside, Tony is severely wounded instead of being killed, a remarkable ending for a *giallo* villain. It is compelling to probe into Tony's personality. Having unmasked himself to his sister by removing his blond wig, he tells her that she is the only one he loved since they were children. When he sexually molests her and before he is about to kill her, he is shot in his crotch by Mark as he is about to force Gloria to take her panties off at knifepoint. As a consequence, Tony is rendered both symbolically impotent, dropping the phallic weapon he is carrying, and physically impotent. He slumps down, vomiting blood over his sister's white undergarments as though in raping her he has, for the very first time, ravaged a virgin. It becomes an emblematic wish fulfillment that he could never legitimately accomplish. The film is thus an elaborate revenge story. Tony attempts to kill his sister because he can't possess her, and while trying to rid himself of his incestuous desire, he is castrated.

Critic Robin Wood claims that basic repression is something we all must live with, for it is associated with our capacity for self-control and our acknowledgment of and concern for others. But for Tony it is not basic repression that is the root of his conflict, it is the concept of *otherness* that is at the heart of his repression. This type, as Wood explains, functions not only as something external to the self, but also as what is repressed (but never eliminated) in the self and projected outwards to be hated and disowned. Tony feels that while his sister is alive he will never be free from his repressed desires. Bava's revelatory concluding scene between Gloria and her brother's "coming out" opens the action to a polysemy of significations without a functioning anchorage. One possible response to this incestuous yearning is that Gloria's brother has projected onto the murdered women, and onto his sister in particular, his innate repressed femininity in order to repudiate it as inferior. His masculinity has ambiguously been called into question in his aborted lovemaking with Sabrina, which might have constituted a supreme insult to him. Tony's repressed wish to have intercourse with his sibling is so appalling to him that he must disown its loathsomeness. In fact, he has kept this secret since childhood and in so doing has seriously threatened his sanity. This psychological summation constitutes what might be considered much of the film's backstory. When Tony apprises his sister about his feelings toward her, his motivations remain vague, but they are precisely what provoke his killing spree. Yet this "otherness" in Tony, which he sees as an evil, also makes him an object of pity. That which he has repressed returns as a threat to Gloria when made manifest and is repellent to her. In his spiritual agony he confesses to her that he is not good at "normal" love, that is, conforming to the dominant heterosexual social customs.[8] Still, Tony's lack of normality, as well as the homosexual orientation of Flora and Roberto, isn't introduced to counterpoint their "otherness" to the remaining "straight" characters. Alex and Gloria's disastrous relationship posits no traditional, heterosexual, exemplary model, making this *giallo* rather daring. It is such a deliriously and dolorously misanthropic world which Bava films, that the viewer might be hard put to tell the difference between the "normal" people and those represented as "the other."

Bava's various loose ends to *Le foto di Gioia* are a trait he shares with Dario Argento, whose

> films are driven more by the surface associations of elements ... evil houses ... with *profondo rossos* (deep reds) ... sets of architectural richness; broken glass; and wildly inappropriate funk jam music ... than by inductive logic.[9]

Much of the above is present in *Le foto*: the evil house where the dead are photographed, the primary colors of blue and red, the tectonic affluence of Gloria's home, the broken glass and strong rhythmic swing of electric bass and drums. Argento, echoing Bava's similar lack of character motivation, has maintained, "Motivation doesn't matter to me.... I'm interested in seeing what goes on in people minds ... the psychology."[10] Both directors might agree that to ask a madman to speak logically about what motivates him isn't always a tenable position. This is probably the reason Inspector Corsi isn't given the chance to solve the whodunit since Bava takes the story out of the realm of ratiocinative detection. In *Le foto*, there isn't even an amateur detective to solve the mystery, for Roberto's discovery of the killer's identity and his inability to convey the information disqualify him.

Despite the non-traditional approach *Le foto* takes regarding its characters, it creates a meta-discourse which at once evokes and circumvents those traditional British murder mystery tropes from which Bava and others found their inspiration. Several consequential arguments can be drawn from this regarding the murderer himself. One of the seminal English mystery writers the *giallo* mined was Agatha Christie. In Bava's film we have the perfect complement to Christie's *And Then There Were None* (1939). The use of a character, thought dead, who reappears at the conclusion only to be the murderer himself bears a close resemblance to Christie's Judge Wargrave. In the novel, Judge Wargrave is supposedly murdered, as is Tony, only to reappear at the conclusion, and like Christie, Bava has Tony reappear very much alive at the finale by Gloria's swimming pool. Filmic comparisons are also prevalent.

Like Argento's Peter Neal of *Tenebrae* (1982) and Inspector Alan Santini in *Opera*, Bava's Tony shares something in common with the other two; Tony, Santini and Neal counterfeit their deaths to destroy the remaining persons on their list for revenge and to facilitate their escape. *Foto di Gioia* offers another link to *Tenebrae* in that the original murderer, Christiano Berti, fetishizes the killing by taking photos of the female victims just as Tony does. But whereas Berti's photos are for his private enjoyment, Tony, as a photographer, arranges the corpses around a six-foot photo of Gloria as though she is presiding over those whom he thinks are attempting to assume her place. By sending them to his sister's office and home, he both boasts of his accomplishments in ridding her of "rivals" and intimidates her.

Besides Argento, *Le Foto di Gioia* also references Hitchcock. The wig-wearing murderer recalls Norman Bates in *Psycho* (1960). Like Norman, Tony has no parental figure in his life. Norman, to keep his deceased mother's presence alive, becomes her by donning her clothing and wearing a wig. Tony uses a wig and female attire as a disguise, but also perhaps to emulate Gloria, calling her the greatest and the most attractive woman he knows. More significantly, Gloria has taken on a maternal role for him. She encourages him at his work, and like Norman, Tony seeks approval from her. Tony ultimately chooses to kill his sister instead of her lover, Alex, so no one can possess her, unlike Norman who has killed his mother and her lover. Apropos of this, Jacqueline Reich maintains that the *giallo* is "a genre dominated by sexually ambiguous villains ... offering diverse points of cross-gender identification."[11] Although Tony cannot have intercourse with his sister, he does display his carnal nature by using a knife as phallic replacement to caress her mouth, breasts, belly and pubic region as he strips her with it in a savagely taunting manner. It is, therefore, understandable that he should hate the very thing he loves because he recognizes the implications that his desires drive him to and so becomes desperate to rid himself of the longing and loathing. This issue, developed in *Psycho*, becomes an underlying impetus for Tony's murderous rampage.

Mark, another dysfunctional character, is also in love with Gloria, but far from repressing his desires, like Tony, he acts them out via telephone and symbolically through amplified phallic tools: a telescope, an illuminated wand and a rifle. Like Tony, he sees any man as a rival for Gloria's affections, particularly when Alex returns home with Gloria after a drink at a bar. Mark takes out his rifle and from the window points it at Alex making a shooting sound, thereby utilizing a phallic extension of male aggression to symbolically rid himself of a competitor. His "besting" of Alex is akin to a masturbatory fantasy that makes him feel potent. The same is true of his seemingly innocuous telescope which he uses as an extension of his sexual organ to become intimate with Gloria from afar as though reliving a wet dream without having to be near her. One has only to recollect Norman's Peeping Tomism in *Psycho* as he spies on Marion Crane in the bathroom of her motel room.

Le Foto di Gioia moreover recalls Michael Powell's *Peeping Tom*, another sexual psychopath, suggesting such men are more likely than not to be homicidal maniacs. Bava's Tony, Hitchcock's Norman and Powell's Mark Lewis have a similar love-hate relationship with members of their families: with Tony it is with his sister Gloria, with Norman it is with his mother and with Mark it is with his father, a psychologist who has made his son the subject of clinical experiments on fear. Mark conducts his own psychological experiments by murdering women while filming them to capture their fear and so imitate, even more aberrantly, his father's work. Mark then plays the films back, sickened yet fascinated by what he has done and what his father has done to him. Tony, like Mark, conducts his own deadly experiments. Both men dispatch women and then photograph their murders, one on photographic paper, the other on celluloid; Tony publicizes the pictures to intimidate his sister while Mark shows them to Helen Stephens, a woman who befriends him.

Norman Bates and Mark Lewis form a trajectory to Tony, all three are misfits with sadomasochistic traits alternating between love and hate for themselves, for what they have become and for what their families have done to them. Likewise, Tony's warped desire to protect Gloria from those around her necessitates a bizarre form of sadomasochism. The sadistic impulses are enunciated through the ingenious means he employs in dispatching various individuals, but the relentless compulsion to do so contributes to the masochistic facet of Tony's twisted psyche. While he enjoys inflicting punishment, he is constrained by his pathology to loathe what he has become to the point of killing the fetishistic object he worships. His cruelty toward women only intensifies his unsatisfied misogynistic disposition toward Kim, Sabrina and Susan.

Is the *giallo* misogynistic? In the end it depends whom you are talking to. In antiquity, the Greeks considered misogyny to be generated by *gynophobia*, a fear of women, a condition proposed by late 20th-century feminist theorists whose speculations equated almost exclusively male hegemony with the rise of misogyny as both a cause and result of patriarchal social structures.[12] Are the films' misogyny due to the "blurring of gender roles and sadomasochistic identificatory practices" as Carol Clover argues?[13] Mikel J. Koven disagrees with their reported misogynistic premise insinuating that the *giallo* is quite democratic in choosing victims of both sexes and instead calls them "misanthropic."[14] To add to his argument, Koven cites Steven Thrower's belief that the *giallo* also has a number of female killers, making a distinction between misogyny and women as victims and misanthropy and the general disdain of humanity. Women in the *gialli* can be as misogynistic as their male counterparts, murdering their own kind because of fear, hatred, sadistic impulses or revenge as well as to acquire power and money. Let the readers be the judge, for either one enjoys these films for their own sake, disregarding the cultural and social conditions that influenced their content, or detests them for their violence in general and specifically for their brutality against women.

As has been done in the nine previous essays, consideration is turned now to Propp's narrative structure of folk tales as delineated in his *Morphology*.

1. **A member of the family leaves home (I).**

In *Le foto*, the leaving home concerns Gloria's departure for work. What appears to be a more commonplace occurrence of having a career is not so for Gloria, having frightening repercussions in her life. Gloria, a former model for stag magazines, has become head of one, and at the death of her wealthy husband determines to live for herself and return to work having given the running of the business to Evelyn who is anxious to see Gloria again take control of the magazine.

2. **An interdiction is addressed to the heroine (II).**

The interdictions in the film are of two types; one is an indirect "order or command" through the murders themselves that begin with the model, Kim. The string of killings is associated with an absentation: it is the first anniversary of Carlo's death and marks Gloria's return to the magazine that "prepares for the misfortune, creating an opportune moment for it." Gloria, after a year of mourning and feeling lonely, explains to Kim the rationale of resuming control of *Pussycat*. Gloria's first interdiction comes in the form of Kim's brutal murder, and several points must be considered.

(a) The threat of bodily harm, immediate or not, is a way of imposing an indirect interdiction on Gloria which is just as emphatic as a straightforward warning "without the interdiction being addressed." Tony does this through murdering people around his sister, photographing their corpses with Gloria's picture and sending them to her, indirectly inculpating her and women in general for his psychosis.

(b) The murders, a warning to Gloria not to let others become close to her, is revealed by Tony at the film's conclusion: (i) Kim, in his view, was trying to take Gloria's place as a model by becoming close to his sister and, therefore, supplant her as the object of his idealized love. (ii) Sabrina, he believes, was trying to take Gloria's place in bed. He sees his girlfriend, Susan, as trying to use him to get to his sister.

A second weakened interdiction comes from Flora by way of a "request or a bit of advice" to Gloria to buy the magazine from her. Whether the request is simply that of a rival magazine to buy out a competitor, or Flora's taking advantage of Gloria's bereavement to buy the magazine at a cheaper price, or whether Flora, as a spurned lover, wants revenge on Gloria and is willing to pay a good price to gloat over her, is not certain; her aggressive behavior may encompass all three reasons. This, however, is not the first time Flora has asked to buy the magazine, which Gloria has staunchly refused to sell. That Gloria does not at first acquiesce has nothing to do with money but with the older woman's amorous advances and treatment of her. Flora had gotten Gloria her first job as a model; otherwise, she contends, Gloria would have remained a prostitute because she didn't know where her next meal was coming from to feed herself and her brother. But when Gloria wanted to quit Flora's modeling job, she argues that Flora did everything to ruin her, even to turn Carlo against her with lies.

A third group of four minor interdictions arise from well-meaning friends and will be discussed in the following section.

3. The interdictions are violated (III).

It is a moot point whether the antagonist should enter the story once an interdiction is violated, but Tony certainly does, although in the *giallo* the antagonist's identity is not revealed until the conclusion. Despite Gloria's seeming to need the support of a retinue of people in times of danger or emotional distress, she emerges somewhat more of a dauntless heroine than a passive individual since she invariably violates interdictions that her friends pressure her to fulfill. Consider four interdictions she breaks: (1) An interdiction which results from the first murder comes from Mark and is quite direct. Immediately after Kim is slain, Mark, who has seen the incident from across the way, informs Gloria not go to the pool. Gloria defies the injunction at the possible risk of her life. At the conclusion, in a parallel situation, she will repeat the action by going to the poolside and discover Tony's "body" but finds it is really she who is the intended victim. (2) Gloria also ignores Evelyn's warning, coming on the heels of Mark's telephone call, not to pay attention to him. Gloria's response is to ignore this second directive, and she even fantasizes about Mark's raping her. (3) A third interdiction comes from Flora who tries to force Gloria to sell the magazine which she first refuses. Gloria's refusal places her life and those around her in jeopardy because Tony sees her resuming control of the magazine as a way of his losing his sister's affection and preoccupation with him. (4) When the *Pussycat* staff objects to Gloria's selling the magazine to Flora, she defies the directive and finally sells to her rival realizing she is getting rid of all the bad memories.

4. **The villain receives information about his victims (V).**

Tony is in a privileged position as brother of Gloria; he knows exactly what she is doing so that his probing for information about her or the women at the magazine or about Roberto with whom he shares an apartment is not difficult since he works with them and has their confidences. In most cases the information the villain receives is elliptically conveyed, that is, a presumed receiving of information not presented to the audience through the diegesis directly. For example, Tony learns that Roberto has discovered that he is the murderer. We are only told this at the very end of the film when Gloria's brother reveals it before he is about to kill his sister.

After Tony's failed attempt at lovemaking with Sabrina, her casually asking him for a better modeling job corresponds to Propp's "careless act," giving Tony the impression he is being used sexually for his connections to Gloria and, therefore, a reason for murdering her.

There is no indication of the circumstances that prompt Tony to call Kim a "bitch," but his twisted reasoning deduces that she is trying to supplant him in Gloria's eyes. This information, whether received directly or imagined by him is the ultimate reason for Kim's death. Every woman in Tony's view represents an unattainable object of desire, like his sister, and therefore a humiliation that must be eradicated through murder.

5. **The villain attempts to deceive the victim in order to take possession of her (VI).**

The villain's disguise is simple; as the younger brother of the head of the magazine he has Gloria's full confidence as well as that of those who work there. Tony is a paranoid schizophrenic and his delusions dwell on the belief that the *Pussycat* group is out to harm his sister and this directly affects him. His schizophrenia is a "disorder of thought" where he experiences visual hallucinations.[15] These hallucinations cause changes in his color perception and drive him to view women as monsters. The other side of Tony's pathology comprises a "blunted affect" whereby he doesn't register much emotion when photographing women, performing sexually or being told that the magazine is being sold. Ironically the illness itself enables him to deceive his victims by maintaining a normal outward appearance.

6. **The villain causes harm or injury to a member of a family (VIII).**

Tony is the only blood relation Gloria has left. Gloria's extended family is the magazine. She seems to have a close bond to Roberto, Evelyn, and even Kim, but beyond that she is equally friendly to the other women models in the magazine asking them to dinner in her home. With Kim, Gloria shares her private life and assuredly her intimates, like Evelyn and Roberto, know her story. Consequently, the harm Tony causes is to Gloria's personal friends on the magazine. The patterns of villainy implemented by the killer can be traced to two within the 18 disparate subcategories listed by Propp. The first is that "The villain commits murder" (#14). The murder necessitates a "Sudden disappearance" of the victims (#7) who are photographed after being slaughtered, with the exception of Tony who simulates his death. The other victims include Kim, Sabrina, and Susan. They are intimidated before being slain at night by the villain (#18), while Roberto is killed by Tony suddenly one night in a hit-and-run. Lastly the heroine both at her home and in a department store is persecuted at night not only by the villain but by Roberto, as he demands entrance to Gloria's home, compelling her to flee into the darkness.

7. **One member of a family either lacks something or desires to have something (VIIIa).**

Normally, in Propp's view, this element is peculiar to the middle of the tale. In the *giallo* it is transferred to the end. This is quite natural since *Le foto di Gioia* is a whodunit and the audience must wait until the outcome to discover Tony's incestuous desires and his motivation for the murders. The object lacking in Tony's life is a sexual partner, if in the traditional sense we mean a girlfriend or a wife. Naturally, Tony's desire for Gloria is socially taboo, but it is the motivating force behind the story that leads to the intimidation of the heroine and others, such as Evelyn and Roberto. The family member desires what he cannot have which in turn causes him to see all women as inferior substitutes for his sister resulting in their deaths to expunge his transgressive shame. Tony is punished for the desire to desire and hence madness is the result.

8. **The heroine is tested and attacked which prepares the way of her receiving a helper/donor (XII).**

This function likewise has many subcategories with Propp listing ten. The eighth subcategory states that "A hostile creature attempts to destroy the heroine." The means used here are not physical, that is, until the conclusion, but are psychological. The "family" at the magazine is being dispatched, but it is obvious that the killer is tormenting Gloria and that she is his ultimate victim. After the first murder a "Donor greets and interrogates the heroine" (#2) in the form of Inspector Corsi, but he is incapable of solving the mystery and apprehending the killer; therefore, he becomes a spurious benefactor who confesses that his hardest job is to get people to trust him. The only thing he discovers about Kim's murder is that the killer is a blond, either a man or a woman, wearing a wig or not. Corsi can't tell. He informs Gloria that the photo sent to her is either a warning or an attempt to implicate her. The second interview he has with her after Sabrina's body is discovered results in Corsi telling her not to worry or to look for motives because the police are paid to do that. In these ersatz interrogations Corsi doesn't ask the questions as much as informs the characters what he has discovered. The real donor is Mark who watches over her and finally saves her life.

9. **The heroine is branded (XVII).**

In this designation a brand is defined as a marking. The brand in this instance is a wound received by Gloria during an encounter with Tony at the film's conclusion as he orgiastically takes his knife and purposely cuts her lip and chest as he moves down her semi-naked body with his blade ripping into her undergarments. As in the horror film, this release of the villain's sexuality is presented as perverted, monstrous and excessive. Both Tony's defying the incest taboo and the excess of his speech, his physical appearance in women's clothes, and his phallic knife become, according to Woods, the logical outcome of his repression.[16]

10. **The villain is defeated (XXX).**

Mark, bound to a wheelchair, is the most unlikely individual to be the heroine's protector, for this psychologically scarred character, filled with remorse at the death of Einzia, his fiancée, in a car accident, is also the same self-centered young man who makes explicit sexual telephone calls to Gloria. But Mark comes to her defense and punishes the villain without battling him because of his handicap. In shooting Tony in the crotch, he doesn't mortally wound him but physically emasculates this psychologically impotent villain. News of Tony's condition is reported by Inspector Corsi to Gloria recovering at a hospital and, ironically enough, Tony now will be permanently confined to a wheelchair supplanting Mark who is beginning to walk. Although an amateur "law enforcer" brings Tony to justice, Bava does not designate Mark as the traditional amateur hero. The power of the law's "hegemonic forces" puts Tony away for psychiatric treatment.[17]

Mention might be made of the concluding "resurrected villain" trope. Once Corsi leaves the hospital room where Gloria is recovering, she is urged to sleep by the nurse. There is a long wide-angle shot of the nurse walking down the corridor making the passageway seem elongated, empty and menacing. At the elevator door the lower part of a wheelchair emerges and proceeds down the same corridor the nurse has just left. This is followed by a point-of-view shot from the wheelchair's occupant with flowers he is holding. Suspense intensifies through the rapid cutting from point-of-view shots of the chair's occupant to the wheels moving along the corridor. Suddenly the frame is suffused in a red tint as an indication of the killer's viewpoint. Originally the tinted shots were solely from the assassin's viewpoint, but now this scene is interspersed with a close-up of Gloria fitfully asleep in her room signifying that the killer's movement and point of view have now been transferred to her dream. This bit of ambiguity deceptively generates the impression that the audience might, in reality, be looking through Tony's eyes and not through Gloria's dream.

The doorknob of Gloria's room begins slowly to turn and open revealing a bouquet of flowers. The bouquet is put aside and a knife, in a vertical position, is seen, the camera then tilting up to Tony's face. Sardonically, the man whose genitals have been destroyed now uses the phallic knife pointed upward as though in an erection to fulfill the threat he has made to his sister the night he was shot. Gloria wakes up with a start and seems relieved. There is then a cut to Mark in his wheelchair as he apologizes for frightening her while still sincerely and politely professing his love. In the end Mark will be healed of his psychological impotence, but Gloria will not be free of her brother with an incurable wound to his manhood.

Conclusion: A Postscript of Sorts, Not a Requiem for a Genre

The reader's challenge is to replicate the experiment by reading the [film] and to draw their own conclusions.—John Barton

During the '60s Italy experienced its own cinematic New Wave in the midst of the country's booming economy and its concomitant materialism, skepticism and estrangement due in part to the youth revolution and the need to break away from its conventional class-conscious educational system. In the filmmaking industry, the revolution affected traditional storytelling at a time when neo-realism had ceased to be the *sine qua non* of Italian cinema with the emergence of Fellini, Pasolini, Lattuada, Germi, Monicelli, and Risi. While the *giallo* wasn't part of the New Wave's *Weltanschauung*, oddly enough, to a degree, it assimilated some of its sensibilities. Mira Liehm, in her book *Passion and Defiance*, propounds four major characteristics of the Italian New Wave that are not dissimilar to the *giallo*. I would, very briefly, like to pursue this connection to recapitulate what has been said throughout these chapters from a slightly different perspective.

The first attribute Liehm identifies with New Wave filmmaking is "a subjective approach that resulted from the denial of an objective reality identified with the establishment." That is, the objective reality created by 19th-century fiction gave way to a personalized view of the world without the comfort of the empirical reality of the previous century. The reality posited in the New Wave was subjective in that it existed differently for each person and in some cases may or may not have existed. Yet if we think of the *giallo* as being part of the "vernacular or popular cinema,"[1] the opposite of the highbrow films of Antonioni, Pasolini, and Fellini, much of it represents a subjective approach to reality that views life through the filter of an individual on the verge of losing hold on reality. The heroine of *The Girl Who Knew Too Much* lives in a fictional world of her own making which may or may not exist in reality.

That she is proven correct, up to a point, in no way mitigates the nightmarish situations the viewer is subjected to. This subjective reality is borne out in other *gialli* like *The Strange Vice of Mrs. Wardh* and *Lizard in a Woman's Skin*, where the altered reality experienced by its bourgeoisie protagonists begins to blur the divisions between actuality and fantasy.

Ms. Liehm's second characteristic of the Italian New Wave, "the rejection of closed plots," doesn't rule out the *giallo*. Although justice does triumph and evil is vanquished in these whodunits, not all the films have sutured endings; some leave the conclusion indeterminate. For illustration, take the heroine of Martino's *The Strange Vice of Mrs. Wardh*, who, at the close, is left on her own, fearful of trusting any man, betrayed by a husband, a lover and a former lover, all operating through the economy of greed. The return to normalcy in this film isn't quite the conventional happy ending that populist cinema demands, and happiness is tenuous at best. Evil has been subjugated, but its lingering effects are devastating. At the conclusion of Argento's *Opera*, it only appears that the status quo has returned, but the reality for Betty, subjected to disorienting nightmares, is to retreat psychologically into the unconscious mind's defense mechanism against feelings of anxiety and to distort reality to maintain her self-worth. Even in *Delirium: Photo of Gioia*, Gloria's existence, left with a demented brother who has tried to kill her and a voyeur/psychologically paralyzed lover who wants to be a part of her life, doesn't bode well for future happiness. In *The Bloodstained Shadow*, although Stefano D'Archangelo's trauma has concluded, it results in the death of his brother, Paolo, and the knowledge that he indirectly brought it about. Likewise, in *Seven Shawls of Yellow Silk*, Peter Oliver has solved the crime, but in the end he is companionless as his girlfriend and his new love interest are brutally murdered.

If we limit Mira Liehm's third trait of New Wave cinema to "the film's structure [is] ... an expression of the film's idea,"[2] then the *giallo* can be accommodated to her description since every genre has its own particular structure from which general principles/ideas may be deduced, including the New Wave which contains characteristics that transcend the specific genres it has embraced. Her example, to support this rather broad statement, is a bit ingenuous in announcing that the New Wave favors the sequence shot over the traditional subdivision into shots and sequences, for not every New Wave film, including those of Chabrol, Truffaut, Robbe-Grillet, and so on, makes extensive use of this as a signature trait, much less Francesco Rosi, Marco Bellocchio, Ermanno Olmi, Bernardo Bertolucci, and Valerio Zurlini, to name but a few Italian New Wave practitioners, unless one centers on the films of Antonioni. *L'Avventura* (1960), for example, is a mystery film, a whodunit of sorts that hardly uses the language of the *giallo* as it "systematically subverted the filmic codes, practices and structures in currency at its time."[3]

Yet when Liehm speaks of New Wave cinema's "disconnected, loose, violent, shocking … and provocative" signifiers to articulate the director's dissatisfaction with the more traditional values, the *giallo* does demolish many of these same concepts: religion, family, fidelity, trust, love and honor (*The Case of the Bloodstained Shadow*).

The *giallo* mirrors the New Wave in its convoluted structure, its surreal situations (*Lizard in a Woman's Skin*), its lack of a logical progression of ideas (*Delirium: Photos of Gioia*), producing jarring plot developments and violent and shocking images meant to provoke, creating a film language that expresses what the characters undergo existentially (*The Case of the Bloody Iris*). The world the *giallo* invents is a vision of despair, paranoia and even dread, much like the New Wave but through an abrasive editing style that is meant to jar the audience's complacency. The *giallo* is so constructed that rather than favor the sequence shot as in *L'Avventura*, its minimalism is found in its deductive reasoning that structures a narrative which is never logically presented, obscuring what has led the protagonists (law enforcement/lovers) to come to the conclusions they entertain in solving the crime (*Strip Nude for Your Killer*). Non-traditionally, the antagonist is presented through a fractured editing style, a synecdoche of signifiers, that obfuscates his/her identity while the formal, systematic crosscutting not only increases tension but does even more, at times, by reaching the level of poetic intensity through its parallel structures (*Opera*). As in the New Wave, settings reinforce alienation through large spatial areas that simulate human vulnerability (*The Case of the Bloody Iris*), the variety of bizarre camera angles functions as objective correlatives to the emotional and physical states of the protagonists while generating psychological stress through the manipulation of space. Framing at times creates claustrophobic and untenable situations that describe the characters' mental states while restricting the visual information the viewer receives (*The Girl Who Knew Too Much*). Even the foreground clutter of objects, preempting a sizable component of the frame, produces a muddle of angular patterns as characters appear trapped in their substantial vortexes.

The fourth and final characteristic given by Liehm is "the rejection of the social … status quo."[4] While the *giallo* seems to privilege the establishment and the centricity of Italian bourgeois society and ideology, in reality it attacks this class. In Bianchi's *Strip Nude for Your Killer*, it is management that preys on the working women in their fashion house, exploiting them as sex objects for their own pleasure, as well as for their clients' gratification. Likewise, *Seven Bloodstained Orchids* allows the blue-collar cinemagoer to savor the middle and upper-middle classes' lifestyles while it subjects the bourgeoisie to horrific situations that border on the surreal, like death by electric drill. In Pastore's *Seven Shawls of Yellow Silk*, the establishment undermines itself in its attack on its workers through a domestic black cat's poisonous claws.

A Postscript of Sorts, Not a Requiem for a Genre 215

Too often the law also is rendered impotent in most of these films, *Lizard in a Woman's Skin* and *Seven Shawls of Yellow Silk* being the exceptions, while the protagonists are left to solve the crime themselves. In Argento's *Opera*, the establishment in the person of the police inspector, Alan Santini, is not the solution to the problem but the cause. In *Seven Bloodstained Orchids* and *Solamente Nero*, it is religion that initiates the conflict rather than act as an arbitrator of peace and justice. Although these films seem to speak for individualism against conformity through their portrayal of the '70s counterculture, they likewise do not side with this class, as seen in *The Strange Vice of Mrs. Wardh*, *The Bloody Iris*, *Lizard in a Woman's Skin*, and *Seven Bloodstained Orchids*, but use them as foils to the protagonists and dominant culture.

Ultimately, the *giallo* now occupies a small niche in cinematic history cherished by film buffs, historians and critics. What will continue to resonate in these stylish whodunits will be the cinematography, the haute couture and mod interior design of individuals with money to burn, the political incorrectness of patriarchal attitudes toward women, stories redolent of bygone pulp thrillers, the memorable and astonishingly well-composed music, and the heroines and heroes that can be tough as well as tender when the occasion demands. These characteristics are what, for many viewers, cement the *gialli* together and make coming back to them as pleasurable as reading an old mystery thriller for the second or even third time.

Chapter Notes

Introduction

1. Bart D. Ehrman, *Misquoting Jesus: The Story Behind Who Changed the Bible and Why* (New York: HarperSanFrancisco, 2005), 207, 216.
2. Keith Clements, *Friedrich Schleiermacher: Pioneer of Modern Theology*, ed. Keith W. Clements (Minneapolis: Fortress Press, 1991), 49.
3. Friedrich Schleiermacher, *Hermeneutics: The Handwritten Manuscripts*, ed. H. Kimmerle, trans. J. Duke and J. Forstman, American Academy of Religion Texts and Translations Series (Missoula, MT: Scholars Press, 1977), 112.
4. John G. Cawelti, *Adventure, Mystery, and Romance: Formula Stories as Art and Popular Culture* (Chicago: University of Chicago Press, 1976), 13.
5. Philippa Gates, "The Maritorious Melodrama: Film Noir with a Female Detective," *Journal of Film and Video* 61, no. 3 (Fall 2009): 24–39, 26.
6. Philippe Met, "'Knowing Too Much' About Hitchcock: The Genesis of the Italian Giallo," in *After Hitchcock, Influence, Imitation, and Intertextuality*, ed. David Boyd and R. Barton Palmer (Austin: University of Texas Press, 2006), 198.
7. Jeremy Butler, *Television: Critical Methods and Applications* (Mahwah, NJ: Lawrence Erlbaum, 2006).
8. Donato Totaro, "The Italian Zombie Film: From Derivation to Reinvention," in *Fear Without Frontiers: Horror Cinema Across the Globe*, ed. Steven Jay Schneider (UK: Fab Press, 2003), 162.
9. V. Propp, *Morphology of the Folktale*, trans. Laurence Scott (Austin: University of Texas Press, 1968), 21.
10. Allan Dundes, introduction to V. Propp, *Morphology of the Folktale*, xiv.
11. Robin Wood, *Sexual Politics & Narrative Film* (New York: Columbia University Press, 1998), 15–16.

Chapter 1

1. Troy Howarth, *The Haunted World of Mario Bava* (UK: Fab Press, 2002), 67.
2. Colette Balman, "The Girl Who Knew Too Much," in *100 European Horror Films*, ed. Steven Jay Schneider (London: British Film Institute, 2007), 94, mentions the film's "Multiplicity of its intertextual referencing."
3. Robert Stam, Robert Burgoyne, and Sandy Fitterman-Lewis, eds., "The Politics of Reflexivity," in *New Vocabularies in Film Semiotics* (New York: Routledge, 1992), 201–203.
4. Anthony Whiting, *The Never-Resting Mind: Wallace Stevens' Romantic Irony* (Ann Arbor: University of Michigan Press, 1996).
5. Christian Metz, "Story/Discourse: Notes on Two Kinds of Voyeurism," in *Movies and Methods*, vol. 2, ed. Bill Nichols (Los Angeles: University of California Press, 1985), 544–548.
6. Les Daniels, *Living in Fear: A History of Horror in the Mass Media* (New York: Scribner, 1975), 2.
7. Donald Spoto, *The Art of Alfred Hitchcock* (New York: Doubleday, 1992), 243, 245.
8. Sigmund Freud, "On Psychopathology," in *The Pelican Freud Library*, vol. 10, ed. Angela Richards et al. (Harmondsworth: Penguin), 112–113.
9. Otto Fenichel, *The Psychoanalytic Theory of Neurosis* (London, 1946), 71, 348.
10. Shlomith Rimmon-Kenan, *Narrative Fiction: Contemporary Poetics* (London: Methuen, 1983), 71.

11. Noel Carroll, *The Philosophy of Horror or Paradoxes of the Heart* (New York: Routledge, 1990), 130.

12. Alan Jones, *Profondo Argento: The Man, the Myths & the Magic* (UK: Fab Press, 2004), 19.

13. Mary Ann Doane, *The Desire to Desire* (Bloomington: Indiana University Press, 1987), 20ff.

14. Philippe Met, "Knowing Too Much About Hitchcock: The Genesis of the Italian *Giallo*," maintains that since the voice-over is that of a male and not the heroine's voice, "This gendering ... is redolent of the archetypal noir figure of the private eye as narrator and ... that Nora is possibly crafting her own crime thriller," in *After Hitchcock: Influence, Imitation and Intertextuality*, ed. David Boyd and R. Barton Palmer (Austin: University of Texas Press, 2006), 204.

15. David Alan Black, "Genette and Film: Narrative Level in the Fiction Cinema," *Wide Angle* 8, nos. 3/4 (1986): 19–26.

16. Samuel Taylor Coleridge affirms this connection in *Writings on Shakespeare*, ed. Terrence Hawks (New York: Putman, 1959), 158.

17. Vladimir Propp, "Functions of the Dramatis Personae," chap. 3 in *Morphology of the Folktale*, trans. Laurence Scott (Austin: University of Texas Press, 2003), 25–65.

18. Propp, *Morphology of the Folktale*, 30–31.

Chapter 2

1. Cindy Hendershot, "The Cold War Horror Film: Taboo and Transgression in the Bad Seed, the Fly, and Psycho," in *Journal of Popular Film and Television* 29, no. 1 (Spring 2001): 20–21. Also see Georges Bataille, *The Accursed Share*, vols. 2 and 3, trans. Robert Hurley (New York: Zone, 1993); Bataille, *Erotism: Death and Sensuality*, trans. Mary Dalwood (San Francisco: City Lights, 1986); Bataille, *The Impossible*, trans. Robert Hurley (San Francisco: City Lights, 1991).

2. Sigmund Freud, "The Taboo of Virginity," in *Standard Edition: Contributions to the Psychology of Love, III*, vol. 11, 198–199.

3. Kim Newman, *Nightmare Movies* (New York: Harmony Books, 1988), 105.

4. Gary Needham, "Playing with Genre: An Introduction to the Italian *Giallo*," *Kinoeye* 2, no. 11 (June 10, 2002), accessed May 31, 2007, http://www.kinoeye.org/02/11/needham 11.php. Also in *Fear Without Frontiers*, ed. Steven Jay Schneider (UK: Fab Press, 2003), 135–144.

5. Laura Mulvey, "Visual Pleasure and Narrative Cinema," in *Women and the Cinema*, ed. Karyn Kay and Gerald Peary (New York: E.P. Dutton, 1977), 413.

6. Adalgisa Giorgio claims that Italian universities did not absorb feminism into the curriculum in the '70s. If this is so then the portrayal of women in films must also be affected particularly in genres such as the *Giallo* where the female is either the victim or the deranged killer. See Adalgisa Giorgio, *A History of Women's Writing*, ed. Letizia Panizza and Sharon Wood (Cambridge: Cambridge University Press, 2000).

7. Lucia Chiavola Birnbaum, *Liberazione della Donna: Feminism in Italy* (Middletown, CT: Wesleyan University Press, 1986), 82.

8. Silvia Montefoshi, "Maternal Role and Personal Identity on the Woman's Movement and Psychoanalysis," first published as "Ruolo Materno e Identità Personale: A Proposito di Movimento delle Donne e Psicoanalisa," *Nuova DWF*, nos. 6–7 (1978), trans. Carol Lazzaro-Weis in *The Lonely Mirror*, 103.

9. C.G. Jung, *The Archetypes and the Collective Unconscious*, trans. R.F.C. Hull (Princeton, NJ: Princeton University Press, 1977), vol. 9, part 1, 18, para. 40; 17, para. 33; 22, para. 45.

10. *Classic Film Scripts, L'Age d'Or* and *Un Chien Andalou* by Luis Buñuel, trans. by Marianne Alexandre (New York: Simon & Schuster, 1968), 28.

11. Silvia Vegetti Finzi, "The Female Animal," first published as "L'Animale Femminile" in *I Labirinti dell'Eros* (Florence, 1985), trans. Giuliana De Novellis in *The Lonely Mirror*, 145.

12. Noel Carroll, *The Philosophy of Horror*, 137–138.

13. Christian Metz, "Story/Discourse: Notes on Two Kinds of Voyeurism," in *Movies and Methods*, vol. 2, ed. Bill Nichols (Berkeley: University of California Press, 1985), 545–546.

14. Roman Jakobson, "Shifters, Verbal Categories, and the Russian Verb," in *Selected Writings*, vol. 2, *Word and Language* (The Hague: Mouton, 1971), 132.

15. Christian Metz, "Le Dire et le Dit au Cinéma: Vers le Déclin d'un Vraisemblable?" *Communications* 11 (1968), 22–33.9.

16. Herbert Eagle, *Russian Formalist Film Theory* (Ann Arbor: Michigan Slavic Publications, 1981), 17.

17. Linda Ruth Williams, *The Erotic Thril-*

ler in *Contemporary Cinema* (Edinburgh: Edinburgh University Press, 2005), 352.

Chapter 3

1. M.M. Bakhtin used the term *Chronotope* to designate the spatio-temporal form, which regulates the rudimentary requisites of every narrative in his essay "Forms of Time and of the Chronotope in the Novel," in *The Dialogic Imagination: Four Essays*, ed. Michael Holquist (Austin: University of Texas Press, 1981).
2. Walter Rankin, *Grimm Pictures: Fairy Tale Archetypes in Eight Horror and Suspense Films* (Jefferson, NC: McFarland, 2007), 14.
3. Barry Keith Grant, "American Psycho/SIS: The Pure Products of America Go Crazy," in *Mythologies of Violence in Postmodern Media*, ed. Christopher Sharrett (Detroit: Wayne State University Press, 1999), 27.
4. Chris Petrak, "Mute Swan: A Varied Symbol in Myth and Law," *Tails of Birding*, February 2, 2008, accessed February 10, 2010, http://tailsofbirding.blogspot.com/2008/02/mute-swan-varied-symbol-in-myth-and.html.
5. Adrien Clerc, *Alfred Hitchcock et Lucio Fulci: Deux Univers Mitoyens*, luciofulci.fr., 2007–2009, accessed June 4, 2010, http://www.luciofulci.fr/pages/fulciologie_alfred hitchetlucioful.html.
6. Sigmund Freud, *On Dreams*, trans. James Strachy (New York: Norton, 1952), 29–30.
7. Slavoj Žižek, *Looking Awry: An Introduction to Jacques Lacan Through Popular Culture* (Cambridge, MA: MIT Press, 1991), 58.
8. Patricia MacCormack, "Lucio Fulci," *Senses of Cinema*, March 2004, accessed May 23, 2010, http://archive.sensesofcinema.com/contents/directors/04/fulci.html.
9. Dylan Evans, *An Introductory Dictionary of Lacanian Psychoanalysis* (New York: Routledge Press, 1996).
10. Norman O. Brown, "Apocalypse: The Place of Mystery in the Life of the Mind," *Harper's*, May 1961.
11. Charles Fourier, *La Phalange*, quoted by Daniel Bell in "Charles Fourier: Prophet of Eupsychia," *American Scholar*, Winter 1968–1969, 50.
12. Robin Wood, "An Introduction to the American Horror Film," in *Movies and Methods*, vol. 2, ed. Bill Nichols (Berkeley: University of California Press, 1985), 195–220.
13. A. H. Maslow, "Eupsychia—The Good Society," *Journal of Humanistic Psychology*, no. 1 (1961): 1–11.
14. Shlomith Rimmon-Kenan, *Narrative Fiction: Contemporary Poetics* (London: Methuen, 1983), 71.
15. MacCormack, "Lucio Fulci."
16. Freud, *On Dreams*, 44.
17. Arnold Hauser, "Space and Time in the Film," in *Film: A Montage of Theories*, by Richard Dyer MacCann (New York: E.P. Dutton, 1966), 188.

Chapter 4

1. Luca M. Palmerini and Gaetano Mistretta in *Spaghetti Nightmares* (Key West, FL: Fantasma Books, 1996), 68.
2. Michael Sevastakis, "A Dangerous Mind: Dario Argento's *Opera*," *Kinoeye* 2, no. 12 (June 24, 2002), accessed July 27, 2010, http://www.kinoeye.org/02/12/sevastakis12.php.
3. Maitland McDonagh, *Broken Mirrors/Broken Minds: The Dark Dreams of Dario Argento* (New York: Carol Publishing, 1994), 245.
4. DVD Shriek Show, *7 Blood Stained Orchids*, "Interview with Umberto Lenzi."
5. Daniela Colombo, "The Italian Feminist Movement," in *Women's Studies International Quarterly* 4, no. 4 (1981): 461–469.
6. Daniele Magni and Silvio Giobbio, *Cinici Infami e Violenti: Guida ai Film Polizieschi Italiani Anni '70* (Milan: Bloodbuster, 2005).
7. ELS = extreme long shot.
8. Propp, *Morphology of the Folktale*, 26–27.

Chapter 5

1. Linda Hutcheon, *Narcissistic Narrative: The Metafictional Paradox* (London: Methuen Press, 1984), 1.
2. John Barth, *The Literature of Exhaustion*, first printed in *The Atlantic*, August 1967.
3. Sergei Eisenstein, *Film Form*, trans. Jay Leyda (New York: Harcourt, Brace and World, 1949), 72–75.
4. Gary Needham, op. cit., chap. 3.
5. Andre Gaudreault, "Narration and Monstration in the Cinema," *Journal of Film and Video* 39 (Spring 1987): 32.
6. Jan Clark and Jim Crawley, *Transference and Projection: Mirrors to the Self* (Buckingham, MD: Open University Press, 2002), 38.
7. Ken Dancyger, *The Technique of Film and Video Editing: History, Theory and Prac-*

tice (Burlington: M.A., 2007), 97–109. Also see Patrick McGilligan, *A Life in Darkness and Light* (New York: Regan Books, 2003), 594.

8. Tzvetan Todorov, *Genres in Discourse*, trans. Catherine Potter (Cambridge: Cambridge University Press, 1990), 33.

Chapter 6

1. See Chapter 2 regarding feminism in Italy.

2. Edgar Allan Poe, "The Philosophy of Composition," in *The Oxford Book of American Essays*, ed. Brander Matthews (New York: Oxford University Press, 1914), 106.

3. Henri Bergson, "Laughter," in *Comedy* (New York: Doubleday, 1956), 147.

4. Thomas Pfau, *Romantic Moods; Paranoia, Trauma, and Melancholy, 1790–1840* (Baltimore, MD: Johns Hopkins University Press, 2005).

5. Barry S. Sapolsky and Fred Molitor, "*Sex and Violence in Slasher Films*," in *Mass Media and Society*, ed. A. Wells and E.A. Hakanen (Greenwich, CT: Ablex Publishing, 1997).

6. Jacqueline Rose, *Sexuality in the Field of Vision* (London: Verso, 1986), 72.

7. Tammy M. Clarksville, *Women Hippies*, accessed on July 11, 2011, http://www.teenink.com/nonfiction/travel_culture/article/122225/Women-Hippies.

8. John Hooper, "Italian Firm's Women-Only Job Cull Inflames Gender Controversy," *Guardian*, June 30, 2011, guardian.co.uk.

9. Andrea Weiss, *Vampires and Violets* (New York: Penguin, 1993), 70.

10. Mikel J. Koven, "La Dolce Morte," *Kinoeye* 3, no. 12 (October 27, 2003), accessed July 28, 2011, http://www.kinoeye.org/03/12/koven12.php.

11. D.H. Lawrence, "Making Love to Music," in *Sex, Literature and Censorship* (New York: Twayne, 1953), 40.

12. Robert Stam, Robert Burgoyne, Sandy Flitterman-Lewis, *New Vocabularies in Film Semiotics* (New York; London: Routledge Press, 1992), 167.

Chapter 7

1. See Neil Malamuth and Edward Donnerstein, eds., *Pornography and Sexual Aggression* (New York: Academic Press, 1984).

2. Walter Chaw, *Film Freak Central* review of *Strip Nude for Your Killer*, accessed October 12, 2011, http://www.filmfreakcentral.net/dvdreviews/stripnudeforyourkiller.htm.

3. Susan Sontag, "The Pornographic Imagination," in *Styles of Radical Will* (New York: Delta Books, 1969), 66.

4. Paul Willemen, "The Zoom in Popular Cinema: A Question of Performance," *Rogue*, accessed December 21, 2011, http://rouge.com.au/1/zoom.html.

Chapter 8

1. *Solamente Bido* (2002) filmed interview of Antonio Bido directed by Gary Hertz for Blue Underground.

2. Joseph Eynaud, *The Italian Detective Novel: The Literary and Cinematic Giallo*, accessed June 1, 2012, http://www.italianisticaultraiectina.org/publish/articles/000004/index.html.

3. Daniel L. Schacter, *The Seven Sins of Memory* (New York: Houghton Mifflin, 2001), 4.

4. Christian Metz, "History/Discourse: Note on Two Voyeurisms," *Edinburgh '76 Magazine*, 24.

5. James W. Prescott, "Body Pleasure and the Origins of Violence," *Bulletin of the Atomic Scientists*, November 1975, 14.

6. David G. Winter, "Power, Sex, and Violence: A Psychological Reconstruction of the 20th Century and an Intellectual Agenda for Political Psychology," in *Political Psychology* 21, no. 2 (June 2000): 383–404, 387, accessed May 31, 2012, http://www.jstor.org/stable/10.2307/3791797.

7. See J.H. Mace, "Does Involuntary Remembering Occur During Voluntary Remembering?" in *Involuntary Memory*, ed. J.H. Mace (Oxford: Blackwell, 2007), 50–67.

8. Mark A. Vieira, *Hollywood Horror: From Gothic to Cosmic* (New York: Harry Abrams, 2003).

9. Ayn Rand, *The Art of Fiction: A Guide for Writers and Readers* (New York: Plume, 2000).

Chapter 9

1. Jones, *Profondo, Argento*, 157.

2. McDonagh, *Broken Mirrors/Broken Minds*, 210.

3. Chris Gallant, ed., "Opera," in *Art of Darkness: The Cinema of Dario Argento* (UK: Fab Press, 2001), 210.

4. Edward De Grazia and Roger K. Newman, *Banned Films: Movies, Censors and the First Amendment* (New York: Bowker, 1982), 332.

5. Colette Balmain, "Female Subjectivity and the Politics of 'Becoming Other,'" *Kinoeye* 2, no. 12 (June 24, 2002).
6. Sigmund Freud, *On Dreams*, trans. James Strachey (New York: Norton, 1952), 109.
7. Linda Ruth Williams, "An Eye for an Eye," *Sight and Sound* 4, no. 4 (April 1994): 16.
8. Maitland McDonagh, *Broken Mirrors/Broken Minds*, 202.
9. Xavier Mendik, "Detection and Transgression: The Investigative Drive of the Giallo," in *Necronomicon: The Journal of Horror and Erotic Cinema*, vol. 1, ed. Andy Black (London: Creation Books, 1996), 35.
10. Leopold von Sacher-Masoch, *Venus in Furs* (New York: Penguin, 2000), 36.
11. Alexander Astruc, "The Birth of a New Avant-Garde: La Camera Stylo" [1948], in *The New Wave: Critical Landmarks*, ed. Peter Graham (Garden City, NY: Doubleday, 1968), 17–23. Astruc wrote, "Direction is no longer a means of illustrating, of presenting a scene, but a true act of writing. This filmmaker/author writes with his camera as a writer writes with his pen."
12. See Maitland McDonagh, *Broken Mirrors/Broken Minds*, 245, 253. Her interview is a reprint of her article "The Evil Eye of Dario Argento," *Gorezone*, July 14, 1990. Also see Maya Deren, "Notes, Essays, Letters," *Film Culture* 36 (Winter 1965): 1.
13. Maximilian Le Cain, "Kenneth Anger," *Senses of Cinema*, January 2003, accessed September 27, 2009, http://archive.sensesofcinema.com/contents/directors/03/anger.html.
14. McDonagh, *Broken Mirrors/Broken Minds*, 252.
15. Ibid., McDonagh's interview with Argento, 243.
16. Jones, *Profondo Argento*, 168.
17. David Alan Black, "Genette and the Film: Narrative Level in the Fiction Cinema," *Wide Angle* 8, nos. 3/4 (1986): 21.
18. Propp, *Morphology of the Folktale*, 28.

Chapter 10

1. Mirko D. Grmek, *History of AIDS: Emergence & Origin of a Modern Pandemic*, trans. Russell C. Maulitz and Jacalyn Duffin (Princeton, NJ: Princeton University Press, 1993), 42.
2. Ravi Mehta and Rui (Juliet) Zhu, "Blue or Red? Exploring the Effect of Color on Cognitive Task Performances," *Science* 323, no. 5918 (February 27, 2009): 1226–1229, accessed January 21, 2015, doi:10.1126/science.1169144.
3. Robin Wood, "An Introduction to the American Horror Film," in *Movies and Methods*, 197.
4. Sigmund Freud, *On Dreams*, trans. James Strachey (New York: Norton, 1952), 90.
5. Interview by Gavin Schmitt, in *Killer Interviews*, 2009, accessed July 24, 2009, http://killerreviews.com/dispinterview.php?intid=1260.
6. Jacqueline Rose, *Sexuality in the Field of Vision* (London: Verso, 1986), 72.
7. Raymond Bellour, "Alternation, Segmentation, Hypnosis: An Interview," *Camera Obscura*, nos. 3/4 (Summer 1979): 70–103.
8. Wood, "An Introduction to the American Horror Film," 197, 199, 203.
9. Aaron Smuts, "The Principles of Association: Dario Argento's *Profondo Rosso*," in *Kinoeye* 2, no. 11 (June 10, 2002), accessed June 18, 2009, http://www.kinoeye.org/02/11/smuts11.php.
10. Maitland McDonagh, *Broken Mirrors Broken Minds*, 245.
11. Jacqueline Reich, "The Mother of All Horror: Witches, Gender, and the Films of Dario Argento," in *Monsters in the Italian Literary Imagination*, ed. Keala Jewell (Detroit, MI: Wayne State University Press, 2001), 89.
12. See Kate Millett, *Sexual Politics* (Boston, MA: New England Free Press, 1968).
13. Harry M. Benshoff, *Monsters in the Closet: Homosexuality and the Horror Film* (New York: Manchester University Press, 1997), 231. Also see Carol J. Clover's *Men, Women and Chain Saws: Gender in the Modern Horror Film* (Princeton, NJ: Princeton University Press, 1992).
14. Mikel J. Koven, *La Dolce Morte: Vernacular Cinema and the Italian Giallo Film* (Lanham, MD: Scarecrow Press, 2006), 66.
15. Ibid.
16. Robin Wood, "An Introduction to the American Horror Film," 213.
17. Koven, *La Dolce Morte*, 107.

Conclusion

1. Koven, *La Dolce Morte*, 29.
2. Mira Liehm, *Passion and Defiance: Film in Italy from 1942 to the Present* (Berkeley: University of California Press, 1984), 188–189.
3. Gilbert Adair, "Michelangelo Antonioni," *The Independent*, August 1, 2007.
4. Liehm, *Loc. Cit.*

Bibliography

Astruc, Alexander. "The Birth of a New Avant-Garde: La Camera Stylo." *The New Wave: Critical Landmarks*, ed. Peter Graham, 17–23. Garden City, NY: Doubleday, 1968.

Bakhtin, M.M. "Forms of Time and of the Chronotope in the Novel." In *The Dialogic Imagination: Four Essays*, ed. Michael Holquist. Austin: University of Texas Press, 1981.

Balman, Colette. "Female Subjectivity and the Politics of 'Becoming Other.'" *Kinoeye* 2, no. 12 (June 24, 2002). Accessed May 24, 2008. www.kinoeye.org/02/12/argento bibliography12.php.

———. "The Girl Who Knew Too Much." In *100 European Horror Films*, ed. Steven Jay Schneider. London: British Film Institute, 2007.

Barth, John. "The Literature of Exhaustion." *The Atlantic*, August 1967, 29–34.

Bataille, Georges. *The Accursed Share*. Vols. 2 and 3. Trans. Robert Hurley. New York: Zone, 1993.

———. *Erotism: Death and Sensuality*. Trans. Mary Dalwood. San Francisco: City Lights, 1986.

———. *The Impossible*. Trans. Robert Hurley. San Francisco: City Lights, 1991.

Bell, Daniel. "Charles Fourier: Prophet of Eupsychia." *American Scholar*, Winter 1968–1969, 41–58.

Bellour, Raymond. "Alternation, Segmentation, Hypnosis: An Interview." *Camera Obscura*, nos. 3/4 (Summer 1979): 70–103.

Benshoff, Harry M. *Monsters in the Closet: Homosexuality and the Horror Film*. New York: Manchester University Press, 1997.

Bergson, Henri. "Laughter." In *Comedy*. New York: Doubleday, 1956.

Birnbaum, Lucia Chiavola. *Liberazione della Donna: Feminism in Italy*. Middletown, CT: Wesleyan University Press, 1986.

Black, David Alan. "Genette and Film: Narrative Level in the Fiction Cinema." *Wide Angle* 8, nos. 3/4 (1986): 19–26.

Brown, Norman O. "Apocalypse: The Place of Mystery in the Life of the Mind." *Harper's*, May 1961.

Buñuel, Luis. *Classic Film Scripts: L'Age d'Or and Un Chien Andalou*. Trans. Marianne Alexandre. New York: Simon & Schuster, 1968.

Butler, Jeremy. *Television: Critical Methods and Applications*. Mahwah, NJ: Lawrence Erlbaum, 2006.

Carroll, Noel. *The Philosophy of Horror or Paradoxes of the Heart*. New York: Routledge, 1990.

Cawelti, John G. *Adventure, Mystery, and Romance: Formula Stories as Art and Popular Culture*. Chicago: University of Chicago Press, 1976.

Chaw, Walter. "Strip Nude for Your Killer." *Film Freak Central*. Accessed October 12, 2011. http://www.filmfreakcentral.net/dvdreviews/stripnudeforyourkiller.htm.
Clark, Jan, and Jim Crawley. *Transference and Projection: Mirrors to the Self*. Buckingham, MD: Open University Press, 2002.
Clarksville, Tammy M. *Women Hippies*. Accessed July 11, 2011. http://www.teenink.com/nonfiction/travel_culture/article/122225/Women-Hippies.
Clements, Keith. *Friedrich Schleiermacher: Pioneer of Modern Theology*. Ed. K.W. Clements. Minneapolis, MN: Fortress Press, 1991.
Clover, Carol J. *Men, Women and Chain Saws: Gender in the Modern Horror Film*. Princeton, NJ: Princeton University Press, 1992.
Coleridge, Samuel Taylor. *Writings on Shakespeare*. Ed. Terrence Hawks. New York: Putman, 1959.
Colombo, Daniela. "The Italian Feminist Movement." *Women's Studies International Quarterly* 4, no. 4 (1981): 461–69.
Dancyger, Ken. *The Technique of Film and Video Editing: History, Theory and Practice*. Burlington, MA: Focal Press, 2007.
Daniels, Les. *Living in Fear: A History of Horror in the Mass Media*. New York: Scribner, 1975.
De Grazia, Edward, and Roger K. Newman. *Banned Films: Movies, Censors and the First Amendment*. New York: R. R. Bowker, 1982.
Deren, Maya. "Notes, Essays and Letters." *Film Culture* 36 (Winter 1965).
Doane, Mary Ann. *The Desire to Desire*. Bloomington: Indiana University Press, 1987.
Eagle, Herbert. *Russian Formalist Film Theory*. Ann Arbor: Michigan Slavic Publications, 1981.
Ehrman, Bart D. *Misquoting Jesus: The Story Behind Who Changed the Bible and Why*. New York: HarperSanFrancisco, 2005.
Eisenstein, Sergei. *Film Form*. Trans. Jay Leyda. New York: Harcourt, Brace and World, 1949.
Evans, Dylan. *An Introductory Dictionary of Lacanian Psychoanalysis*. New York: Routledge Press, 1996.
Eynaud, Joseph. *The Italian Detective Novel: The Literary and Cinematic Giallo*. Accessed June 1, 2012. http://www.italianisticaultraiectina.org/publish/articles/000004/index.html.
Fenichel, Otto. *The Psychoanalytic Theory of Neurosis*. London: Routledge and Kegan Paul, 1946.
Finzi, Silvia Vegetti. "The Female Animal." *I Labirinti dell' Eros*. Florence, 1985. Trans. Giuliana De Novellis in *The Lonely Mirror*.
Freud, Sigmund. *On Dreams*. Trans. James Strachey. New York: Norton, 1952.
_____. "On Psychopathology." In *The Pelican Freud Library*, vol. 10, ed. Angela Richards et al. Harmondsworth: Penguin.
_____. "The Taboo of Virginity." *Standard Edition: Contributions to the Psychology of Love, III*, vol. 11, 198–99.
Gallant, Chris, ed. "Opera." In *Art of Darkness: The Cinema of Dario Argento*. UK: Fab Press, 2001.
Gates, Philippa. "The Maritorious Melodrama: Film Noir with a Female Detective." *Journal of Film and Video* 61, no. 3 (Fall 2009): 24–39.
Gaudreault, Andre. "Narration and Monstration in the Cinema." *Journal of Film and Video* 39, no. 1 (Spring 1987): 29–36.
Giorgio, Adalgisa. *A History of Women's Writing*. Ed. Letizia Panizza, and Sharon Wood. Cambridge: Cambridge University Press, 2000.
Grant, Barry Keith. "American Psycho/SIS: The Pure Products of America Go Crazy." In *Mythologies of Violence in Postmodern Media*, ed. Christopher Sharrett. Detroit: Wayne State University Press, 1999.

Grmek, Mirko D. *History of AIDS: Emergence & Origin of a Modern Pandemic.* Trans. Russell C. Maulitz and Jacalyn Duffin. Princeton, NJ: Princeton University Press, 1993.
Hall, Richard H. *General Characteristics of Schizophrenia.* 1998. Accessed July 23, 2009. http://web.mst.edu/~rhall/neuroscience/07_disorders/schizo_general.pdf.
Hauser, Arnold. "Space and Time in the Film." In *Film: A Montage of Theories*, ed. Richard Dyer MacCann. New York: E.P. Dutton, 1966.
Hendershot, Cindy. "The Cold War Horror Film: Taboo and Transgression in the Bad Seed, the Fly, and Psycho." *Journal of Popular Film and Television* 29, no. 1 (Spring 2001): 20–21.
Hertz, Gary. *Dr. Solamente Bido: Interview of Antonio Bido.* Blue Underground, 2002.
Hooper, John. "Italian Firm's Women-Only Job Cull Inflames Gender Controversy." Accessed June 30, 2011. http://www.theguardian.com/world/2011/jun/30/italian-firm-women-job-cutsat.
Howarth, Troy. *The Haunted World of Mario Bava.* UK: Fab Press, 2002.
Hutcheon, Linda. *Narcissistic Narrative: The Metafictional Paradox.* London: Methuen Press, 1984.
Jakobson, Roman. "Shifters, Verbal Categories, and the Russian Verb." In *Selected Writings*, vol. 2, *Word and Language*. The Hague: Mouton, 1971.
Jones, Alan. *Profondo, Argento: The Man, the Myths and the Magic.* UK: Fab Press, 2004.
Jung, C.G. *The Archetypes and the Collective Unconscious.* Vol. 9, part 1, trans. R.F.C. Hull. Princeton, NJ: Princeton University Press, 1977.
Khairy, Wael. "Hitchcock's Symphony: Psycho a Shot-By-Shot Commentary." *Film Analysis*, June 17, 2010. Accessed March 13, 2011. http://cinephilefix.wordpress.com/2010/06/17/hitchcocks-symphony-psycho-a-shot-by-shot-commentary.
Koven, Mijkel J. "La Dolce Morte." *Kinoeye* 3, no. 12 (October 27, 2003): 1. Accessed July 28, 2011. http://www.kinoeye.org/03/12/koven12.php.
_____. *La Dolce Morte: Vernacular Cinema and the Italian Giallo Film.* Lanham, MD: Scarecrow Press, 2006.
Lawrence, D.H. "Making Love to Music." In *Sex, Literature and Censorship.* New York: Twayne, 1953.
Le Cain, Maximilian. "Kenneth Anger." *Senses of Cinema*, January 2003. Accessed September 27, 2009. http://archive.sensesofcinema.com/contents/directors/03/anger.html.
Lenzi, Umberto. *Seven Blood Stained Orchids.* "Interview with Umberto Lenzi." DVD Shriek Show Production.
Liehm, Mira. *Passion and Defiance: Film in Italy from 1942 to the Present.* Berkeley: University of California Press, 1984.
MacCormack, Patricia. "Lucio Fulci." *Senses of Cinema*, March 2004. Accessed May 23, 2010. http://archive.sensesofcinema.com/contents/directors/04/fulci.html.
Mace, J.H., ed. "Does Involuntary Remembering Occur During Voluntary Remembering?" In *Involuntary Memory*, 50–67. Oxford: Blackwell Publishing, 2007.
Magni, Daniele, and Silvio Giobbio. "Cinici Infami E Violenti." In *Guida ai Film Polizieschi Italiani Anni '70.* Milan: Bloodbuster, 2005.
Malamuth, Neil, and Edward Donnerstein, eds. *Pornography and Sexual Aggression.* New York: Academic Press, 1984.
Maslow, A.H. "Eupsychia: The Good Society." *Journal of Humanistic Psychology* 1 (1961): 1–11.
McDonagh, Maitland. *Broken Mirrors/Broken Minds: The Dark Dreams of Dario Argento.* New York: Carol Publishing, 1994.
McGilligan, Patrick. *Alfred Hitchcock: A Life in Darkness and Light.* New York: Regan Books, 2003.
Mehta, Ravi, and Rui Zhu (Juliet). "Blue or Red? Exploring the Effect of Color on Cognitive

Task Performances." *Science* 323, no. 5918 (February 5, 2009): 1226–1229. Accessed January 21, 2015. http://dx.doi.org/10.1126/science.1169144.
Mendik, Xavier. "Detection and Transgression: The Investigative Drive of the Giallo." In *Necronomicon: The Journal of Horror and Erotic Cinema*, vol. 1, ed. Andy Black. London: Creation Books, 1996.
Met, Philippe. "'Knowing Too Much' About Hitchcock: The Genesis of the Italian Giallo." In *After Hitchcock, Influence, Imitation, and Intertextuality*, ed. David Boyd and R. Barton Palmer. Austin: University of Texas Press, 2006.
Metz, Christian. "Le Dire et le Dit au Cinéma: Vers le Déclin d'un Vraisemblable?" *Communications* 11 (1968): 22–33.
———. "Story/Discourse: Notes on Two Kinds of Voyeurism." In *Movies and Methods*, vol. 2, ed. Bill Nichols, 543–549. Los Angeles: University of California Press, 1985.
Millett, Kate. *Sexual Politics*. Boston: New England Free Press, 1968.
Montefoshi, Silvia. "Maternal Role and Personal Identity on the Woman's Movement and Psychoanalysis." *Nuova DWF*, nos. 6–7 (1978). Trans. Carol Lazzaro-Weis in *The Lonely Mirror*.
Mulvey, Laura. "Visual Pleasure and Narrative Cinema." In *Women and the Cinema*, ed. Karyn Kay and Gerald Peary. New York: E.P. Dutton, 1977.
Needham, Gary. "Playing with Genre: An Introduction to the Giallo." *Kinoeye* 2 (June 2002). http://www.kinoeye.org/02/11/needham11.php.
Newman, Kim. *Nightmare Movies*. New York: Harmony Books, 1988.
Palmerini, Luca M., and Gaetano Mistretta. *Spaghetti Nightmares*. Key West, FL: Fantasma Books, 1996.
Petrak, Chris. "Mute Swan: A Varied Symbol in Myth and Law." *Tails of Birding*, February 2, 2008. Accessed February 10, 2010. http://tailsofbirding.blogspot.com/2008/02/mute-swan-varied-symbol-in-myth-and.html.
Pfau, Thomas. *Romantic Moods: Paranoia, Trauma, and Melancholy, 1790–1840*. Baltimore: Johns Hopkins University Press, 2005.
Poe, Edgar Allan. "The Philosophy of Composition." In *The Oxford Book of American Essays*, ed. Brander Matthews. New York: Oxford University Press, 1914.
Prescott, James W. "Body Pleasure and the Origins of Violence." *Bulletin of the Atomic Scientists*, November 1975, 10–20.
Propp, V. *Morphology of the Folktale*. Trans. Laurence Scott. Austin: University of Texas Press, 1968.
Rand, Ayn. *The Art of Fiction: A Guide for Writers and Readers*. New York: Plume, 2000.
Rankin, Walter. *Grimm Pictures: Fairy Tale Archetypes in Eight Horror and Suspense Films*. Jefferson, NC: McFarland, 2007.
Reich, Jacqueline. "The Mother of All Horror: Witches, Gender, and the Films of Dario Argento." In *Monsters in the Italian Literary Imagination*, ed. Keala Jewell. Detroit: Wayne State University Press, 2001.
Rimmon-Kenan, Shlomith. *Narrative Fiction: Contemporary Poetics*. London: Methuen, 1983.
Rose, Jacqueline. *Sexuality in the Field of Vision*. London: Verso, 1986.
Sacher-Masoch, Leopold von. *Venus in Furs*. New York: Penguin, 2000.
Sapolsky, Barry S., and Fred Molitor. "Sex and Violence in Slasher Films." In *Mass Media and Society*, ed. A. Wells and E.A. Hakanen. Greenwich, CT: Ablex Publishing, 1997.
Schacter, Daniel L. *The Seven Sins of Memory*. New York: Houghton Mifflin, 2001.
Schleiermacher, Friedrich. *Hermeneutics: The Handwritten Manuscripts*. Ed. H. Kimmerle. Trans. J. Duke and J. Forstman. American Academy of Religion Texts and Translations Series. Missoula, MT: Scholars Press, 1977.
Schmitt, Gavin. "Interview with Simon Boswell." *Killer Interviews*, 2009. Accessed July 24, 2009. http://killerreviews.com/dispinterview.php?intid=1260.

Schneider, Steven Jay, ed. *Fear Without Frontiers: Horror Cinema Across the Globe.* UK: Fab Press, 2003.
Smuts, Aaron. "The Principles of Association: Dario Argento's *Profondo Rosso.*" *Kinoeye* 2, no. 11 (June 10, 2002). Accessed June 10, 2009. http://www.kinoeye.org/02/11/smuts11.php.
Sontag, Susan. "The Pornographic Imagination." In *Styles of Radical Will.* New York: Delta Books, 1969.
Spoto, Donald. *The Art of Alfred Hitchcock.* New York: Doubleday, 1992.
Stam, Robert, et al. "The Politics of Reflexivity." In *New Vocabularies in Film Semiotics.* New York: Routledge, 1992.
Todorov, Tzvetan. *Genres in Discourse.* Trans. Catherine Potter. Cambridge: Cambridge University Press, 1990.
Totaro, Donato. "The Italian Zombie Film: From Derivation to Reinvention." In *Fear Without Frontiers: Horror Cinema Across the Globe,* ed. Steven Jay Schneider. UK: Fab Press, 2003.
Vieira, Mark A. *Hollywood Horror: From Gothic to Cosmic.* New York: Harry Abrams, 2003.
Weiss, Andrea. *Vampires and Violets.* New York: Penguin, 1993.
Whiting, Anthony. *The Never-Resting Mind: Wallace Stevens' Romantic Irony.* Ann Arbor: University of Michigan Press, 1996.
Willemen, Paul. "The Zoom in Popular Cinema: A Question of Performance." *Rogue.* Accessed on December 21, 2011. http://rouge.com.au/1/zoom.html.
Williams, Linda Ruth. *The Erotic Thriller in Contemporary Cinema.* Edinburgh: Edinburgh University Press, 2005.
_____. "An Eye for an Eye." *Sight and Sound* 4, no. 4 (April 1994).
Winter, David G. "Power, Sex, and Violence: A Psychological Reconstruction of the 20th Century and an Intellectual Agenda for Political Psychology." *Political Psychology* 21 (June 2, 2000): 383–404. Accessed May 31, 2012. http://www.jstor.org/stable/10.2307/3791797.
Wood, Robin. "An Introduction to the American Horror Film." In *Movies and Methods,* vol. 2, ed. Bill Nichols, 195–220. Berkeley: University of California Press, 1985.
_____. *Sexual Politics & Narrative Film.* New York: Columbia University Press, 1998.
Žižek, Slavoj. *Looking Awry: An Introduction to Jacques Lacan Through Popular Culture.* Cambridge: MIT Press, 1991.

Index

Numbers in **_bold italics_** refer to pages with photographs.

abortion/abortionists 130, 132, 144, 146, 147, 148, 149, 153, 166, 169
action-image 174
Adam and Eve 28, 29
Adricel (Adriano Celentano) 6
L'Age d'or (1930) 32
AIDS 193
Airoldi, Cristina 27
Albertini, Giampiero 115
Alexandra Palace 60
Alice's Adventures in Wonderland 60
Allain, Marcel 135
alternating syntagma 75, 78, 139, 176, 198
Amanda (Giuliana Cecchini) 133
analepsis 19, 32
And Then There Were None (1939) 204
Anger, Kenneth 45, 181
anni di piombo 73
anthrozoology 97
anti–Semitism 117
Antonioni, Michelangelo 132, 212, 213
aphasic stoppage 19
Apollonian and Dionysian 57
Argento, Dario 2, 11, 29, 67, 70, 81, 88, 92, 93, 103, 109, 171, 172, 173, 174, 176, 178, 180, 181, 182, 184, 186, 188, 203, 204, 213, 215
Ariadne (mythology) 18
Aristotle 29, 162, 181
Astruc, Alexandre 181, 221*ch*9*n*11
Austria 31, 35, 39, 40
L'Avventura (1960) 213, 214

Bachianas Brasileiras 196
Bacon, Francis 55
Baker, Stanley 46, **_49_**, 61
ballet mécanique 103
Balman, Colette 217*ch*1*n*2
Barberini, Urbano 171, **_190_**
Barberito, Aldo 73
Barth, John 88
Bast (mythology) 95

Bataille, Georges 26
Bava, Lamberto 2, 192
Bava, Mario 2, 3, 5, 87
Bellocchio, Marco 213
Benussi, Femi 132
Berstorf Glassworks 101
Bertolucci, Bernardo 213
Bianchi, Andrea 130
Bido, Antonio 164
Biggers, Earl Derr 1
biologism 197
The Birds (Hitchcock, 1963) 61
Birth of a New Avant-Garde 181
The Birth of Tragedy 57
Bluebeard 14
Bolkan, Florinda 45, **_49_**
Bosic, Andrea 83
Boswell, Simon 192 196
Bovaryism 33
Brait, Carla 109
Brandon, David 193
Brown, Norman O. 51
Brown, Penny 49
Bullo, Gianfranco 153
Buñuel, Luis 32, 178
"bus" 155

le camera stylo 181, 221*ch*9*n*11
Capolicchio, Lino 152
Capponi, Pier Paolo 69
Capucine 97
Carman, Bliss 108, 109
Carnimeo, Giuliano 108, 110, 121, 122, 126
Carre, Ben 108
Carroll, Noel 10, 36
Casini, Stefania 152, **_155_**
Cassola, Francesca 177
Castelnuovo, Nino 130, **_135_**
The Cat and the Cannery (1927) 81
The Cat People (1942) 155
Cataldi-Tassoni, Coralina 172

227

catharsis 158, 162, 181
Catholic Church 114, 146
Catullus 6
Cavara, Paolo 88
Chabrol, Claude 213
Charleson, Ian 172
Chi l'ha vista morire? (*Who Saw Her Die*, 1972) 151
Un Chien andalou (1929) 178
Christie, Agatha 1, 17, 204
chronotope 219*ch*3*n*1
Cipriani, Stelvio 157
Clover, Carol 206
cognitive task performance 194; *see also* psychological use of primary colors
Columbo 73
Corazzari, Bruno 67
Corbellini, Vanni 193
Corinthians 50
Corrigan, Shirley 87, **102**
Cortese, Valentina 11, **15**
Coubert, Chana 6
Counterculture 49, 53, 110, 114, 115, 215
Cupid and Psyche (Canova) 172
Cyclops 195

La Dama rossa uccide sette volte (*The Red Queen Kills Seven Times*) 87
David, Jacques-Louis 34
Davidson, Avram 101
The Death of Marat 34
De Carmine, Renato 91
Degrave, Jean 59
Deleuze, Gilles 174
De Mendoza, Alberto 27, 58
De Palma, Brian 38
Deren, Maya 45, 181
De Sica, Manuel 89
Deuteronomy 71
The Devil Bat (1940) 88
diegesis 138, 208
Di Leo, Fernando 73
Diogene, Franco 133
Di Paolo, Dante 16
displaced diegetic insert 131, 139, 176
Don Camillo (1952) 151
Donne, John 115
Dressed to Kill (1980) 38
Dunes, Alan 3
Duse, Attilo 153
Dutch angle 55, 68, 89, 96, 124
Duvivier, Julien 151

Eberz, Ursel 58
Ecplexis 181
Eisenstein, Sergi 90
erotetic 10, 14, 15, 19, 20
The Ethics of Psychoanalysis 51
Exodus 71
exploitation cinema 2
extradiegetic narrator 7, 10, 14, 91, 116, 144
Eyes in the Night (1942) 88

Falk, Rosella 75
Fantomas 135
Farinelli, Evi 110
Fellini, Frederico 212
feminism 29, 30, 70, 218*ch*1*n*6
Fenech, Edwige 26, 28, **33**, 108, **113**, **118**, 132, **135**, **138**
Fenichel, Otto 10
film noir 103, 121, 123, 134, 193
final girl 70, 92, 94
Finzi, Silvia 33
Fireworks (1947) 45, 181
Flaubert, Gustave 33
focalization 10, 37
focalizer 10, 12, 14, 50, 80, 94, 98, 99, 152, 176, 184, 198, 199
Foro Italico 19
Le foto di Gioia (*Delirium: Photos of Gioia*, 1987) 2, 192–211, **194**, 213, 214
Four Flies on Grey Velvet (1971) 88
Fourier, Charles 51
A Fragment of Seeking (1946) 181
Francesco, giullare di Dio (*Francis, God's Jester*, 1950) 151
Freud, Sigmund 10, 26, 27, 28, 29, 48, 52, 54, 57, 99, 109, 196
Freytag, Gustav 162
Fulci, Lucio 45, 151
Furore 6

Gall, Edy 46
Garrone, Maurizio 182
Gastaldi, Ernesto 118
Il gatto a nove code (*Cat O'Nine Tails*, 1971) 88
Genesis 27, 29, 114
Genn, Leo 46
Genoa 119, 126
German Expressionism 182
Germi, Pietro 212
Giorgelli, Gabriella 69
Giorgio, Adalgisa 218*ch*2*n*6
Glass, Uschi 66, **75**
Goblin 154, 161
Godard, Jean-Luc 11
Gothic traits 5, 6, 8, 17, 80, 81, 95, 121, 138
Grandi, Serena 192, **194**
Grant, Barry Keith 45
gynophobia 206

Hammer Studios 164
Harrington, Curtis 45, 181
Hathaway, Henry 88
Hendershot, Cyndy 26
Hesiod 195
heterodiegetic narrator 7, 15, 16, 20
Hill, Craig 151
Hilton, George 27, 108
Hitchcock, Alfred 6, 8, 9, 11, 19, 27, 61, 69, 88, 102, 167, 204, 205
Holy Sonnet 14 115

homodiegetic narrator 186
Humanae Vitae (1968) 146
hysteron proteron 9, 13, 18

iconic/indexical signs 122
Incontrera, Annabella 94, 109, **118**
Inferno (1980) 93
intertextual transtextuality 6
intradiegetic narrator 186
invocatory drive 81, 143
iris shot 175

Jamesian reflector/center of vision 6, 144
Jones, Alan 186
jouissance 51
Julian, Rupert 171
Jung, Carl/Jungian 31, 123, 182

Kennedy, Mike 49
Koscina, Silvia 87
Koven, Mikel J. 117
Krimi 1

Lacan, Jacques 81
Lado, Aldo 151
La Neve, Filippo 130
Lang, Fritz 11, 38, 182
La Scala Opera House 172
Lattuada, Alberto 212
Lawrence, D.H. 119
Leda and the swan 47
LeFanu, Sheridan 8
Leni, Paul 81, 95
Lenzi, Giovanna 88
Leroux, Gaston 171
Lesbia 6
lesbianism 52, 53, 61, 62, 115, 117, 118, 197
Leviticus 71
Lewis, Matthew Gregory 80
Lewton, Val 11, 155
Liehm, Mira 212, 213, 214
Lionello, Oreste 109
Litany of the Blessed Virgin 164
low-key lighting 8, 9, 103, 143, 176
Una lucertola con la pelle di donna (*A Lizard in a Woman's Skin*, 1971) 45–65, **49**, 87, 103, 213, 214, 215
Lugosi, Bela 88
Lys, Lya 32

M (1930) 58
Macbeth (opera) 172, 173, 174, 175, 176, 179, 186, 187, 189
MacCormack, Patricia 51, 56
Madama Butterfly 183
Madame Bovary 33
"magick" 181
La Mala ordina (*Manhunt*, 1972) 73
Malaspina, Romano 87
Malfatti, Marina 70
mammoni 141

The Man Who Knew Too Much (1934, 1956) 6, 8
Manichaean dialectic 38
Marani, Imelde 92
Marano, Ezio 58
Marchall, Isabelle 87
Marsillach, Cristina 171, **179**
Marxist-Freudian perspective 52
masculinist culture 30
Maslow, Abraham 53
Mayniel, Juliette 153
McNamara, William 178
Mell, Marisa 67, 75
Mendoza, Alberto de 27, 58
Meshes of the Afternoon (1943) 181
Met, Philippe 2, 218ch1n14
metatextuality 6
Metric montage 90
Metropolis (1927) 38
Metz, Christian 36
Michelsen, Katrine 191, **194**
Mickey Mousing 99
Milan 131, 147
Milano calibro 9 (*Caliber 9*) 73
mimetic stratum 16
Mioni, Sergio 153
Miraglia, Emilio 87
misandristic 41
mise-en-abîme 13
mise-en-scène 9, 17, 39, 80, 81, 89, 101, 121, 156
misogyny 2, 206
Modot, Gaston 32
La moglie del prete (*The Priest's Wife*, 1971) 151
Mondadori 1
Mondino, Enzo 112
money shot 140
Monicelli, Mario 212
The Monk (1796) 80
Montefoshi, Silvia 218ch2n2
Monti, Silvia 48
Morphology of the Folktale 21
Morricone, Ennio 48
Mulvey, Laura 29, 112
Murano, Venice 152, 153, 167
Murnau, F.W. 182
The Mysteries of Udolopho 6
Mystical Body of Christ 114

narratemes 21
Needham, Gary 92
Nicolai, Bruno 110
Nicolodi, Daria 173, 193
Nietzsche, Friedrich 57
Night of the Demon (1958) 17
Nistri, Piero 49
Non si sevizia un paperino (*Don't Torture a Duckling* 1972) 151
nondiegetic sound 81, 91, 97, 99, 161, 183, 184, 198
North by Northwest (1959) 6

Index

Northanger Abbey 6
Nouvelle Vague 2
Nucci, Laura 154
Nude per l'assassino (1975) 130–150, **135**, **138**
nunsploitation 151

ocularization 37, 38, 198
Odi et Amo 6, 47
The Old Dark House (1932) 17, 81
Olmi, Ermanno 213
oneiric 59, 61, 99, 121, 177, 182
Opera (*Terror at the Opera*, 1987) 2, 93, 103, 171–191, 204, 213, 214, 215, **179**, **190**
Ortolani, Ritz 68
Ostia 18, 19
ostinato (music) 58
over-cranking 177, 185

Palmenhaus Gardens 35, 36
Pasolini, Pier Paolo 212
Passion and Defiance 212
patriarchal perspective 7, 25, 29, 30, 31, 49, 52, 61, 62, 109, 115, 126, 132, 145, 195, 206, 215
Pavlo, Lilana 94
Peeping Tom (1960) 132, 205
Pellegrini, Claudio 132
perceptual and psychological facets 10, 15, 68
Perche quelle strane gocce di sangue sul corpo di Jennifer? (*The Case of the Bloody Iris*, 1972) 108–129, **113**, **118**, 132, 214
Perrault, Charles 14
phallic representation 16, 18, 26, 57, 74, 112, 138, 160, 177, 193, 195, 196, 202, 204, 205, 210, 211
phallocentrism 46
Phantom of the Opera (1925) 171
Phantom of the Opera (novel) 171
The Philosophy of Composition 109
Le Pied de Fanchette ou le soulier couleur de rose 138
Pigozzi, Luciano 109
plot point 91, 100
Poe, Edgar Allan 109
Poetics 162
point d'écoute 39, 138
La Polizia ringrazia (*Execution Squad* 1972) 73
poliziottesco 73
Pond, Ersi 49
Pope Paul VI 146
pornography and violence 132, 140, 142
Powell, Michael 132, 205
Profondo rosso (*Deep Red* 1975) 68, 203
Propp, Vladimir 3, 21, 22, 23, 24, 39, 62, 64, 83, 84, 85, 86, 104, 105, 106, 126, 129, 147, 148, 149, 167, 169, 170, 186, 187, 188, 189, 206, 208, 209
Protestant Cemetery 79
Psalm 135, 159
Psycho (1960) 204, 205

psychological use of primary colors 92, 93, 194, 198, 203
Pygmalion & Galatea 113
pyramidal structure of a play 162

Quattrini, Paola 108, **113**
4 mosche di velluto grigio (*Four Flies on Grey Velvet*, 1971) 88
Quesada, Milo 8

Ra (mythology) 95
Rachmaninoff, Sergei 196
Radcliffe, Ann 6, 7
La Ragazza che sapeva troppo (*The Girl Who Knew Too Much*, 1962) 2, 3, 5–25, **13**, **15**, 212, 214
Raho, Umberto 87
Rand, Ayn 157
Rassimov, Ivan 27, 28
Rear Window (1954) 19
Reich, Jacqueline 204
Rendezvous in Black 66
repetition compulsion 99, 100
Restif, Nicolas-Edme 138
retifism 138
rhymed articulation 59; rhyme scheme 77, 78, 157; rhymed cut 92, 143
rhythmic montage 100
Rigaud, George 45, 109
Rio dei Vetrai 153
Risi, Dino 151
Robbe-Grillet, Alain 213
Robson, Mark 155
Roma, città aperta (*Rome Open City*, 1945) 151
Roman, Leticia 6, **13**, **15**
Romano, Renato 67
Romantic (literary term) 109
Rose, Jacqueline 112
Rosi, Francesco 213
Rossellini, Roberto 151
Rubens, Peter 137
Russian montage 90

Sabato, Antonio 66, 68, **75**
Salerno, Sabrina 193
Sacher-Masoch, Leopold von 180
sadomasochism 205
St. John 146
St. Mark 100
Santissima Trinità al Monte Pincio 9
Sapphic interests 110
Saxon, John 8, **13**
Scalinata di Piazza di Spagna 8, 9, 11, 12, 13, 14, 16, 22, 24
Schizoid (1973) 46
Schleiermacher, Friedrich 1
Schurer, Erna 137, **138**
Schurmann, Petra 75
scopophilia 10, 132, 133, 174
Secret Agent (1936) 19
secure and insecure noise 81

Index

Sei donne per l'assassino (*Blood and Black Lace*, 1962) 87
Serato, Massimo 153
Sette orchidee macchiate di rosso (*Seven Bloodstained Orchids*, 1972) 66–86, **75**, 108, 132, 151, 214, 215
Sette scialli di seta gialla (*Seven Shawls of Yellow Silk*, aka *Crimes of the Black Cat*, 1972) 87–107, **102**, 133, 162, 213, 214, 215
Sini, Linda 70
Soavi, Michele 184
Solamente nero (*The Bloodstained Shadow*, 1978) 151–170, **155**, 213, 214, 215
Sorel, Jean 46
sous rature 35
Souvestre, Pierre 135
A Space Odyssey (1968) 123
Spillane, Mickey 17
Stagnaro, Carola 182
Steadicam 175, 177
Steffen, Anthony 87
Steno (Stefano Vanzina) 73
Una strana orchidea con cinque gocce di sangue (*A Strange Orchid with Five Drops of Blood*) 108
Strangers on a Train (1951) 8, 27
Lo strano vizio della Signora Wardh (*The Strange Vice of Mrs. Wardh*, 1970) 26–44, **33**, 118, 213, 215
Strindberg, Anita 46
Stuart, Giacomo-Rossi 87
Stubing, Solvi 132
Study After Velázquez's Portrait of Pope Innocent X 55
subjective insert 32, 33, 176, 177, 179, 182, 200
Suspicion (1941) 9
Suspiria (1977) 81, 93
swish pan 50, 71, 74, 90, 91, 96, 175
synecdoche 39, 68, 69, 82, 89, 95, 102, 116, 135, 157, 160, 161, 214
syntagma: alternating 75, 78, 139, 176, 198; subjective insert 32, 33, 176, 177, 179, 182, 200

La Tarantola dal ventre nero (*The Black Belly of the Tarantula*, 1971) 88
Teatro Regio 172
Tedeschi, Maria 111
Tenebrae (1982) 67, 92, 204
Theseus 18

1 Thessalonians 95
The Thin Man (1934) 67
The 39 Steps (1935) 19
Thrower, Steven 206
Tourneur, Jacques 17
tromp l'oeil 80, 161
trope 8, 11, 28, 36, 43, 45, 72, 75, 78, 80, 81, 83, 87, 89, 94, 98, 133, 138, 168, 174, 179, 204, 210
Truffaut, François 213
Tuo vizio è una stanza chiusa e solo lo ne ho la chiave Il (*Your Vice Is a Locked Room and I Only Have the Key*, 1972) 28
23 Paces to Baker Street (1956) 88

L'uccello dalle piume di cristallo (*The Bird with the Crystal Plumage*, 1970) 11
Uncle Silas 8

vagina dentata 180; symbols 28, 54, 196
vampire 117, 118
Van Dine, S.S. 1
Velázquez, Diego 137
Venus in Furs 180
vernacular cinema 212
Verri, Wainer 137
Vertigo (1958) 167
Villa-Lobos, Heitor 196
Vitale, Antonella 182
Vivarelli, Piero 6
Vocalise 196
vococentrism 7
voyeurism 178

Wallace, Edgar 2, 17
Whale, James 17
Woburn Abbey 61
Wood, Robin 52, 202
Woolrich, Cornell 66

Yarbrough, Jean 88
Young and Innocent (1937) 6, 19

Zammi, Alfredo 154
zero degree editing 59
zeugma 35, 58, 60
Zinnemann, Fred 88
Zinny, Karl 193
Zurlini, Valerio 213

www.ingramcontent.com/pod-product-compliance
Ingram Content Group UK Ltd.
Pitfield, Milton Keynes, MK11 3LW, UK
UKHW041945140426
5217IPUK00014B/662